THE POLITICS OF AGRICULTURE

CHARLES M. HARDIN

The Politics
of Agriculture

Soil Conservation and the Struggle for Power in Rural America

THE FREE PRESS · GLENCOE · ILLINOIS

To Sallie

Contents

Contents

Foreword

This is an era in which agriculture is deeply involved with government—local, state and national. Beginning over thirty years ago with the depression which followed World War I, there has developed remarkable growth in the relationships between government, agriculture and farmers.

Farm programs authorized by congress and administered by the federal government reach every farm in the nation. These programs affect in varying degrees the prices and distribution of agricultural products to all the people.

Roots of our present period extend back to the generation which followed the Civil War. The Grange movement had its beginning and soon proposed cooperative marketing, distribution and governmental action through regulatory control to curb monopolies, to regulate freight rates, and to return a greater share of the national income to farmers.

These revolutionary ideas were expressed through Populism and Progressivism in the early years of the 20th Century. It was presumed that through organized farmer group action and political power, the government would render the same beneficiary services to agriculture that it was presumed to render other social groups.

The curtain on the modern era was gradually drawn during the administration of Theodore Roosevelt. The first signs of this action were: the first White House Conference on conservation;

the results of the County Life Commission; and later the passage of the Smith-Lever Act creating the Cooperative Extension Service and the Federal Farm Loan system.

At the turn of the century little distinction was made between economics, government and rural sociology. The problems were considered largely economic, resulting in a movement which has been excellently described and analyzed by H. C. Taylor. Trained social scientists and other investigators consider that agricultural economics has had a steady, and on the whole, satisfactory growth and development.

It is considered, I believe, not a separate field applicable only to agriculture, but as an area in which economic knowledge and principles are applied to agriculture as an industry. Agriculture is considered as a complex and specialized part of our society. In the same manner, rural sociology has developed, not as a field unto itself, but an area of study within our society as a whole. Unfortunately, I do not believe that political science as it relates to agriculture has yet reached this development.

Wherever government is involved with its complex problems of policy formation, legislation, administration, and political processes, political science is definitely involved. We understand such phenomena in terms of political science pretty much in the same way that we understand prices and distribution phenomena in terms of economic science.

Thus far, trained professional workers in political science as it relates to agriculture are few, and their contributions have frequently been historical and in some instances written by those unfamiliar with farming, the rural social pattern, and other complex phases of agriculture.

In contrast, in agricultural economics and rural sociology there are those well-trained in their respective fields. Generally speaking, they are sons and daughters of the soil, and as public servants and educators have remained a part of agriculture and its institutions. The time, I believe, has arrived in which political science is ready to follow the pattern set by economics and sociology. In the colleges of agriculture, land-grant colleges, and other educational institutions, we should have scientists, public servants and educators trained to give the necessary and important service in political science as is now available in agricultural economics and rural sociology.

This book, I think, exemplifies this trend. The writer has had rigorous training in economics, but has also had extensive study in political science and government. For the past ten years he has specialized in these fields at Harvard University and the University of Chicago. The author has had rare opportunity for field study, developing this book with intimate personal contact with individuals and movements which have produced the politics of agriculture during the last decade.

The complex of agricultural policy is not merely an ideal in men's minds, but is something real. It is extension work, soil conservation, price supports, rural electrification, etc. It is so real in fact, that agricultural economists, political scientists, administrators and extension workers have made it a special object of study.

Traditional bias of American economics for laissez-faire has led many to seek power over nature rather than an understanding of political power. This may be a predilection for improvements in technology and for preservation of free competition. It is their meaning of individualism. Having ruled out as undesirable or uneconomic anything but a minimum of power of one individual over another, they have too often made the subject strictly academic.

Into a situation still somewhat dominated by such thinking, this volume by Professor Hardin comes as a breath of fresh air, even though some of the things it describes are malodorous. Its freshness comes from the recognition of realities by a student of political science. It recognizes the existence of power and studies it with the objectivity of a student concerned only with understanding the subject and expressing his own personal opinions about it.

All students of agricultural policy would do well to study this book, because it deals with aspects of agricultural policy too often neglected by students of the subject. Although *Politics of Agriculture* is not the same thing as agricultural policy, it is indispensable in understanding that policy and for developing practical programs in its change. Although the book deals to an extent with current problems of soil conservation, the analysis demonstrates the inseparability of all major purposes of policy. This volume renders a real service in recording a part of the history of changing human relations in the American economy which otherwise might be lost.

Points made by Prof. Hardin's studies will continue to be controversial, but the material from which he draws his conclusions can be verified by other investigators. The points will continue to be controversial because they are developed in the field of social science, which deals with the conflicting purposes of man in society. There is no *one* irrevocable *policy* that can be discovered in the same manner in which men discover gold deposits or oil fields. Policy is what men make it and politics is the negotiation and maneuvering of those seeking to achieve or maintain control. Control is power—power to achieve purposes. The democratic process is the best means yet devised by man for keeping abuse of power to a minimum. In our modern America it operates through political parties, corporations, cooperatives, trade unions and farm organizations. Dr. Hardin reveals the operation of this process in the agricultural field of our economy.

The problem in this complex world is how to channel collective action and still retain maximum individual action. The real choice is not whether we are to have politics, but: what *kind* are we going to have? Through the study of past policy we should be better equipped to improve on that policy.

An informative part of this book is the history of the relation of collective action by government to collective action by non-governmental organizations—how non-governmental action is the outcome of government action, and vice versa.

The author's approach is from the point of view of a professional political scientist and his interpretations. But the reader's viewpoint can be improved by Hardin's opinions. This book contains many ideas useful in the development of agricultural political economy, or a synthesis of agricultural political science and agricultural economics.

Democracy is both a matter of philosophical ideals, and a process participated in by human beings. It begins with the individual, generating force through group action and expressing itself in the policies of programs of government. In an age of "Big Democracy" there exist certain aspects of the democratic process which must work well if society is to attain higher levels of general well-being for all. Research by competent students must be carried on extensively. Scholars must be free to investigate, to analyze, to interpret, and clarify their facts. This kind of independent research should be carried on in publicly supported research and educational institutions on the same level as research in experiment stations dealing with technical agriculture. This will require wide support by students of honest thought and a public which will defend such research studies.

Extension work today is largely an educational activity growing out of problems in which farmers have a conscious need for education. Farmers must learn to regard the policy aspects of agriculture and rural life as another problem to be considered in Extension work. It should assist them in their understanding of agriculture's economic and political problems.

There is such a thing as "democracy in administration" as well as democracy in policy formation. The possibilities of the democratic process in administration are definitely related to the understanding of these processes by those who benefit therefrom.

There are three things that must be borne in mind in looking to the future: (1) Politics and politicians are not bad per se. They express their constituencies at least to a degree. (2) Tolerance and consideration of others' views must reach a higher plane than it does today. (3) Philosophy as it deals with the goals and values of life must also make its contribution, along with the social sciences, to the problems of public policy in agriculture.

Some research is going on in our colleges and universities in this field which will have a bearing on the welfare of agriculture and on the lives of farmers. The education of the agricultural student of today is becoming broader. As part of his education he is being prepared not only as an agricultural technician, but also as a citizen and leader in his community. The techniques of education in subject-matter fields are consistently improving, and philanthropic institutions are rendering support to adult education in the field of citizenship.

Dr. Hardin in this book has done a remarkable job as a political scientist in interpreting the politics of agriculture today as he sees it. The reader will have his agreements and disagreements, his reservations and his commendations. But when he finishes he will feel that here is combined both idealism and realism. He will have improved his basis for understanding the problems and processes of agricultural politics in the democratic society.

In addition to farmers and the general public, teachers and extension workers especially, will find this book of inestimable value.

M. L. Wilson,

NATIONAL DIRECTOR OF EXTENSION WORK

PART ONE

THE INTERESTS

CHAPTER I

Politics and Agriculture

I. THE POLITICAL QUESTION

Politics is first nature to the farmer. He used politics to carve out satisfactory land laws and to get homesteads on the public domain. He got the vote and the direct primary. Through politics he went after the railroads and the elevators in Granger legislation. He fought for cheap money. He achieved a far-flung system of research and education for agriculture. Especially in this century, he has piled triumph upon triumph—agricultural credit, advantages for farmers' cooperatives, regulation of markets and commodity exchanges, aids to conservation, rural electrification, rural telephones, and price supports and commodity loans. Indeed, when farmers are not playing politics with and against others, they pursue the art among themselves. The struggle for power within agriculture is something to watch.

But the realization is growing that it is not something to watch merely in amusement or consternation, depending (perhaps) on the state of one's liver. Men live by politics. This rather unhappy truth is borne home to our generation by the state of the world. Yet the drive for power and the problems it raises can be studied domestically as well as among nations. As citizens learn that politics is where one finds it, they begin to ask questions: What makes some people hungry for power? Why do political promises seem undependable compared to business promises? Why don't "good men" go into politics? Why are those who say they have no use for politics often among the most active in seeking favors from government? Who is getting his pockets lined?

This inquisitiveness spells opportunity for political scientists. They can add meaning to the desire for knowledge about politics by shifting the inquiry. How is government organized and by whom? What ultimate ends does it serve and what immediate aims? What means does it employ? How are political decisions made? How do citizens and groups behave politically? What are the political trends? Finally, how do answers to these questions affect the age-old problem of politics: How is power sufficient to the needs to be organized, yet controlled?

Many roads are open to study the political problem. This book examines politics as exhibited by agricultural policy in the United States. Though their numbers are declining in proportion to the total, rural people still account for 40 per cent of our population and farm families themselves one-sixth. Rural America is favorably situated to exploit its political power. Rural and small town people are more heavily represented in the Congress and state legislatures than their numbers warrant. Farmers themselves are organized in a number of powerful groups which are led by men who know how to use influence in high places.

Yet American agriculture is neither a solid block of votes nor a uniform political action group which sets its goals and moves toward them with one mind. Rather, agriculture is internally divided. Farmers are pulled in different directions by partisan allegiance. Sometimes farm organizations oppose each other or are threatened by factionalism. Farm interests organized in the states are often at cross-purposes with similar interests organized nationally. Inter-regional conflicts abound.

Thus one is faced by scores of controversies. Some selection is necessary for orderly analysis. The study of a single phase of agricultural politics—such as soil conservation—will illuminate the whole. What are the dimensions of the soil erosion and conservation problems on private land? [1] How is the problem

1. Conservation programs on public land are not dealt with in this book. See Luther Gulick, *American Forestry Policy*, Duell, Sloan, & Pearce, New York (1951) and Marion Clawson, *Uncle Sam's Acres*, Dodd, Mead & Co., New York (1951).

attacked by public policy? What organized interests are involved in the formulation and administration of conservation programs? What other aspects of agricultural policy are affected by the politics of conservation? Answers to these questions will not only provide a grasp of many issues of agricultural politics but will also throw light on the political question itself.

2. THE SOIL CONSERVATION PHASE

Even a statement of the erosion problem in the United States reveals fundamental disagreements which are significant politically. Who has not been distraught by pictures of ramshackle farm homes sliding into gullies described as monuments to man's abuse of the land—only to be confronted by a contrary interpretation, namely, that the area concerned was subject to accelerated erosion before the white man came? Soil from the great plains darkened the sky of Washington, D. C., while Congress debated the Soil Conservation Bill of 1935. Yet the plains have historically alternated between barrenness and bounty; from the same areas wherein dust storms scandalized the nation in the middle 1930's, bumper wheat crops were produced year after year in the 1940's. Many statements are made of "irreparable damage" to soils; yet state experiment stations have demonstrated that, on some soils and under some conditions, if all the top soil is removed it can be rebuilt and the fertility restored fairly rapidly —although sometimes at considerable cost. Again, the "natural" fertility of soils is sometimes described as a mysterious gift of nature which can only be husbanded, but not improved; contrarily, soil scientists point to tremendous supplementations and improvement of the virgin fertility of some soils.

Experts agree that there is a soil and water management problem of considerable dimensions in the United States, but they differ respecting its magnitude and its analysis. Consider the two estimates below.

THE EROSION PROBLEM IN THE UNITED STATES
(millions of acres)

Charles E. Kellogg[2]		Hugh Hammond Bennett[3]	
Cropland	415		414
Cultivable safely without serious erosion, using present practices	160	Ruined for cultivation and almost ruined	100
Cultivable with best known practices	178	Reduced in fertility ⅒ to ½ by erosion damage	100
Subtract land which should be removed from cultivation for various reasons	77	Erosion menacing land values and continued productivity	100
Add land in plowable brush or timber or needing irrigation or drainage to make cultivable	108		
Total cultivable	466	What remains, relatively undamaged	114

These are eminent men. In 1938 Dr. Bennett was Chief of
the Soil Conservation Service, and Dr. Kellogg was Chief of the
Division of Soil Survey, Bureau of Plant Industry, Soils, and
Agricultural Engineering. Both are agencies of the United
States Department of Agriculture (USDA). In June, 1951,
both men continued to hold the same posts—and, presumably,
the same contrary opinions about the dimensions of the erosion-
control and conservation problem in this country. The disagreement is striking. Dr. Bennett claimed that 100,000,000 acres
were beyond redemption, or virtually so. The only comparable
figure on Dr. Kellogg's side appears to be 77,000,000 acres to
be removed from current cultivation—but part of this acreage
should have been removed only because its cultivation was uneconomic at prices prevailing in 1938. Dr. Bennett finds that
114 million acres remain relatively undamaged and presumably
can be farmed safely with present practices. Dr. Kellogg's comparable figure here is 160 million acres.

But the most important contrast is in the point of view. Dr.

2. Yearbook of Agriculture, *Soils and Men*, USDA, 1938, p. 94.
3. *Ibid.*, p. 592.

Bennett considers the soil our most precious national heritage and observes it wasting away, so that only 114 million acres remain "relatively undamaged." Dr. Kellogg gives an estimate of the amount of cropland in the United States which could be used if the economic need was sufficient. Dr. Bennett's orientation is toward the land which the people are charged to maintain, protect, and preserve. Dr. Kellogg focuses on people and what they have to live with. The two attitudes were further illuminated by book titles. Dr. Kellogg produced *The Soils that Support Us* in 1941, whereupon Dr. Bennett published *This Land We Defend*.[4]

3. UNDERLYING ISSUES

In his celebrated preface to Volume III of the Census of 1880 General Francis A. Walker wrote:

"Down to this time our apparently wasteful culture has, as I have sought to show, been the true economy of the national strength; our apparent abuse of the capital fund of the country has, in fact, effected the highest possible improvement of the public patrimony. Thirty-eight noble states, in an indissoluble union, are the ample justification of this policy. Their schoolhouses and churches, their shops and factories, their roads and bridges, their railways and warehouses, are the fruits of the characteristic American agriculture of the past."

General Walker then argued that, if a policy of exploitation had been in the national interest until 1880, the time was rapidly approaching, if not already at hand, when the nation should give serious consideration to the conservation of its national resources. Yet John D. Black and Maxine Keifer commented in 1948:

"If General Walker had been writing a preface to the Census of 1940, he might have written in precisely the same vein, again saying that the exploitation of the past had been sound national economic policy but that the point has now been reached, and so forth. Con-

---

4. Dr. Kellogg's book was published by Macmillan (New York); Dr. Bennett's (with William C. Pryor) by Longmans, Green and Co., New York (1942).

ceivably some commentator another sixty years from now will be moved to write in the same way." [5]

The quotations suggest that political issues underlie and condition the analyses of conservation policy. Clearly, even within the politics of agriculture, soil conservation cannot be accepted as an overriding policy; for other purposes and problems must be weighed, such as the need for agricultural production, the economic welfare of agriculture in general and of farmers in particular, and the effect of agricultural prosperity or depression on the rest of the economy. Indeed, if we draw the analysis out of narrow concern for agricultural policy, the political question emerges even more sharply. Purposes are numerous, such as providing for national defense, organizing to maintain effective foreign policies, conserving natural resources, providing full employment, harmonizing labor and capital, improving race relations, and spelling out programs which recognize the quest of individuals for security, recognition, and prestige. On each of these matters, advocates of various (and often conflicting) viewpoints are continually urging that the nation accept their complete programs or court destruction. But obviously the nation cannot have all of every proposal at once. The arbitration of conflicting purposes, the compromises reached through negotiation among various advocates, the choice among competing political means—this is the political function.

How this function has been performed with respect to soil conservation policies for private land in the United States is the object of discussion. The first order of business (Part I) is to introduce the actors in this political drama. Field investigators for the House Appropriations Committee reported in 1951:

"The national soil-conservation program as currently administered by the U. S. Department of Agriculture is permeated with duplication, overlap, conflict, and lack of coordination, and what has been aptly described as a state of 'civil war' exists in many areas between the Extension Service, the Agricultural Conservation Program Branch of the Production and Marketing Administration, Soil Conservation Service, and Farmers Home Administration. All of these bureaus,

5. *Future Food and Agricultural Policy*, McGraw-Hill, New York, 1948, pp. 99-100.

with the exception of FHA, are competing for control of this program due to the rising importance of conservation in the national economy—and service to the American farmers suffers. This situation was found to exist in the majority of the States and counties visited." [6]

The following chapters will characterize the colleges of agriculture, including the agricultural extension service and its frequent ally, the farm bureau; the Soil Conservation Service (SCS), and the Production and Marketing Administration (PMA). In the process, the lines of conservation policy will be clarified to prepare the way for the examination in Part II of the efforts to change and redirect that policy. Part III provides political interpretations and offers policy recommendations.

---

6. House *Hearings*, Agricultural Appropriations, fiscal, 1952, Part 1, p. 547, Part 2, p. 688.

CHAPTER II

The Colleges of Agriculture

I. THE COLLEGES AND POLITICS

Administrators of colleges of agriculture [1] scrutinize federal farm programs for effects upon their own interests. They work unceasingly to extend and consolidate their own operations and to counter the threat of competing agencies. In their stand against federal "encroachment," the colleges are sustained by their own strength as established institutions, by their collective power in their Association, by political alliances (especially with the Farm Bureau), and by popular attitudes which hold that educational institutions should be free of national political control.

The colleges have urged decentralization of public programs for agriculture. They have advocated reliance upon research

1. The Morrill Act of 1862 stimulated the establishment of land-grant colleges and universities which now exist in all states and territories. Each such institution has its college of agriculture, which is commonly divided into resident teaching, research (the experiment station), and agricultural extension. Research and extension are important cooperative federal-state activities. Since the Hatch Act (1887) for research and the Smith-Lever Act (1914) for extension, a number of federal laws have authorized federal appropriations for grants-in-aid for these activities. The state experiment stations currently receive some $12,000,000 annually in federal grants; since moneys from state and other sources (primarily, state appropriations) provide $4 for every federal $1, the total budget of all state and territorial stations is in the neighborhood of $60,000,000. The corresponding annual budget for agricultural extension in the states is now approximately $76,000,000, of which about 43 per cent is provided by the federal government.

and education rather than "action" programs—such as price supports and production control. They have also represented conservatism. That is, colleges generally have been reluctant to propose new public policies to ameliorate farm problems; they have preferred to "wait and see," to hope that things would right themselves, and to advocate traditional approaches.

What of the political outlook of college administrators—the presidents, deans, and directors of extension or research? Their rise to eminence has schooled them in the "politics of relationships"—how to deal with state legislatures and interest groups; how to play an interminable poker game with the United States Department of Agriculture (USDA) and its agencies. Yet college administrators often lack a comprehension of the broader political issues of an industrial society and the stresses and strains which these issues impose upon political institutions. Many of them are ill-equipped by training, background, or disposition to appreciate the task of politicians who must reconcile the drive for security with the need for maintaining economic mobility; who must mediate the demands of powerful groups; who must shape foreign policies in accordance with the new distribution of power among nations; and who must weigh defense requirements against home consumption and define policies to deal with both deflation and inflation. Confident in their own rectitude, college administrators are prone to view contrary actions of others—e.g., of the Secretary of the USDA— as motivated only by the crassest political motives.

2. CONFLICT OVER POLICY ORIGINS

Before considering the college position on soil conservation policy, some attention must be paid to the controversy over the historical contributions of colleges in this area. In 1929, H. H. Bennett (later to become Chief of the Soil Conservation Service—SCS) declared that the recently established Spur Branch of the Texas experiment station "is the first real soil erosion station that has been established in the history of the world." [2]

---

2. House *Hearings*, Agric. Approp., fiscal 1930, p. 315.

But Loomis Havemeyer wrote that numerous experiment stations had done research on soil erosion.[3]

The same controversy appears regarding the contributions of agricultural Extension Services. H. H. Bennett told the Subcommittee on Agricultural Appropriations of the House of Representatives:

"You may be interested in knowing it was in this committee, as constituted in 1938 [sic., 1928] that the whole soil conservation program in the United States had its beginning, as I see it." [4]

But Extension personnel tell a different story. Director H. C. Sanders (Louisiana) described his efforts (which, as he showed, were by no means unique) in the interests of soil conservation, beginning in 1923 with his service as an agricultural agent in Bienville Parish.[5] A Pennsylvania Extension Bulletin of 1939 fails to mention the SCS but asserts that as early as 1896 some Pennsylvania farms were practicing strip-cropping "by methods more exacting than those recommended in this publication." [6] S. H. McCrory, Chief of the Bureau of Agricultural Engineering of the USDA, declared that between 1915 and 1932 some 18,000,000 acres of land on some 600,000 farms had been terraced through the efforts of state Extension Services.[7]

The colleges feel, with considerable justice, that SCS claims a priority in soil conservation that it does not deserve.[8] But all

---

3. *Conservation of Our Natural Resources*, Macmillan, New York, 1930, p. 376. This is a revision and re-edition of C. H. Van Hise's classic work first published in 1910 by Macmillan.

4. House *Hearings*, Agric. Approp., fiscal 1950, Part 2, p. 58.

5. Testimony before the House Committee on Agriculture, March 3, 1948 (mimeo.).

6. "How to Reduce Soil Erosion Losses by Strip-Farming," Pennsylvania Extension Service Series No. 212, January, 1939.

7. House *Hearings*, Agric. Approp., fiscal 1934, p. 981.

8. The following are illustrative and not exhaustive. H. W. Wiley reported on the control of soil washing in 1894. ("The Conservation of the Fertility of the Soil," *Report* of the National Conservation Commission, Senate Doc., No. 676, 60th Cong., 2d Sess. [1909], Vol. III, pp. 269, 270.) The Tennessee and Arkansas experiment stations published bulletins on soil washing in 1890 and 1894, respectively. (A. F. Gustafson, *et al.*, *Conservation in the United States*, Comstock Publishing Co., Ithaca [New York], 1949, p. 80.) Successful experimentation in controlling erosion on range land through regulated grazing and the use of engineering methods was

must agree that erosion research and especially the application of soil conservation practices have greatly accelerated since the establishment of federal programs in the 1930's.

3. COLLECTIVE POLITICAL ACTION

The colleges created a joint organization in 1887, now known as the Association of Land-Grant Colleges and Universities. In 1890 Congressman Caruth described it as "the only lobby" he had seen during the session. It had "haunted the corridors of the Capitol, . . . stood sentinel at the doors of the Committee on Education, . . . even interrupted the solemn deliberations of that body by imprudent and impudent communications." Its members had buzzed in the ears of solons.[9] The honorable Congressman seems unduly sensitive to pressure from the colleges during a year which saw passage of the Sherman Silver Purchase Bill, the McKinley tariff, and the Disability Pension Act. Yet his remarks correctly recognize that the Association is a political interest group.

The Association has ordinarily confined its political activities to the protection of existing college functions, the acquisition of new functions, and the increase of appropriations. Its hesitation to take positions upon controversial issues is illustrated by its relationship to conservation policy. The annual *Proceedings* of the Association reveal few references to conservation policy over the years. In 1891 a brief resolution requested the Secretary of

---

discussed in 1901, with reference to Arizona. (R. H. Forbes in 15 *Proceedings* of the Association of American Agricultural Colleges and Experiment Stations, pp. 85-87 [1901]. [Subsequently, the Association of Land-Grant Colleges and Universities; future citations will be to *Proceedings*.]) Field work was begun by the Illinois agricultural experiment station in 1907, results of the first ten years' work being published in Illinois Bulletin No. 207 (1917). Professor M. F. Miller and members of the Missouri experiment station began "pioneer soil-erosion control and specific soil- and water-loss measurements . . . in 1917." (Gustafson, *et al.*, *op. cit.*, p. 122. In 1923 Missouri published its results, "Erosion and Surface Run-off under Different Soil Conditions," Research Bulletin 63. Cf. H. H. Bennett, *Soil Conservation*, p. vii.) The California experiment station built 700 check dams in the San Demas area between 1915–1932. (House *Hearings*, Agric. Approp., fiscal 1935, p. 989.)

9. V. O. Key, Jr., *The Administration of Federal Grants to States*, Public Administration Service, Chicago (1937), p. 180.

Agriculture to work for the withdrawal of forest lands from settlement, and ten years later R. H. Forbes read a paper which advocated social control of the western range.[10] Personal positions in favor of conservation policy were stated in the Section of Agriculture and Chemistry in 1903, but the Association itself took no action.[11] In 1905, E. B. Vorhees noted the conservation problem in his presidential address, and the Section on Experiment Station Work discussed soil erosion as related to soil fertility.[12]

In 1908, with the Roosevelt-Pinchot conservation movement in full swing, the Association created a committee to cooperate with the Committee on Conservation of National Resources.[13] The committee never made a report. In 1909 L. G. Carpenter's address, "The Conservation of Our Natural Resources," deprecated the current alarms. Research and private initiative would solve the problem; if a timber shortage occurred, hundreds of thousands of persons would begin growing timber.[14] His speech was the closest approach to a position by the Association on the conservation movement then agitating the country. Subsequent references are few and scattered. In 1925, President F. D. Farrell of Kansas State College declared: [15]

". . . it seems clear that relatively few of the land-grant institutions have definitely developed courses in conservation as such, and that perhaps even fewer of these are endeavoring to build up among . . . their students, who shortly will be leaders of thought and action, a sound and public-spirited attitude toward . . . conservation."

After the coming of the New Deal's national agricultural programs, frequent discussions occurred in Association meetings respecting the relationship of colleges of agriculture to adminis-

---

10. 15 *Proceedings*, pp. 85-87.
11. 17 *Proceedings*, pp. 95-145.
12. 19 *Proceedings*, pp. 33, 135 ff.
13. 22 *Proceedings*, p. 28.
14. 24 *Proceedings*, pp. 32-34.
15. 39 *Proceedings*, pp. 114 ff. Mr. Farrell noted that there was some research and teaching on the subject. Cf. the table of contents, Section on Engineering, in *Proceedings* for 1916 and 1917; in 1919, Eugene Davenport's address, "Wanted: A National Policy for Agriculture," contained a brief reference to soil conservation.

tration of the new action programs. The colleges of agriculture came close to political success in securing the transfer of conservation administration to the states about 1938, only to experience a reversal by Secretary Wallace in consequence of dramatic appeals by representatives of the Soil Conservation Service.[16] Generally the colleges were more notable for making resounding statements on the subject than for effective political action.

In the 1940's, the Association became more active in agricultural policy matters. The adoption of a new constitution in 1945 provided for more independent action by the colleges of agriculture *vis-à-vis* Washington. The Association created a Committee on Post-war Agricultural Policy in 1943 (later continued as a Committee on Agricultural Policy) whose report, *Postwar Agricultural Policy* (1944), examined the entire range of agricultural and related policies and made recommendations respecting both content and administration. The position was carefully maintained that the report was the responsibility of the committee alone and not of the Association; nevertheless, the report was not merely published for the edification of the nation, as its predecessors had been.[17] It was widely circulated so that by 1945 some 120,000 copies had been distributed; more important, representatives of the committee appeared before Congressional committees and other groups to explain and defend the report.

The report of 1944 recommended that the administration of agricultural conservation programs be decentralized to the colleges of agriculture. It declared:

"Soil conservation is not a thing apart, but rather must be considered in relation to the great variety of farm operations and practices which make for efficient production. Moreover, it must be related to the economic and social factors affecting land use; for example, the indirect causes of soil exploitation include insecurity of tenure, farming of submarginal land, overindebtedness, fluctuation in farm income, and lack of knowledge. Efforts to promote conservation without alleviating these basic causes of land exploitation may be largely wasted."

16. Cf. chap. vi, sec. 1, below.
17. In 1927 and 1931; see the relevant *Proceedings*.

In 1948 two bills were introduced in Congress. Each was directed toward the radical reorganization of administration of public soil conservation and related programs.[18] Senator Aiken's measure would have decentralized administration in a manner highly satisfactory to the colleges of agriculture. Congressman Hope's Bill proposed to consolidate administration of conservation and related programs largely in the Soil Conservation Service as the administrator of a new "National Land Policy." In view of their contradictory provisions, it is understandable that neither bill could pass the 80th Congress.

Internal evidence shows rather conclusively that the Hope Bill was written by the Soil Conservation Service; while the evidence is not equally conclusive, the inference is permissible that the conservation provisions of Title 1 of the Aiken Bill were inspired by colleges of agriculture. The Association of Land-Grant Colleges had taken a vigorous states' rights position in its 1947 meeting. A committee chaired by President Hannah of Michigan State College met with Extension Directors and others in the four extension regions. Testimony was prepared which distinguished "action" programs from agricultural research and education, and argued that the latter should be administered by colleges of agriculture, financed, in part, by federal grants-in-aid. Conservation programs were high on the list which the colleges proposed to take over.[19]

On the whole, the colleges were as well pleased with the Aiken Bill as they were dissatisfied with the proposals of Congressman Hope. Professor H. C. M. Case, head of the Department of Agricultural Economics, University of Illinois, was Senator Aiken's chief adviser. It is reasonable to assume that the colleges had an available channel for their views in the person of Professor Case.[20]

---

18. Cf. the writer's "Current Proposals . . .," *JFE*, November, 1948.

19. President Hannah and Extension Director Sanders (Louisiana) presented the college view to the House Committee on Agriculture, in March, 1948; and President Friley of Iowa State College testified before the Senate Committee in April.

20. If it were possible to compare the specific proposals made by Extension Directors in their regional meetings with the clauses of the Aiken Bill, something more precise might be said on this matter. Nothing reprehensible,

The colleges continued to be influential in the political process. The Task Force on Agriculture of the Hoover Commission was strongly representative of the colleges and its report represented the college position.[21] In 1950 members of the Task Force on Agriculture were apparently instrumental in the rejection by the Senate of President Truman's reorganization plan for agriculture.[22] On February 16, 1951, however, Secretary Brannan's reorganization of the USDA called forth college opposition.[23]

4. THE POSITION OF THE COLLEGES OF AGRICULTURE

In testifying before the House Committee on Agriculture (January 13, 1948), representatives of the Association of Land-Grant Colleges and Universities defined "action" programs as making use of the police power, the power to tax, or the power of eminent domain. Agricultural credit, grants-in-aid, and farm subsidies were also called action programs. The college representatives did not want to administer these; but they claimed a dominant role in administering research, demonstration, and education. The original Soil Conservation Service [24] operations had employed Civilian Conservation Corps camps and had provided grants-in-aid of labor, machinery, and planting materials to farmers. When the war came, unemployment disappeared, the CCC camps were closed, and the SCS became more and more an educational program. But education (it was argued) had been the historic field of the colleges. A recommendation was made that the SCS program be operated through the state agencies, i.e., the agricultural Extension Services, insofar as educational, informational, and demonstrational work is involved, including the extension of technical assistance to farmers.

But the Association spokesmen are also on record in opposi-

---

here or elsewhere, is implied in suggesting that the organized influence of public agencies is brought to bear upon the content of proposed legislation.

21. See below, chap. xii.
22. *Ibid.*
23. See below, chap. xiii.
24. The SCS program is the subject of chaps. iv-vi, below.

tion to the rival program of SCS in the USDA, namely, the
Agricultural Conservation Program (ACP) of the Production
and Marketing Administration.[25] Thus the Committee on Agricultural Policy of the Association prepared responses to questions posed by Congressman Clifford Hope. Noting the Committee's previous recommendation scrupulously to avoid using
conservation as a disguise for making payments to farmers to
increase their incomes, Mr. Hope asked under what circumstances would the committee of the Association recommend payments for soil conservation practices.

The committee held that payments for conservation practices
should be made only if a large element of public interest is
involved, if the practice is likely to yield returns only after a
considerable lapse of time, if the practices are not such as
farmers are likely to carry out themselves without assistance, if
the total annual payments for given farms are limited, and if
payments do not exceed one-half the cost of application. The Association's policy committee was also concerned that administration of the conservation payment program should be established
on a state and local basis with federal inspection, auditing, and
approval when federal funds are involved. Any system of payments should be supplementary to a vigorous program of coordinated research and education. In short, the scope of research
and educational work as developed in the land-grant colleges
should be protected.[26]

A similar viewpoint was urged by Noble Clark, Director of
the Wisconsin Experiment Station and Chairman of the Association's committee, who criticized the competition between
governmental agencies. "Even more inexcusable has been the
policy of using the good name of soil conservation as a false
front for other activities which would have a hard time to win
support on their own." Many people are cynical at the sight
of hundreds of millions of dollars spent under the guise of soil
conservation but largely ineffectively. With agricultural incomes
the highest in history, millions of dollars have been paid farmers

---

25. The PMA program is discussed in chaps. vii-ix, below.
26. House *Hearings*, "Long-Range Agricultural Policy," 80th Cong., 1st
Sess., Part 15, pp. 1789-90.

for simply running a mowing machine over their pastures. States with the most level land and the highest farm incomes have had the largest share of government appropriations for agricultural conservation. Note that these serious charges came from Wisconsin, where friction between the AAA—or its successor, the PMA—and the land-grant college has been extreme at times.[27]

Another important land-grant college figure, Milton Eisenhower, President of Kansas State College,[28] analyzed the subject "Conservation and Public Policy" on December 15, 1947. Mr. Eisenhower had high praise for SCS. Why did this scientifically sound program fail to progress rapidly? Because of our second effort at conservation, namely, the Agricultural Conservation Program (ACP) of PMA. Whereas the SCS program represented an honest effort on the part of public policy-makers, the ACP program used conservation as a disguise of production control and price supporting legislation. "The results were hideously unsatisfactory." "I would say that we have achieved perhaps ten cents worth of conservation for each dollar spent in the program—though the percentage is probably declining because we continue to pay for the same practices on the same farms year after year."

Secretary Clinton P. Anderson immediately answered President Eisenhower. Noting the differences between the dust bowl of the 1930's and the bountiful wheat harvests of recent years, Mr. Anderson asserted that production was aided by conservation practices, and praised the farmer committee system which has carried the conservation program to the farmers. He cited the application of agricultural limestone, 1.5 million tons in 1933, increasing to 28.9 million tons in 1946, and added that the phosphate story was pretty much the same. The country had really received at least a dollar for every ten cents that it put into the agricultural conservation program.

---

27. House *Hearings, ibid.,* Part 3, pp. 399 ff. For friction between AAA and Extension in Wisconsin, see Ernst Kneisel, *Administrative Politics in the AAA,* Unpublished Honors thesis, Harvard University (1947).

28. Mr. Eisenhower became President of Pennsylvania State College in 1950.

5. THE AGRICULTURAL EXTENSION SERVICE

Examination of the position of the colleges in terms of the interests which they are attempting to protect requires a closer consideration of the Extension Service [29]—a cooperative endeavor between the USDA and the land-grant colleges with more man power and finances than any other agency of adult education in the United States. Through its agricultural workers it reaches directly to farmers; through home demonstration personnel it serves farm women; and in its 4-H and rural youth programs, it offers many advantages to rural children and young people.

After the passage of the Smith-Lever Act in 1914, providing the initial federal grants-in-aid for Extension, and stimulated by the requirements of the first World War, the Extension Service grew rapidly in numbers, attained financial support, developed a powerful political ally in the Farm Bureau, and acquired considerable prestige. Until the New Deal agricultural agencies, Extension was the primary channel for all governmental activities which reach farmers. But USDA action agencies rapidly developed line administration reaching from Washington to the farmer, and political friction began.

The Extension Service is organized in a bureau of the USDA and the cooperating services of the several states. The federal Extension Service scrutinizes state programs and plans of work to insure that federal grants-in-aid are spent according to Congressional stipulations. It provides information for the state Extension Services, and maintains a small staff of subject-matter specialists to assist the state services in planning and evaluating their work. The state Extension Services employ staffs of specialists to assist the work in the counties. The typical operation is through state county agent and home demonstration leaders, who work through district agents (each in charge of several counties), to serve the county staffs which include the county

---

29. Cf. John M. Gaus and Leon A. Wolcott, *Public Administration and the United States Department of Agriculture*, Public Administration Service, Chicago (1940) index, and Gladys Baker, *The County Agent*, University of Chicago Press, (1939).

agricultural agent, frequently a home demonstration agent, and (increasingly) an agent for 4-H Clubs.

Decentralization is the key to the program. Washington exercises few sanctions upon the states; college officials, who are extremely sensitive to any threat of federal "encroachment," are all but unanimous in maintaining that no federal domination has ever been involved in the administration of federal grants-in-aid for extension. At the same time (although this generalization obscures interesting variations in a few states), the county staffs are rather independent of the state Extension Services. This independence derives from the typical selection of county agents by county governing boards and also from the fact that counties help defray expenses. To be sure, such agents must meet statutory qualifications and must be approved by state Extension Directors (and also, although this is almost wholly formal, by the Secretary of Agriculture at Washington). Yet, once he has his position, the county agent's problem in retaining it is largely to satisfy his local constituents, a process which sometimes includes the maintenance of a farm organization to sponsor extension work, as required by state law.[30]

6. EXTENSION'S RESPONSE TO FEDERAL PROGRAMS

In many states the Extension Service has fought the SCS and the Agricultural Conservation Program of PMA, but the competition of these two agencies and especially of SCS has also stimulated state Extension Services to develop alternative programs. The best known illustration is the TVA-college unit farm demonstration and area demonstration programs in the Tennessee Valley. Rallying around these programs, the TVA and the seven valley colleges were rather effective in limiting the entrance of SCS into the Valley until 1950-1951.[31]

Elsewhere, state Extension Services have been developing farm and home programs and community planning programs.

---

30. See Chapter iii, below.

31. See Norman Wengert, *TVA and Agriculture: A Study in Regional Decentralization,* to be published by the University of Tennessee Press; and Philip Selznick, *TVA and the Grass Roots,* University of California Press, (1948).

The "balanced farming" approach developed by the College of Agriculture of the University of Missouri is the best example.[32] The Missouri Extension Service has established a state advisory committee of 20, elected by the sponsoring county organizations which (under the law of 1943) are required for the maintenance of county extension programs in that state.[33] This advisory committee endorsed the balanced farming program. The idea was to establish associations or rings of 50 farmers, each of whom would pay $50 to provide a sum which would be matched by local businessmen and the state Extension Service. A special assistant agent would then be employed to develop balanced farm plans on these farms—plans which would help the farmers directly concerned and would also serve as demonstrations to their neighbors. Two balanced farming rings were begun in 1946; by 1949, some 38 rings were in action with 1746 farm families as members.

The balanced farming approach differs from the conservation planning of the SCS [34] in being oriented immediately toward the improvement of farm family living, with soil conservation as an incidental purpose. The program has been criticized as providing special services to individual farmers, especially more well-to-do farmers.* It has been charged with failing

---

32. Cf. "Balanced Farming in Missouri," Extension Service Circular No. 537 (1946) of the Missouri College of Agriculture. Other states have studied the Missouri development with a view to adapting it; cf. "Balanced Farming and Family Living in Kansas," an undated leaflet of the Kansas Agricultural Extension Service, Manhattan.

33. The Missouri county Extension programs are sponsored by 58 Farm Bureaus, 31 county Extension associations, 23 Missouri Farmers Associations, one Grange, and one soil improvement association.

34. See below, chap. iv.

* The balanced farming program may be much more effective in reaching low-income farmers if full use is made of payments available in the Agricultural Conservation Program of the Production and Marketing Administration (ACP of PMA; chap. vii, below). Charles E. Kellogg visited a number of low-income farms in balanced farming rings in Missouri where both his analysis and the opinion of the farmer indicated that ACP payments had accounted for much of the difference between success and failure of balanced farming, especially in the first three or four years. On all such farms, the time was approaching or at hand when such payments could be eliminated—the farms were "over the hump." The possible significance is difficult to exaggerate. Both Extension and ACP are criticized (sometimes by their own personnel) for failing to reach low-income farms effectively. The

to include the homemaker sufficiently, and thus to become a model of farm *and home* planning. The $50 fee is considered perhaps too high; and reduction to $25 has been contemplated, a move that would be combined with the creation of larger associations or rings. The method of working intensively with a small number of farmers has not stimulated the spread of better farm management in the interest of improved farm family living as much as desired. By working intensively with smaller groups of farmers but emphasizing more the balanced farms as demonstrations, the program may be improved. The Missouri model has not spread rapidly to other states. One difficulty encountered by extension nearly everywhere in developing farm and home planning programs lies in the coordination of extension subject matter specialists, each of whom is understandably anxious to push his own line. Finally, the program is adaptable to mixed farming areas, where various combinations of enterprises are typical; but it is not well adapted to areas of highly commercialized, one-crop farming, e.g., in the wheat area of western Kansas.

All these criticisms notwithstanding, the balanced farm program constitutes a constructive effort by Extension to develop a workable alternative to the approach of the Soil Conservation Service. If he applauds extension workers who have produced this alternative, the observer must acknowledge that they were prodded into inventiveness by the SCS. In the welter of criticism of "bureaucratic duplication and overlapping," it is well to note that administrative competition may have its uses.

Missouri experience may indicate that *both together may do what each separately may fail to accomplish.* The writer believes, however, that neither Missouri Extension nor the PMA is fully conscious of these possibilities—the inertia of institutionalized programs is great, here as elsewhere! But if Dr. Kellogg's analysis could become the basis of an exploratory program by Extension and PMA, the writer would withdraw his recommendation to eliminate PMA-ACP payments—at least pending a thorough test to see whether such payments could be shifted to those who really need them and could be made in a manner that would really contribute to the development of sound and economically-rewarding farming systems on low-income farms. (Cf. Charles M. Hardin, "The Politics of Conservation: An Illustration," *Journal of Politics*, Nov., 1951, p. 478.)

7. EMERGENT ISSUES

So the colleges of agriculture and their allies are deeply in politics, as examination of the college position on soil conservation programs shows. More is involved than the nature, objectives, and administrative methods of soil conservation programs. Agricultural price policy is also affected. The relationship of public agencies and private groups is brought out. The degree of emphasis placed upon the "action" approach as against the approach of research and education is at stake. The question is raised of centralized administration (which may then be decentralized) as against political decentralization.[35]

But another development demands attention even while one is pausing to point out the political ramifications that are disclosed by the analysis of issues in one field of public policy. That development is the continuous emergence of political issues. If political interpretation is ever to be written, it must snip off the strands and crystallize the account. But in the real world, the old strands continue and new ones appear. Thus Congressman Whitten, who occupies the strategic position of Chairman of the Subcommittee on Agricultural Appropriations, is keenly aware that the effective coordination of national programs is made difficult by the independence of the state Extension Services. He had a field study of conservation (and related) administration in 48 counties in 13 states (1950). The report of the study indicated (a) that state Extension Services cannot withdraw from conservation administration but (b) that the USDA exercizes virtually no control over the state Services in the conduct of their affairs. Mr. Whitten's observations on this subject called forth an explanation by federal Extension Director M. L. Wilson of the "partnership" nature of Extension work. Mr. Whitten acknowledged the many advantages of the partnership but observed that "we are in the midst of an emergency." Could not the USDA develop memoranda of understandings with state Extension Services? If so,

_____
35. Cf. G. C. S. Benson, *The New Centralization*, Farrar and Rinehart, New York (1941), p. 9.

". . . the Extension Service would be obligated to carry it out just as much as if the Department had a right to direct them to do that, would it not?"

When Director Wilson agreed that if the colleges accepted the memoranda they would be obligated to carry them out, Mr. Whitten said:

"It strikes me that such a plan certainly should be worked out as quickly as possible. A plan should be worked up by the Department of Agriculture, which is charged with the primary duty, and there should be a conference with the Extension people as to what part they should play in it. By a memorandum of understanding it strikes me that we might resolve this so that you could know exactly what to count on, instead of setting up a board and merely inviting the Extension Service to participate." [36]

Reference to the board on which the Extension Service is invited to participate can be clarified by examining Secretary Brannan's memorandum No. 1278, February 16, 1951.[37] Mr. Whitten's activities in stimulating the issuance of this memorandum as well as the statement just quoted provide striking evidence of the influence which a strategically-located Congressman may have upon administration. But the larger significance of his statement lies in what it implies for the cooperative federal-state relationship which has hitherto characterized the Extension Service. The essence of this experience has been agreement; but this has implied that if agreement cannot be reached, the state Extension Services have been free to go their own way, subject to the rather general limitations upon the expenditures of federal moneys contained in grant-in-aid statutes. If the politics of conservation produces a situation in which the state Extension Services are given the alternatives either of agreeing to "a plan worked up by the Department of Agriculture" or forfeiting federal funds, a sharp change in federal-state relationships in agriculture will have occurred. If this happens, college folk and their allies should recognize that the impetus has come from Congress and not (or at least, not directly) from "power-hungry bureaucrats in the Department of Agriculture."

36. House *Hearings*, Agric. Approp., fiscal 1952, Part 2, p. 731.
37. See below, chap. xiv.

Meanwhile, a new challenge emerged from the administration. In June, 1951, Secretary Brannan asked for a Family Farm Policy Review which would be conducted by the state and county agricultural mobilization committees.[38] The purpose was to ascertain the reactions of farmers on the question whether agricultural policies are adequately serving the family farm. Many college and farm bureau leaders concluded at once that the Review had two purposes, first, to report that farmers generally favored USDA programs, and, second, to provide the Democratic party and especially Secretary Brannan with a political issue for 1952. Whatever the upshot of the Review, it serves notice on the analyst that at whatever point he chooses to close the chapter for purposes of interpretation, he must concede that the political story itself continues to unfold.

---

38. Cf. *The Family Farm's Future*, USDA, PA 168, June, 1951, the "Family Farm Policy Review," Mimeo., USDA, June, 1951, and "Brannan Poll Finds Farm Opinion Split," New York *Times*, Oct. 14, 1951. The mobilization committees were established by Secretary Brannan's memorandum, No. 1279, Feb. 16, 1951. *Hearings*, S. 1149, 82nd Cong., 1st Sess., pp. 423 ff.

CHAPTER III

Extension and the Farm Bureau

1. THE POLICY ISSUE

"Why break up a good team?" inquired Edward A. O'Neal of the assembled county agents, and added: "I used to fight your battles in Washington when you didn't have another damned fool to fight them for you." If this was the voice of the American Farm Bureau Federation, President James Patton of the National Farmers Union has strongly criticized the Extension-Farm Bureau alliance. His address of 1943 to the National Association of County Agents bore the title, "Whose Extension Service?" Albert Goss of the Grange declared in his annual Master's address in 1945:

"The nation can well afford to support a widely expanded Extension Service, but before this is done, positive steps should be taken to divorce it from private control, and to insure that it serves farmers in accordance with their need rather than their financial support, or their affiliation with any farm organization."

In a political analysis of the major issues in agriculture, one irrepressible question is: Who formulates policy and controls its administration? The colleges of agriculture want federal policy for research and education (broadly conceived) devolved into their hands. They want to control many of the roads by which the USDA reaches the farmer. The Farm Bureau actively supports the college position. Such decentralization would strengthen the colleges and the Farm Bureau and would weaken the organizations and agencies opposed to them. Do these consequences imply that any major inquiry into farm politics and agricultural administration include an analysis of Extension-Farm Bureau relationships? The customary answer is: No![1] But the writer's position is that the question cannot be omitted.

2. LEGAL TIES AND INFORMAL UNDERSTANDINGS

The American Farm Bureau Federation is composed of Farm Bureaus in 47 states and Puerto Rico.[2] If a substantial number of the 1,500,000 members are businessmen, the great bulk are farmers. Since memberships are one to a family (except in New York), the number of individuals in the Farm Bureau is much greater than even this impressive figure indicates. The American Farm Bureau Federation has become the most important influence in agriculture outside of the United States Department of Agriculture itself [3]—and it has done so with the cooperation and assistance of many state agricultural Extension Services.

In 1951, the Extension-Farm Bureau alliance rested (in part, at least) on state laws in Arizona, Connecticut, Kentucky, Illinois, Iowa, Maine, Minnesota, Missouri, New Jersey, New York, and West Virginia.[4] But state laws are unnecessary for

1. See chapters xi, xii, and xiii below.
2. Only Rhode Island is without a state Farm Bureau.
3. Charles M. Hardin, "The Politics of Agriculture," *Journal of Farm Economics*, Nov., 1950. "The Farm Bureau," *Fortune*, June, 1944.
4. The Iowa statute conditions county agricultural extension organizations upon the formation of county agricultural associations with at least 200 bona fide farmers who pay $1,000 annually in dues toward the program. The county board of commissioners is directed to "appropriate to such organization" a sum double the amount provided by dues up to $3,000 for counties with less than 25,000 population and up to $5,000 for larger counties. The Illinois law permits appropriations to similar associations. In West Virginia, creation of county Farm Bureaus with at least 150 members is authorized. Seven state laws name the county Farm Bureau as the Extension organization; but those in Michigan and New Mexico are permissive and unused. A Kentucky law mentions the Farm Bureau but is permissive. Six state laws mention or require a sponsoring organization but do not specify Farm Bureaus. Many differences exist among these states. For example, there was no

intimate association between Extension and the Farm Bureau, as the situation in Alabama, Arkansas, Mississippi, Tennessee, Kansas, Michigan, Ohio, California, and Utah indicates. How did the alliance come about?

The movement to carry programs of colleges of agriculture to farmers through county agents stimulated the development of cooperating associations of farmers. In reaching thousands of farmers in a county, nearly every agricultural administrative agency works through councils, committees, organizations, or cooperatives. In the early years of the county agent movement, federal financial assistance was not firmly established. A sponsoring group could facilitate administration, add prestige, provide financial assistance, and promote the program before the county boards and (later) state legislatures.

Farm Bureaus began to emerge as county sponsoring associations for Extension programs in the North.[5] States began to authorize county appropriations for such programs if farmers formed associations and made financial contributions. The Smith-Lever Act of 1914 provided the first federal grants-in-aid

state Farm Bureau in Maine until September, 1951. In New Jersey, county boards of agriculture (established by law in 1887) sponsor extension work; 19 such boards are affiliated in the N. J. Farm Bureau and, through it, with the American Farm Bureau Federation. Missouri county Extension programs are sponsored by 58 Farm Bureaus, 31 county Extension associations, one Grange, 23 Missouri Farmers' Associations, and one soil improvement association.

An index of the relationship appears in that in 1947-48, 376 counties in 10 states appropriated funds to county Farm Bureaus—317 of these were in Iowa, Kansas, Missouri, and New York. In 559 counties in 14 states, the Farm Bureau either recommended or approved extension budgets. 446 of these were in Iowa, Kansas, Missouri, New York, and West Virginia. The other counties were in Connecticut, Maine, New Hampshire, Vermont, and Rhode Island in New England, plus Arizona and Nebraska.

Much of this material is drawn from H. W. Gilbertson, "Extension-Farm Bureau Relationships—1948," Extension Service, USDA (1949) mimeo. (Referred to as the Gilbertson Report.) See also Gladys Baker, *The County Agent*, Univ. of Chicago Press (1939) and O. M. Kile, *The Farm Bureau Movement*, Macmillan (New York) 1921; articles in *Farm Policy Forum*, Jan., 1952.

5. In Broome County, New York, in 1911, Agricultural Agent John H. Barron was financed jointly by the USDA, the Chamber of Commerce, and the Lackawanna Railroad. He was to work closely with the agricultural committee of the chamber of commerce. The "new information bureau and service was called the 'Farm Bureau.'" The Gilbertson Report, p. 4.

for agricultural extension work but required that federal grants
be matched by contributions from state or local governments—or
from individuals.[6] Soon Farm Bureaus were invited to meet in
state agricultural conferences with county agents. Then state
federations of Farm Bureaus were formed (Missouri, 1915; Illinois, 1916; etc.). World War I greatly expanded both Extension and its affiliate. By 1918, 732 Farm Bureaus in 29 states
had 318,000 members. The American Farm Bureau Federation
was created in 1920. The following year, 46 state Farm Bureaus
had 967,279 members.

Meanwhile, the Farm Bureau was changing. Impressed by
the role of government in the War and then motivated by the
1920-21 depression, many farm leaders favored joint political
and economic action. The new AFBF and state Farm Bureaus
were well-designed to influence government; state and local
Farm Bureaus were equally adapted to develop farm cooperatives. The federal Extension Service, which had assiduously
promoted Farm Bureaus even to the disparagement of other
farm organizations, suddenly found that its partner in advancing
adult education had unforseen potentialities. Farm Bureau entrance into politics and business placed its association with Extension in a very different light. The disillusion of some Extension personnel at the time still echoed in unprintable epithets
as they recalled the matter twenty years later.

3. PROS AND CONS

After the American Farm Bureau Federation was formed and
a number of state Farm Bureaus acquired both business and
political functions, the True-Howard Agreement was formulated to define relationships between Extension and the Farm
Bureau.[7] It declared:

6. "In 1919," says Gilbertson, "about one-fifth of the cost of carrying on
Extension work in the 33 Northern and Western States was contributed
from membership dues." But only some 6 per cent of total Extension expenditures were contributed from similar sources in the 1920's. By 1947-48, this
figure had fallen to 2.6 per cent.

7. The principals were chief of the States Relations Service of the USDA
and President of the American Farm Bureau Federation. Subsequent directives of Secretaries of Agriculture have repeated the proscriptions in the
agreement.

"The county agents will aid the farming people in a broad way with reference to problems of production, marketing, and formation of farm bureaus and other cooperative organizations, but will not themselves organize farm bureaus or similar organizations, conduct membership campaigns, solicit memberships, receive dues, handle farm bureau funds, edit and manage the farm bureau publications, manage or take part in other farm bureau activities which are outside their duties as Extension agents."

Many Extension and Farm Bureau spokesmen hold that this agreement has been strictly maintained. Farmers Union and Grange leaders say that it has been violated in letter and spirit.

The most vigorous and persistent criticism has come from the National Farmers Union which has published facsimiles of letters (signed by Extension personnel and mailed in the "penalty envelope") that appear to be infractions of the True-Howard Agreement.[8] The Union charges that Extension has aided Farm Bureau membership drives.[9] Extension has been accused of employing the AAA program to build Farm Bureau membership.[10] Farmers have been led to believe that Farm Bureau provides them with services which are paid for by the public.[11] Extension has favored Farm Bureau business services over those offered by other farm organizations and private firms.[12] The Farm Bureau-Extension relationship is also declared to result in discrimination against farmers who are not Bureau members.[13]

In 1948 a committee of the Land Grant Colleges and the

8. See the *National Union Farmer*, especially for September 15, 1943, and *Hearings*, S. 1251, 80th Cong., 1st Sess., pp. 385 ff.

9. This material is largely drawn from mimeographed statements of Farmers Union testimony on the Granger Bill, H. R. 3222, 81st Cong., 2nd Sess. (1950). NFU Headquarters, 3501 E. 46th Avenue, Denver, Colorado. See statements of J. Lewis Henderson and Chester A. Graham.

10. Statement of Henderson and E. T. Fortune, President of the Kansas Farmers Union (cf. n. 9). Compare the assertions of John Boutwell and denials of Ransom E. Aldrich in *Hearings*, Jt. Committee on Reduction of Nonessential Federal Expenditures, Part 3, February, 1942, 77th Cong., 2nd Sess., pp. 763-774.

11. Statement of Archie Wright (cf. n. 9).

12. Statement of Meda E. Hauf (cf. note 9) and of President Heinkel of the Missouri Farmers Association, mimeo, 1950: The Missouri Farmers Association, Inc., Columbia, Missouri.

13. Statements of Archie Wright and E. T. Fortune (cf. n. 9).

USDA dealt with the relationship. Where the True-Howard agreement had been strictly followed, no "special relationship difficulties have risen." The committee acknowledged the service rendered by Farm Bureau to Extension and a "definite trend toward the elimination of specific operating agreements between the two agencies." Nevertheless, the committee took note of objections by other farm organizations that the Farm Bureau had been given undue advantages. No public agency, it thought, should be associated in this way with a private organization engaged in lobbying and in commercial activities. It recommended the removal of all "legal connections and exclusive operating relationships between Farm Bureaus and the Extension Service." [14]

One committee member, Dean H. P. Rusk, of the College of Agriculture, University of Illinois, dissented. The Smith-Lever Act of 1914 had established a cooperative program which many states had tried to make effective through the provision of local associations to sponsor Extension work. In Illinois, where county Farm Bureaus had contributed $582,997 to the program in 1947, the True-Howard Agreement had been strictly observed. He considered that formal agreements with responsible farm organizations safeguarded the grant-in-aid principle. Extension Services without Farm Bureau affiliations may be safe and sterile, while others may be goaded into greater usefulness by their Farm Bureau partners. Playing favorites and indulging in political give-and-take may occur where no formal tie with the Farm Bureau exists. The Dean also urged that a blanket proscription of all formal agreements would put an end to some mutually helpful arrangements which are generally admitted to be beyond criticism.

Vice President Romeo Short of the American Farm Bureau Federation laid down the official position. "The operation of Cooperative Extension relationships is a matter that should be handled by citizens of the respective States." Mr. Short said that

---

14. *Extension Programs, Policies, and Goals* (1948). Jointly appointed in 1946 by the Secretary of Agriculture and the Association of Land Grant Colleges and Universities, the committee of ten included eight college officials and two employees of the USDA; both of the latter had had distinguished careers in colleges of agriculture before joining the Department.

the Gilbertson report found only one county Extension employee out of 12,300 to have served as a leader in a Farm Bureau membership campaign in 1948. Only 5 such officials in three states had participated in similar campaigns. Reports showed that the 1948 violations had all been corrected.[15]

4. BILLS OF DIVORCEMENT

In 1949-50, Congressman Granger (D., Utah) introduced bills to divorce Extension from the Farm Bureau.[16] In 1948 at least one Midwestern Farm Bureau had campaigned for Republican candidates; the Granger Bill even more than the Brannan Plan was grounded on the assumption that the election had weakened the Farm Bureau politically. The Bill proposed to enact the True-Howard Agreement and to forbid payment of federal grants-in-aid to states where either law or informal agreement:

"(1) establishes, requires, or permits a farm bureau, county farm aid association, or other organization or association as an official cooperating or sponsoring agency for the Extension Service;

"(2) requires the organization of farmers as a prerequisite to the conduct of cooperative agricultural work in any county or locality; or

"(3) provides for furnishing to, or accepting from, any private organization or association any housing, publicity, telephone, clerical, or other services in connection with cooperative agricultural extension work. . . ."

In May and July, 1950, the first Congressional hearings in history which center upon the Extension-Farm Bureau relationship were held.[17] The *National Union Farmer* reported: [18]

---

15. Mimeo., May 18, 1950. American Farm Bureau Federation, 221 N. La Salle St., Chicago. The National Farmers Union retorted by challenging the accuracy of the Gilbertson report. Mr. Gilbertson (it was understood) "had to rely on replies sent in by Extension Directors . . . The report is not . . . the result of any field investigation." Statement of Benton J. Stong, May 17, 1950 (mimeo). NFU, 3501 E. 46th Avenue, Denver, Colorado.
16. H. R. 3222, 81st Cong., 2nd Sess.
17. The hearings, before the House Committee on Agriculture, have not been published.
18. June, 1950.

"Testifying in favor of the basic purpose of the Granger Bill were the Farmers Union, the National Grange, the Missouri Farmers Association, Kansas Friends of the Extension Service, the National Association of Land Grant Colleges and Universities, the U. S. Department of Agriculture represented by veteran Extension Director M. L. Wilson, the National Livestock Exchange and the National Association of Mutual Insurance Agents."

Opposed was the American Farm Bureau Federation, which reported that "the measure was promptly killed when ten Republican Congressmen joined with eight Democrats to defeat it, 18 to 8." [19] The Farm Bureau was saved further Congressional embarrassment, at least for the time. The Utah Farm Bureau attempted to defeat Congressman Granger in 1950, but he was re-elected.

If national legislation is indefinitely postponed, what of action by the states? A number of state legislatures have stricken the provision which made the Farm Bureau the legal association for sponsoring the Extension program.[20] The most recent example is Kansas legislation of 1951 which provides for a sponsoring association to be chosen in county elections wherein all farmers are eligible to vote.[21] New York will probably end the alliance as soon as it can discover another manner of establishing an effective local organization to sponsor Extension's program. The Iowa and Minnesota legislatures have allowed

19. American Farm Bureau Federation, *Official News Letter*, August 21, 1950.

20. Examples are South Dakota (1935), Nevada and Vermont (1947), and Montana in 1949. Of these, the Montana and South Dakota Farm Bureaus have been relatively small organizations in states in which the Farmers Unions have traditionally been the strongest general farm organizations. The Farm Bureau is the strongest farm organization in Nevada, but there are only 3200 farms and ranches in the state. Of these states, therefore, Vermont provides the most significant test. Here legal separation is a fact, but actual separation at the county level is reportedly proceeding very slowly.

21. Bills to divorce Extension from the Farm Bureau in Kansas were introduced for many years and killed in committee. In 1949, the bill (endorsed by Director Williams of the Extension Service of Kansas State College) reached the floor where friends of the Farm Bureau succeeded in tabling it. Late in 1950, a district court in Kansas ruled that a county Farm Bureau had no authority to pay dues to the state Farm Bureau. (*National Union Farmer*, Dec., 1950). "Handbook for County Agricultural Extension Councils," Kansas State College (1951).

bills to end the alliance to die in committee. In Illinois there is
no apparent disposition to change the law. On the other hand,
the Missouri legislature required county sponsoring organizations as a condition of Extension programs in 1943.

5. THE DIVORCE—ANTICIPATIONS AND PROBABLE CONSEQUENCES

Divorcing Extension from the Farm Bureau would probably
not improve the competitive position of the Farmers Union or
the Grange at this late date. Nearly every state has its dominant
general farm organization—usually the Farm Bureau which has
typically grown into a position that is very difficult to challenge.[22]
Where numerically strong Granges and Farm Bureaus co-exist,
the latter are usually of more political significance.[23] Where
the leading general farm organization of a state has been challenged by another, the second organization has been the Farm
Bureau in recent years.[24]

By the same reasoning, to divorce Extension from the Farm
Bureau would not help create a situation in which colleges of

22. The Farm Bureau derives its strength from membership in the
powerful AFBF in view of farmers' interest in national farm policy. The
Farm Bureau · is well financed nationally and in most states. The AFBF
maintains a staff of regional membership directors; and many state Farm
Bureaus have established strong membership recruiting staffs. Thus Arkansas
has recently set up district membership directors, hired from the Extension
Service. The Farm Bureau insurance program, farm supply companies
(cooperatives), and other services are impressive and growing; existence of
such services in the Farm Bureau handicaps the growth of rival farm organizations. All this says nothing of the force of custom or prestige, which appear
to favor the Farm Bureau.

23. In Ohio and the northeast generally, except Pennsylvania, many
farmers belong to both the Grange and the Farm Bureau. Here the Grange
has significant social functions, but the Bureau is more important politically.
In the writer's judgment, only in Washington, Oregon, California, and
North Carolina are the Grange and the Farm Bureau really competitive.
In all these, both organizations are fairly strong numerically and both are
probably generally understood by their members to be instruments of political
action.

24. Farm Bureaus are providing fairly effective challenges to the Farmers
Unions in North and South Dakota, to the Grange in Washington and
Oregon, and to the Missouri Farmers Association—all these are essentially
developments of the last decade.

agriculture could balance two or more general farm organizations against each other. Colleges in Oregon, Montana, Missouri, and North Carolina may derive some advantages at present from having more than one fairly strong general farm organization in their states. A few similar situations may develop elsewhere, but probably not many.[25]

It is also doubtful that Extension would reach more people or more low income people if the alliance could be eliminated everywhere. Some Extension employees prefer to deal with Farm Bureau members (exemplified by one ex-county agent's remark about unorganized farmers: "If you don't bother them, they won't bother you.") But it may also be argued that Extension reaches more people by operating through the well-organized Farm Bureaus than it would otherwise—in any event, it seems clear that county agents must operate through some kind of organization. Again, some Extension personnel perform special services for the politically influential (this is sometimes called "chicken culling"); but pressure for this kind of work may exist with or without the alliance. Among Extension workers there is a frequent—and often quite outspoken—preference for commercial farmers.[26] But this preference seems no greater in states where Extension is in alliance with the Farm Bureau. The concern among many Extension workers because they fail to reach low income farmers effectively is noticeable as much in one kind of state as in the other.

---

25. One of the curious relationships in this area is that organizations other than the Farm Bureau are or have been indifferent toward colleges of agriculture or even inimical toward them. Many state Farmers Unions have been or are suspicious of such colleges; the Farmers Unions also maintain their own educational programs and tend to operate in their own orbit rather apart from the colleges. Somewhat the same statement seems applicable to the Granges in Washington and California. For many years the Missouri Farmers Association was unfriendly toward the college, although this relationship has improved greatly since about 1935. On the other hand, Farm Bureaus everywhere are strongly oriented toward colleges of agriculture.

26. A familiar justification might be paraphrased as follows: "The only reason for having a publicly supported agricultural Extension program is that it improves the efficiency of production and distribution of food. This objective is in the public interest. Therefore, Extension should concentrate its program upon commercial farmers."

6. THE DIFFICULTIES OF DIVORCE

Fortune recognized the legitimacy of lobbies based upon the right of citizens to assemble and petition government but (speaking specifically of the Farm Bureau) declared: [27]

"Certainly nothing in the Bill of Rights suggests that petitioners should be aided by public funds; plain common sense recommends against it. . . ."

This is a powerful argument, but there are difficulties in acting upon it.

The social ties that bind Extension to the Farm Bureau are strong. Extension personnel and Farm Bureau leaders exhibit that "equality of conditions" which struck deTocqueville as the most significant characteristic of American society. They are similar in background, experience, and outlook. They share the same values. Extension (in common with most agricultural agencies) tends to serve chiefly the commercial farmers—the third of census farmers who produce 80 per cent of the commercial product. The Farm Bureau is officered by such farmers. A well-worn path exists between desks in Farm Bureau offices and those of the Extension Service.

Common interest unites Extension and the Farm Bureau. For understandable reasons, both are suspicious of centralized authority for agricultural policy formation and administration. In a number of states, both were unfriendly toward the Farm Security Administration.[28] Extension saw a rival agency in FSA which reached a different clientele and which might induce the rise of a new farm organization (or perhaps stimulate the formation of Farmers Unions). The Farm Bureau feared the same kind of development. Both were suspicious of new approaches, the enlargement of the agricultural "public," and the unsettling consequences for the organization of influence in agriculture. Both Extension and the Farm Bureau have opposed the Soil

---

27. "The Farm Bureau," June, 1944.
28. Since 1946, the Farmers Home Administration.

Conservation Service. Both have attacked—and been attacked by—the Agricultural Adjustment Administration.[29]

In view of the existence of social ties and of common interests, the separation of Farm Bureau from Extension presents a profound problem. Can the Farm Bureau be prevented from supporting Extension appropriations? Can legislative separation remove from Extension workers' minds the stimulation of employment possibilities in the Farm Bureau? Can legislation nullify the advantages involved in mixing professional activities with an exchange of social amenities with those persons heavy with the symbol of success in our society?

The ties of interest and common outlook are as binding in many states with only informal understandings between Extension and the Farm Bureau as they are where the alliance rests upon law. The existence of such ties makes the prospect of successful divorce discouraging. On the other hand, most of the common arguments against divorce can be answered. Thus the need for Extension to have a "power base" is often cited; but Extension Services in such states as Oregon and Montana have been successful in securing appropriations without effective support of powerful Farm Bureaus. The financial contributions of Farm Bureaus in Illinois, Iowa, and New York are considerable; but the existence of flourishing Extension programs in most other states shows that this source of funds is not essential. Finally, Extension badly needs a sponsoring agency if its program is to be effective and if the county staff is to be spared the frustration of having to operate in an "unstructured" situation; but again the success of a number of Extension programs which are operated in little or no relationship to county Farm Bureaus is certainly significant.

7. WHAT POLICY?

The writer favors an effective divorce of Extension from the Farm Bureau.[30] As the foregoing indicates, no illusions are held

---

29. Now the Production and Marketing Administration; cf. Ch. IX, section 2.

30. This recommendation is not a "scientific" conclusion but a matter of judgment.

that divorce will be easy to obtain [31] or that divorce is wholly good and alliance wholly undesirable. To be sure, other farm organizations deserve to have a competitive situation in which Extension is not prompted by state law to favor the Farm Bureau; yet the actual benefits other farm organizations may derive are doubtful. One might also wryly observe that legal divorce would remove a certain debility under which Extension and the Farm Bureau now operate. So long as the alliance rests on statutes in a number of states, both will be subject to chastening criticism. Remove these laws, and some present tendencies toward self-righteousness in both Bureau and Extension may become quite overwhelming!

Recognizing the strength of the common sense argument by

---

31. Two steps would be involved, legal divorce and an actual (and much more difficult) separation. Legal divorce is hard enough to achieve. Thus the moribund Granger bill raised many problems. Should Extension be confined to cooperation only with local agencies formed solely to sponsor its program? Would groups have to form themselves spontaneously to sponsor each demonstration? How often could the same group work with Extension without becoming an "official sponsoring agency" by "informal agreement"? Would Extension be able to cooperate with soil conservation districts in view of their membership in state associations and the National Association of Soil Conservation Districts? To forbid Extension's acceptance of publicity from any private organization might severely handicap the dissemination of educational material. The bill also forbids preferential treatment of individuals. This provision strikes at a widely recognized problem, but it might place obstacles in the way of conducting demonstrations or working with local "leaders."

Federal law might remove the possibility of matching federal grants by contributions from individuals. It might deny federal monies to states in which county extension staffs are appointed by other than governmental officials (county governing boards, the state Extension Director, or some combination of the two). It might also deny such grants to states wherein county Extension budgets are controlled by other than public officials. Whether federal law can advisedly go further, the writer is not prepared to say. The legislation advocated would certainly not "centralize control of the Land-Grant College system and provide a precedent for Federal domination of our entire educational system" as Romeo Short said of the Granger bill in his statement of May 18, 1950. Any legislation which does not circumscribe Extension with minute regulations will leave open the use of informal understandings and agreements. It is in this area—the more difficult one of attaining actual separation—that the real problems emerge. The task of the law seems to be to declare principles that will clarify the role of Extension and sustain its personnel in performing that role. Cf. A. D. Lindsay on the function of law in *The Modern Democratic State*, Oxford University Press (1947), Vol. 1, pp. 88-89.

Fortune, the writer finds the most compelling reason for divorce in the opinion of the Joint Committee Report [32] that no public educational agency should be united with an organization engaged in business and politics. The relevance of this argument is underscored by the changing character of Extension.[33] The celebrated statement "To make two blades of grass grow where one grew before" is still descriptive of much Extension work. But Extension Services in some 40 states are currently developing programs in public policy education.[34] In order to proceed in this field, Extension must be able to discuss controversial issues. What are the consequences of public programs for the distribution of the factors of production and of income among farmers? What effects do such programs have upon the organization and distribution of political power? What are the consequences of farm politics for the purposes of public policy? The ability to probe these and similar questions is a requisite of education in the field of public policy.

Can Extension attain this degree of freedom? Relationships to the Farm Bureau are of considerable significance to this question; but the significance is not always the same and is probably never conclusive. Sometimes Farm Bureaus have talked or acted in a high-handed manner toward the colleges. In the 1943 Iowa margarine incident, the then state Farm Bureau president was a leader in the attack upon the controversial bulletin.[35] In another state, the Farm Bureau president reportedly told the Dean

---

32. See Note 14, above.
33. Cf. the *Survey* of the Land-Grant Colleges and Universities, Office of Education, U. S. Department of the Interior, (1930), Vol. II, p. 539; Gladys Baker, *The County Agent* (1939); George A. Works and Barton Morgan, *The Land Grant Colleges* (1939); testimony of Director Willard Munson of Massachusetts, *Hearings,* S. 2228, 74th Cong., 1st sess. (1935); the Joint Committee *Report on Extension Programs, Policies, and Goals, op. cit.;* John D. Black, *Federal State-Local Relationships in Agriculture,* National Planning Association, 1950.
34. Materials are available in the federal Extension Service, USDA, and the Farm Foundation, 600 S. Michigan Avenue, Chicago, Illinois.
35. Charles M. Hardin, "Federal-State Relationships in Agricultural Research and Education," (1950) prepared for the Commission on Financing Higher Education; typescript, Political Science Department, University of Chicago.

of the College of Agriculture: "You know that we own you, body and soul, and you have to do what we say." [36]

Relationships are commonly more subtle. In one state the college of agriculture had reportedly long dominated the Farm Bureau. When the Extension Director wanted to make speeches analyzing the case for flexible price supports for agriculture, however, he hesitated because of his anticipations of unfavorable reactions from the Farm Bureau. In another state, the Dean of the College of Agriculture was encouraged to make similar speeches by the Farm Bureau president. (He was criticized for making them by the chairman of the State Production and Marketing Administration.) In a third state, which is engaged in a vigorous program in public policy education, it was said: "So far we have not carried on discussions, the trend of which was to oppose positions held by the Farm Bureau. We have had searching staff conferences on what the consequences might be if we were to carry on such discussions."

But the evidence does not all tend in one direction. The writer recently requested the judgment of a number of informed persons respecting which colleges of agriculture had been most effective in analyzing public policy issues since 1920. Among states repeatedly named were several in which strong Extension-Farm Bureau tie-ups obtain. Iowa is an outstanding example. If significant changes in the economics staff at Iowa State College followed the margarine incident of 1943, there were also important changes in Iowa Farm Bureau leadership; moreover, the experience weighs heavily upon the consciences of Iowans today.[37] Analyses in colleges of agriculture in Iowa, Illinois, and Indiana (and probably other states) contributed to the shift of the American Farm Bureau Federation toward flexible support prices in 1947. It is arguable—and argued—that the college analysts were more effective in these states because of the pres-

---

36. This and following material is derived from interviews; sources cannot be identified.

37. This is an excellent example of the influence of the belief in the "rules of the game" as held by what David B. Truman calls "potential groups." Cf. *The Governmental Process*, Knopf, New York (1951) index.

ence of strong Farm Bureaus than they would have been without them.[38]

Nevertheless, the writer persists in the judgment in favor of separation. The Farm Bureau is an organized political group which takes positions on numerous public issues and vigorously supports or opposes various policies and programs. The Farm Bureau in a number of states openly attacks the Farmers Union.[39] In carrying on such activities, the Farm Bureau is playing its authentic role as a political organization. But what is the role of the colleges of agriculture? It seems clear to the writer that the colleges need to be effectively separated from the Farm Bureau in order to clarify their own roles in society— and to clarify these roles both to themselves and to the public.

The 1950 hearings on the Granger Bill brought out what common experience attests, namely, that many farmers and others identify the Extension Service with the Farm Bureau. This identification contributes to the assumption that "Extension is just another agency with an angle." This assumption lends undue weight to the principle of relativism—a principle

---

38. It should not be forgotten that other interests than the Farm Bureau may act to inhibit college discussion of controversial issues. The Iowa Farm Bureau was associated with powerful commodity groups in its stand of 1943 in the margarine incident. Some of the commodity groups reached effectively into the staff of the college of agriculture. Interviews have provided numerous other illustrations of attempts by commodity groups to restrain colleges of agriculture in their research, publication, and teaching. The writer is fully conscious of the importance of such groups (and also at times of proprietary businesses) to the question whether colleges of agriculture can maintain an effective degree of freedom and objectivity in the discussion of controversial issues; these considerations, however, cannot be examined further in the present book.

39. In a jury trial in federal district court in Salt Lake City, the Farmers Union was awarded $25,000 damages from the Utah Farm Bureau because of the latter's allegations that the Farmers Union was "Communist dominated." Cf. *National Union Farmer* for May, 1951. At least two other state Farm Bureaus have helped make similar attacks. In all three states, the Farm Bureau and Extension are very close; even if they were not, this kind of attack calls the alliance in question wherever it exists. In speaking of the Farm Bureau's playing an "authentic political role," the writer does not want to be construed as condoning attacks of this nature. Whatever the provocation, and some Farmers Union members are extreme in the epithets they apply to the Farm Bureau, there ought to be some limits beyond which men of conscience will not go in political attacks.

which democratic theory should honor but not make a fetish. In extreme form, relativism implies that the value of ideas is measured only by the political power that supports them. Force is then the only thing that counts. It involves no depreciation of the significance of power in political analysis to argue that an objective of constitutional states is to increase the role of intelligence in service of the public interest—however tentatively that phrase is defined.[40] This objective is served by education, viewed as a process which cracks the husks of custom and modifies the demands of passion so that men can make rational choices.[41] Extension is an educational agency. It needs considerable freedom to clarify its function in the contemporary American scene. It also needs favorable conditions for public acceptance and support of this function, once clarified. As a Farm Bureau president (in a state wherein the Farm Bureau and the Extension Service are all but indistinguishable) remarked to the writer: "Extension workers ought to be free agents."[42]

---

40. Cf. Pendleton Herring, *The Politics of Democracy,* (Rinehart and Co., New York, 1940), p. 424.

41. Following R. G. Collingwood, *The New Leviathan,* Oxford University Press (1947).

42. This remark is a tribute to its maker's respect for the "rules of the game," (cf. n. 37). But it may also reflect the judgment that agriculture in the United States is a minority decreasing in numbers, that farm leaders must anticipate the day when decreased numbers will be reflected in diminished political power, and that it clearly serves the long run interests of organized agriculture to establish the educational independence of agricultural Extension in the eyes of the public.

CHAPTER IV

The Soil Conservation Service—
The Land Doctors

1. SCS—A PANORAMA

Few agencies have enjoyed so rapid or sustained growth as the Soil Conservation Service (SCS). Its announced goal, that every acre should be handled according to its needs, has become the basic soil conservation objective of the USDA. It has joined hands with soil conservation districts which have spread rapidly in rural America. It has impressed Congress, secured considerable appropriations, and widely (and apparently successfully) advertised itself to the general public. Yet it remains controversial, with powerful critics in the colleges of agriculture, the Farm Bureau, and among other USDA bureaus.

The Soil Conservation Service has roots in the erosion investigation work established by an amendment to the USDA appropriation act for fiscal 1930, which provided $160,000 for such investigations to be conducted cooperatively between the USDA and the colleges under the direction of a five-man board composed of one representative from three federal bureaus and two experiment stations. A number of erosion experiments were established, and the project was beginning to take on some logrolling, pork-barrel aspects when 1933 arrived. Among New Deal programs, erosion control was pushed through the Soil

Erosion Service, set up in the Department of the Interior (reportedly to escape the unwieldy board-administration in the USDA), financed by presidential grants from money supplied under authority of the National Industrial Recovery Act. A major objective until World War II of this and other agricultural programs was work relief.

Hugh Hammond Bennett came from the USDA to administer the program, developed the demonstration-project approach, recruited a large staff of natural scientists concerned with numerous aspects of soil management (particularly, physical soil management), and spent some $12,000,000 before the transfer back to agriculture as the Soil Conservation Service in 1935. This transfer was underwritten by the Soil Conservation Act of 1935 which gave the SCS bureau status and endowed it with considerable powers.[1]

---

1. Act of April 7, 1935, ch. 85, secs. 1-5, 49 Stat. 163. The Act recognizes wastage of soil and moisture resources as a menace to national welfare and declares a Congressional policy to provide for the permanent control of erosion, etc. It provides that the Secretary of Agriculture "shall coordinate and direct all activities with relation to soil erosion. . . ." It authorizes the Secretary (1) to conduct surveys, researches, etc., to disseminate the results, and to carry on demonstrations; (2) to carry out preventive measures; (3) to cooperate or enter into agreements with any agency or person and to extend financial aid to the same, subject to the conditions he deems necessary to carry out the purposes of the Act; and (4) to acquire lands or rights or interests therein by any means, including condemnation in order to carry out the purposes of the Act. Preventive measures may be taken on lands controlled by the United States or on other lands, upon obtaining consent or the necessary rights or interests therein. As conditions for granting benefits, the Secretary may require (1) "The enactment and reasonable safeguards for the enforcement of State and local laws imposing suitable permanent restrictions on the use of such lands and otherwise providing for the prevention of soil erosion;" [this is the provision which underlies the land-use regulations provided by the Standard State Soil Conservation Law, discussed in the next chapter]; (2) agreements or covenants respecting the use of such land, and (3) contributions, money or otherwise. The Act further provided for the covering of the employees concerned into the Civil Service at the end of eight months. Then the Act provided that "The Secretary . . . shall establish an agency to be known as the 'Soil Conservation Service,' to exercise the powers conferred on him by" the Act. This provision has probably restrained more than one Secretary from radically reorganizing the Soil Conservation Service. It helps explain why the SCS is kept intact in the Feb. 16, 1951, reorganization, but made subject to the "coordination and direction" of the Assistant Secretary. See below, ch. xiv.

Subsequent development may be summarized as follows: The SCS acquired a number of programs and a cooperative stake in others, all dealing with land management. Since 1938 the SCS has had general control of all USDA activities relating to land-management on private lands; since 1939 (by presidential order) SCS work on the public domain has been transferred to the United States Department of the Interior. The SCS operates through seven regional offices (with regional conservators), state offices, district offices (with District Conservationists), and work unit offices which contact farmers directly.

The demonstration project program has given way to cooperation with soil conservation districts. These districts are defined as local units of government, "Bodies corporate and politic." They are created under 48 states' enabling acts which modify in more or less degree a "Standard State Soil Conservation Districts Act" prepared in 1936 jointly by the USDA and the colleges. Under these acts, farmers typically petition for a district to a state soil conservation committee which conducts a referendum. After a favorable vote among affected land owners and subject to the state committee's discretion, districts are established. The districts have considerable paper powers, e.g., to acquire and dispose of real and personal property, to sue and be sued, and, in some states (and generally with considerable qualifications) to pass land-use regulations. With the exception of two states, soil conservation districts are without the power to tax. Most districts are governed by boards of five farmer supervisors. Originally, most states followed the standard act in providing for the election of three by farmers in the district and the appointment of two by the state soil conservation committee. The tendency is toward electing all members in the district, and some states have followed Wisconsin's lead in vesting governance of the committee in the county governing board.

The "complete farm plan" is the essence of district and SCS work. It is made through agreement between farmer and district governing body; actually, it is the product of the SCS and the farmer. The five-year plan is designed to treat every acre according to its "land use capabilities" as these are developed in a conservation survey by the SCS. Farmers receive technical assistance, some seedlings and slips of soil-conserving plants not otherwise available, and frequently the assistance of heavy machinery in the hands of the district. Before the war SCS could offer farmers considerable labor through CCC camps and WPA.

There were over 2300 soil conservation districts in the country in 1951. The late E. C. McArthur, first president of the National Association of Soil Conservation Districts, declared: "The Soil Conservation Service is the very lifeblood of the districts." [2]

2. ACHIEVEMENTS AND THE TASK AHEAD

Appropriations for SCS have increased rapidly. The increase seems largely explainable in terms of (a) the appeal of soil conservation, (b) the concrete services performed to individual farmers—frequently very influential farmers—and the consequent pressure on Congress for more money for SCS, (c) the political skill with which SCS has marshalled its supporters to get larger appropriations, and (d) the formation of soil conservation districts. In 1951 the SCS budget was approximately $55,000,000. In addition thirty-three states in 1951 provided money for soil conservation districts. Texas has set up a $5,000,-000 revolving fund, largely for the purchase of equipment, such as terracing machinery. Annual appropriations of states for soil conservation districts other than Texas approximated $2,700,000 in 1951. While this figure remained small in comparison with the Congressional appropriation, it had grown rapidly. [3]

What has SCS done with the money? How much of the conservation job, as defined by SCS, has been accomplished? What are the prospects and what will be the cost of completion? SCS operations include conservation surveys, farm planning, and application. In appraising the proportion of the job

---

2. Senate *Hearings*, Agric. Approp., fiscal 1948, p. 1112.

3. Calculated from a table, House *Hearings*, Agric. Approp., fiscal, 1952, Part 2, p. 795. The sum had to be calculated as most states appropriate for bienniums. A few states account for most of this figure. Not counting the Texas appropriation, however, the 1951 figure provided by the states marks a threefold increase over 1947.

completed, SCS calculates 5 per cent for the survey, 25 per cent for the farm plans, and 70 per cent for the application. Dr. Bennett declared in the House Appropriation Hearings for 1952, "We are about one-fifth through with the job." At the rate SCS is now working, he estimated that the job would be completed in 35 years. An accelerated program could cut this figure to 20 years. This would require $1,120,000,000, or an average of $56,000,000 for technical services for 20 years.[4] But total appropriations would be considerably higher. Thus the National Association of Soil Conservation Districts proposed some $80,000,000 for the SCS for fiscal 1953.[5] Even this is a much lower sum than would be required if an analysis of 1943 is employed. In that year 3,634,932 man-years of skilled and unskilled labor were estimated to be needed for the completion of the application of conservation and related practices to land in farms in the United States. At $3,000 per man-year, this would cost nearly $11,000,000,000. In addition, 327,411 years of motor equipment and 1,089,978 years of horse equipment were estimated as needed.[6]

Perhaps an estimate can be made of the cost per farm of a complete conservation program. From the beginning of the program in 1933 through fiscal 1948 SCS had spent some $345,-900,000 for soil erosion control. This sum does not include outlays for flood control, land-utilization, or Wheeler-Case operations; nor does it include outlays for the Civilian Conservation Corps camps and WPA labor in the 1930's (the latter are more properly charged to relief expenditures than to soil conservation). At the end of fiscal 1948, SCS reported 571,163 farms with active conservation plans. Dividing $345,900,000 by this figure gives $605 per farm planned. But what of applications? At this time, applications were reported on 52 per cent of the acreage planned. Arbitrarily applying 52 per cent to the number of farms planned gives 297,005 farms; dividing this figure into

---

4. House *Hearings*, Agric. Approp. fiscal 1952, Part 2, p. 784.
5. *Ibid.*, p. 1283.
6. SCS, USDA, "Soil and Water Conservation Needs Estimates for the United States," June, 1945, *mimeo*, Table 2. Only a fraction of the outlay involved would require national appropriations, of course.

the total expenditures gives $1164 per farm with plans put into effect.[7]

Can a closer estimate of acres actually treated be had? In February, 1951, SCS reported some 150,000,000 acres to which soil conservation practices had been applied. Perhaps twice this much acreage has been planned; [8] but the aim of planning is, of course, application. At the end of fiscal 1950, South Carolina and Georgia reported soil conservation work applied to 29 and 30 per cent of the farm land in the state, respectively; four states reported 19 to 22 per cent; 15 states reported 10 to 18 per cent; and this left 27 states with less than 10 per cent completed. There was considerable regional concentration in the work completed. Thus the eight southeastern states, from Maryland to Florida and West to Mississippi, plus Arkansas, Louisiana, Oklahoma, and Texas, had 43 per cent of the total applied acreage in the country. On the other hand, Illinois, Indiana, Iowa, and Ohio had applied conservation practices to only 5 per cent of the land in farms—yet these four states have some 11 per cent of the value of farm land and buildings according to the 1945 census of agriculture.

In recent years the SCS program has been accelerated. Dr. Bennett declared that in 1942 one man-year of technical help was required to treat 2,150 acres; in 1950, this figure had risen to 3,240. In 1946 SCS had treated some 55,000,000 acres; in 1950 some 128,000,000 acres. But two questions arise: *First,* how much of the acreage treated represents extensive practices? In 1946, some 24,500,000 of the 55 million were "range properly stocked." Surely this practice cannot compare in its demands

---

7. A figure of $1000 was given as the average cost to the government of planning, and carrying out the plan upon, a farm. One-third was estimated for planning, two-thirds for application. In addition, the SCS estimates that farmers contribute two dollars for every government dollar. Cf. Senate *Hearings,* Agric. Approp., 1948, pp. 358-59.

8. W. R. Parks interprets SCS policy as pushing farm planning work at the expense of application work in order to make a record to induce Congressional appropriations—"to ring the cash register" is his expressive phrase. District supervisors, however, have sometimes succeeded in shifting SCS emphasis toward application. *Effort to Synthesize National Programming with Local Administration in Soil Conservation Districts,* University of Wisconsin, Unpublished Ph. D. thesis (1948), pp. 87 ff.

upon the technician's time with running terrace lines and lay-
ing out strip crops. Actually in 1950 the SCS reported strip-
cropping applied to only 5,760,000 acres—although it had estimated in 1943 that 96,000,000 acres of farm land required
strip-cropping. Does the proportion of extensive practices (stock-
ing range land properly, establishing rotation grazing for range
land, the management of crop residues, etc.) still equal some
44 per cent of the entire acreage reported as treated?

Second, does duplication in reporting exist among various
agencies concerned with the application of soil conservation
practices to private land and, if so, how much? Both the Agricultural Conservation Branch of the Production and Marketing
Administration and representatives of various state Agricultural
Extension Services have asserted that SCS claims credit for
work which was actually the result of their agencies' activities.

Clearly a large and costly job remains. But how large and
how costly? Answers to these questions depend on which estimate one examines and how he interprets it.

3. ENGINEERS ON THE LAND

In 1944, Chief H. H. Bennett told the House Sub-committee on Agricultural Appropriations: "Contouring still continues
to be the central theme of our conservation work, and I think
it will come to be . . . looked upon as being as valuable to
human life as the discovery of the utility of the wheel and
fire." Congressman Plumley said, "I think you are being
modest." [9] In his 1947 statement on SCS work in the South,
Dr. Bennett mentioned that there were 60 or 70 practices which
the "land doctors" of SCS had in their scientific arsenal; but
he drew most of his illustrations from terracing, contour farming, and strip-cropping.[10] In 1951, SCS technicians were described as graduate engineers and agronomists "in the engineering field." Many of them had had "experience with State high-

9. Agric. Approp., fiscal 1945, p. 1020.
10. "Soil Conservation and Better Land-Use in the South," in "Study of
Agricultural and Economic Problems of the Cotton Belt," Special Subcommittee on Cotton, House of Representatives, 80th Cong., 1st Sess.

way departments, with counties, or with private engineering firms." [11]

There is considerable criticism on part of SCS of the soil survey as carried on by the Division of Soil Survey, Bureau of Plant Industry, Soils, and Agricultural Engineering, USDA, in cooperation with the agricultural experiment stations of colleges of agriculture; [12] the criticism is returned by the latter.[13] No attempt will be made to appraise these technical matters. Another kind of criticism will be examined, however; namely, that the SCS farm planning fails to plan the farm from the standpoint of production economics.

This criticism is frequently voiced by land-grant college personnel. Its validity is important for the writer's conclusions which suggest an alternative approach to that of the SCS.[14] Yet the conclusion is extremely difficult to verify, since assertions of college workers that it is true have to be discounted considerably as prejudiced. Nevertheless, some evidence suggests that the SCS approach neglects economic analysis. This evidence is derived from a study of in-service training procedures and other SCS materials.

H. C. Diener and R. H. Musser (the latter being regional conservationist in the Midwest),[15] in *Soil Conservation*, May, 1944, describe a training school for sub-professional workers— recruited mainly from county agents and agricultural graduates. The school lasted for 28 days and included 10 days in the classroom studying soils, plant relationships, land capabilities, etc. What of economic analysis in this program? Twenty hours were allotted to the study of "The effect of conservation planning on the farm business."

In the SCS report, "Regional Training for Professional Employees" (1948), the share of production economics in the five weeks' course appears more impressive in the Milwaukee region (No. 3, Upper Mississippi). In the fourth and fifth weeks,

11. House *Hearings*, Agric. Approp., 1952, p. 793.

12. Cf. reference cited in n. 10, above.

13. *Soil Science*, February, 1949. Charles E. Kellogg, "Soil and Land Classification," *JFE*, Nov., 1951.

14. See chap. xiv below.

15. The Upper Mississippi Region, headquartering in Milwaukee.

some 16 hours of intensive work is devoted to the economics of farm planning. Further, in the soil conservationist's handbook [16] in this region, much of the material is devoted to figures, tables, and analyses all directed to improving the farm management planning of SCS technicians.

But this emphasis upon economics of farm planning does not necessarily carry over into administration. A series of memoranda and supplements, beginning March 1, 1946, details the duties and functions of personnel, from the regional office to work unit technicians and conservation aids. Some 69 pages (mimeographed) are employed. Certainly, in the frequent mention of farm planning, economic analysis is implied; yet it seems notable that only in the original memorandum is economic planning clearly—if briefly—mentioned. Thus, among the P-2 farm planner's duties is the following:

"Assist farmer to determine livestock set-up. Figure requirements for feed, pasture, and woodland products. Develop budget analysis where needed."

A memorandum of the same region on work load analysis, dated November 16, 1948, emphasizes conservation measures completed. In the difficult endeavor to measure accomplishment and to develop some criteria for judging the efficiency of personnel and units, the stress is placed upon the amount of, and the technical quality of, conservation practices. To be sure, farm management practices might be more difficult to measure; but the administrative procedure seems to depreciate the importance of economic farm planning.

If this is true in the upper Mississippi region, it seems that other SCS regions would show even a more marked tendency to depreciate economic analysis. Region 3 has been noted for emphasizing the economic approach. Excepting those connected with the flood control work, SCS had in September, 1948, two

---

16. *Ready References for Conservation Farm Planning.* One entire section of 38 pages is devoted to farm management data, as distinguished from erosion-control and conservation data *per se*. It is rather interesting that the hand book contains little reference to the land-use capability tables, which appear to be mentioned only on two pages (48-49) in the section on Soil, and towards the end of the book, in five pages devoted to a model lecture on conservation planning.

professional economists working on economic research; both were in Region 3.[17] Thus for Region 6 (Albuquerque) an undated "Training Guide" (mimeographed) systematically breaks down the special skills and knowledge required for SCS field positions. This is an imaginative document and should be highly useful in facilitating in-service training. But the 18 pages dealing with professional soil conservationists include less than one page, under the heading "Training in Range Management and Ranch Planning," which is pointed toward analysis of the co-operator's business as such. A similar lack of emphasis upon farm economic aspects is notable in the "Regional Personnel Handbook" of Region 5 (Fort Worth: April 11, 1949, mimeographed).

To be sure, the foregoing is inconclusive, but it points in the same direction as that indicated by the general orientation of SCS, namely, toward physical erosion control and soil and moisture conservation. SCS officials tend to answer either that the farmer takes care of the economic aspects of his planning or that SCS farm planners perform an adequate amount of economic analysis, even if it is not reflected in SCS documents. Land-grant college personnel and representatives of TVA criticize SCS for not including a sufficient amount of farm management analysis. But the college critics would be the first to redouble their claims that SCS was duplicating agricultural extension work, were it to include farm management planning.

If it is true that the SCS approach underemphasizes economics, one would expect to find that SCS farm plans have little meaning to most farmers; one would also suppose that many of the practices planned and applied by SCS have been abandoned, for example, if farmers are faced by a shortage of labor and therefore fail to maintain their terraces and grass waterways properly, or if farmers are attracted by prices to exploit their soil regardless of the departure involved from practices and rotations which SCS technicians may have prescribed.

Very little evidence bears on these points one way or another.

----

17. In the past, SCS has had a larger economic research staff, the members of which have been none too happy. There has been considerable emphasis upon the kind of economic analysis which will justify the agency's program.

Many persons declare that farmers are anxious to have SCS engineers run terrace lines for them and that they will accept the complete farm plan—on paper—but then file it away in a bureau drawer. Eugene A. Wilkening intensively interviewed farmers in a community of Yadkin County, North Carolina. Of his interviewees, 35 had SCS plans. But only one "spontaneously referred to his . . . plan and showed it to the interviewer. Even he did not understand the land capability classes for his farm although he was above average in education and interest in better methods of farming." [18] In 1947 there were 593 cooperators with SCS in Goodhue County, Minnesota, or 19.5 per cent of all farmers in the county.

"Not all of these cooperators were active. The agency's most critical problem is follow-up work with those who have agreed to participate. With the present staff, the caseload is entirely too large for effective operation." [19]

The problem of getting farmers to develop and employ farm plans is a pressing one; but it is not peculiar to SCS—it is also encountered by the Farmers Home Administration, the TVA, and the Extension Service. The question was pointedly raised by Congressman Whitten in an exchange with H. H. Bennett in 1951. Dr. Bennett wanted to speed up the conservation job. Congressman Whitten agreed, but stressed that it was necessary to educate people, to "get the folks with you," to get the farmers' cooperation. Dr. Bennett's reply was that farmers were ready for conservation, and he cited the backlog of 200,000 applications for SCS farm plans.[20] But clearly, if we have *no* information whether present plans are carried out *as plans* or how well conservation practices, once applied, are maintained, Mr. Whitten has by no means been answered. The issue is whether planning each acre according to its capabilities will be as effective as planning economic farm operations, with due attention

---

18. "A Socio-Psychological Analysis of the Acceptance of Certain Agricultural Programs and Practices in a Piedmont Community of North Carolina," Unpublished Ph. D. thesis, University of Chicago, 1949, p. 113.
19. Alexander and Nelson, "Rural Social Organization in Goodhue County," Minnesota Experiment Station Bulletin 401, February, 1949, p. 56.
20. House *Hearings,* Agric. Approp., fiscal 1952, p. 784.

to resource conservation, but with the chief aim of maximizing farmers' incomes.[20a]

If the advocates of "balanced farm planning," or farm and home planning as alternatives to the SCS conservation plan are to be convincing, they need to do three things. *First,* they need to redirect their agricultural extension programs *away from* the single-practice approach and *toward* the whole-farm approach. From numerous interviews with Extension personnel during the last decade, the writer believes that this step marks a radical and difficult departure for Extension. *Second,* some corresponding means of estimating or evaluating program results needs developing. SCS stresses single practices in its reports—miles of terraces built, acres of contour farming established, etc. But Extension also emphasizes single-practices— numbers of farmers adopting hybrid corn, numbers adopting the practice of rotating the garden plot, etc. It is much more difficult to appraise the results of balanced farming programs— for the real achievement here is revealed in the growth of analytical ability of farm men and women as reflected in improved economic management of their resources. *Third,* Congressmen have to be convinced that programs are successful even though their success is demonstrated in less tangible ways than figures of miles of terraces built, acres of strip-cropping established, etc.

Finally, another aspect of the SCS approach bears mentioning. This approach involves a conservation survey as the result of which the farmer is given a map of his farm which shows it divided into "land capability classes"—for each of which the permissible uses are spelled out.[21] Suppose a farmer has solely Class IV land, suitable only for occasional or limited cultivation. This may mean that the farmer cannot follow the SCS complete farm plan and still make a living. The question arises, Which gives way, the rigid SCS concepts or the farmer's eco-

---

20a. A recent analysis of "Conservation Problems and Achievements on Selected Midwestern Farms" (Special circ. 86 Ohio Agric. Exper. Sta. July, 1951; N. C. Regional Publ. No. 23) stresses the significance of sound economic analysis and development in the effective application of "conservation" plans to farms.

21. See, e.g., "Soil and Water Conservation Needs Estimates for the United States," *op. cit.,* pp. 1-2, and below, chap. vi, sec. 3.

nomic needs? To the writer's knowledge, this question has never been adequately explored.

4. THE ADMINISTRATIVE LINE

SCS has been and remains a highly centralized agency. This is true in spite of the tendency to increase the proportion of professional personnel in the local offices dealing directly with farmers. In Washington, the SCS is divided into two main areas—operations and research. Divisions under "operations" include agronomy, range, engineering, biology, nursery, forestry, land management, cartography, project plans, soil conservation surveys, and water conservation. Except for the last three, each of which has several professional employees (mid-1949), the other divisions have one professional man each. In recent years, considerable delegation has taken place to the seven regional offices (reduced from the original 10).

The regional offices, except for research, correspond to the organization in Washington. Employment authority has been delegated to regional offices, except for research technicians. SCS makes lump sum appropriations to regional offices which allocate to states on the basis of three criteria, (1) known land problems, (2) opportunities, and (3) soil conservation districts. In recent years Congress has directed that some resources be allocated to each district. Regional allocations to states are made in consultation with state conservationists who then allocate within states, in consultation with district conservationists. Sometimes aid is withdrawn from districts which do not show sufficient progress.

States are divided into work groups, numbering from two in Delaware to 24 in Texas, for which the paper work is handled by state offices. Work groups assist one or several districts, a situation held advisable in that districts range from approximately 17,000 to 5,000,000 acres, and from 17 to 25,000 farms. Work groups are headed by district conservationists and serve 12,617 work units (February, 1949), the offices from which farm planners go directly to farms. The work unit is headed by a conservationist who supervises an assistant-in-training to head a work unit somewhere else, plus one (or, perhaps several) part-time conservation aides of sub-professional standing. There may be an engineer in the work unit office, if, for example, special drainage problems are involved and the work unit conservationist lacks the necessary training. Or the engineer may be attached to the work group office, where there will also ordinarily be a soil scientist, who does the mapping in conservation surveys, and occasionally a forester or agronomist.

The regions are divided into zones, each of which has a team of two zone conservationists, one an engineer and one with training in soils or agronomy. These men assist work unit technicians in keeping abreast of technical advances. They help with complex problems and afford inspection and on-the-job training. They cannot reach each work unit yearly, but try to visit those needing help the most. These men are regional staff members; the chain of command runs from the regional conservator through the state conservationist, the district conservationist, to the work unit. But zone technicians' counsel is usually accepted. This sketch of administration is largely derived from interviews. A few observations are in order.

SCS is a line agency operating from Washington to the farmer. SCS has been one of the USDA "action" agencies accused of "by-passing" the states—i.e., the colleges of agriculture. Early tendencies in the SCS, the Farm Security Administration, and the Agricultural Adjustment Administration, were to develop their own lines of administration from Washington through regional offices to the farmer. Regional offices have always been anathemas to the colleges of agriculture and the Farm Bureau. While Farm Security, AAA, and BAE regional offices have been abolished, those of SCS continue to be the main centers of program formulation. Retention and the continued strength of regional offices is evidence of the political strength of SCS.

The line administration fits the SCS conceptions and the code that it has developed.[22] The theory of the application of science to soil conservation seems to require an administration in which the basic concepts of the SCS program are carried down to the farm and there applied with considerable conformance.

22. Chap. vi, sec. 3, below.

The contrast to the highly decentralized Extension Service is striking. The SCS form of administration may be less well suited than that of Extension to the development of the farmer's ability to manage his resources; but there can be little doubt that SCS gains in its ability to present a united front for the strengthening of its program. That is, SCS can define the conservation job (however loosely), can assert that it has the method of doing that job (if inquiry into actual accomplishments is not too sharp), and can estimate the time and expense of completing the job (if these estimations are not carefully probed). All this can be done with one disciplined voice on part of SCS as an organization, with the invaluable help of strategically placed Congressmen, and with the formidable assistance of the soil conservation districts now organized in a national pressure group.

SCS has sought to distinguish itself from the Extension Service in order to nullify the charge that it is merely duplicating what Extension does. This has meant that SCS has developed a unique program. As noted later, the unique program requires uniquely-trained administrators—as part of the SCS code. These administrators are "land doctors" who are distinguished from ordinary agriculturalists (meaning the Extension county agents) as the cardiac specialist is distinguished from the general practitioner.[23] At the same time, development of a unique program has also come to involve the creation of an extremely broad program designed to accomplish everything necessary to achieve the conservation and development of soil and moisture resources. Thus SCS personnel guides and in-service training memoranda suggest that these "specialists" must really be "universalists," since they must be experts in soil science, engineering, agronomy, and animal husbandry—and (some would add) in farm management, sociology, and psychology. To anyone who has attempted to master any of these fields, the conception of what is required of a well-trained "soil conservationist" becomes very broad, indeed!

The question of the role of soil conservation districts needs pointing up for development in the following chapter. What

---

23. Cf. The *Report* of the Chief of the SCS, 1946, p. 3.

can districts actually do in the way of self-determination of programs, given the SCS program and administration? Here it is noteworthy that the SCS administrative organization is not designed to coincide with soil conservation districts. As early as 1941, the trend was well-established in the Fort Worth region; now it appears to be a national phenomenon. It may be that efficiency is served by the present organization, but it should be asked whether the assignment of technical personnel to offices corresponding with soil conservation districts would not enable the latter to participate more actively in the development of local programs.

CHAPTER V

Soil Conservation Districts

I. ANTICIPATIONS—AND WHAT HAPPENED

The development of the idea of soil conservation districts reflected the determination of a number of persons influential in agricultural policy in the mid-1930's that land-use programs should become the farmers' own. There is some evidence that the SCS did not welcome the district program at first. In 1935, Chief H. H. Bennett foresaw the control of erosion on public lands through demonstration projects and on private lands through local erosion-control associations. He argued, however, that

". . . the Federal Government would provide technical direction and supervision and would establish regulations protecting any erosion-control measures which might be installed."

This remark was made during consideration of a bill which later became the Soil Conservation Act of 1935. At that time the bill authorized the Secretary of Agriculture to make regulations deemed proper for carrying out the Act. Infractions were to be punished by fines up to $100. True, Dr. Bennett called for close cooperation with the states, since they had the power to tax and to pass zoning regulations. But he also praised an Italian law of 1928 under which the cooperation of private land owners was forced and the owner was required to pay his share of the cost of control measures installed.[1] The anticipations implicit in this analysis, together with many others, have been unfulfilled in the actual development and operation of soil conservation districts.

Districts were conceived as being adaptable to "natural" communities and divisions based upon topography, especially upon watersheds—rather than being confined to "arbitrary" political boundaries. But districts have more and more come in on county lines. On January 1, 1949, there were 2046 districts in continental United States. Of these 1060 corresponded with counties and 118 were mainly groups of counties. This left 868 districts as parts of counties, although even here the county boundaries may have been considerably influential upon the district area in those examples where two or three districts together correspond to counties.

Districts have not been produced by spontaneous combustion. Their early skepticism aside, SCS soon assiduously pushed the establishment of districts. This statement is made on the basis of scores of interviews, including many with SCS personnel and with farmer supervisors of districts. This has been a perfectly natural thing for SCS to do, just as it has been equally natural for SCS to maintain that districts are formed spontaneously. Year after year SCS has testified before appropriations committees to the need for more funds to service districts; Congress has lent an attentive ear; and SCS has been able to build up its organization and prestige. About 1939, SCS established the policy of cooperating only with farmers in soil conservation districts.[2]

Thus SCS has been the prime mover in district establishment.[3] Other administrative organizations, and not the reluctance

1. *Hearings,* Sub-committee of the House Committee on Public Lands, 74th Cong., 1st Sess., pp. 14, 17-18, 23.

2. Officially, this was USDA policy, but it was established at the behest of SCS.

3. W. Robert Parks indicates, however, that the early aggressive role of SCS in stimulating district formation has been considerably modified, *op. cit.,* pp. 207-9. In February, 1951, some 2300 districts existed. The Secretary's memorandum of February 16, 1951, No. 1278, for the first time expressed a national obligation, assigned to the Assistant Secretary of Agriculture, to

of farmers themselves, have been the chief obstacles to district establishment where they were slow in formation. State Extension Services have often cooperated in establishing districts; but in some states, particularly Missouri, Pennsylvania, and Oregon, state extension services have either opposed district establishment or have, at least, "failed to cooperate" therein.[4] Other state

---

encourage "the creation and development of soil conservation districts." Mr. Dykes, Deputy Chief, SCS, noted that the memorandum "does put the responsibility on the State PMA committee and the State conservationist of the SCS to do what they can in jointly encouraging district formation." New districts were anticipated in Tennessee, California, and Pennsylvania. Some 150 new districts were anticipated in fiscal 1952—"and no new money" to provide technicians to service them. House *Hearings, Agric.* Approp., fiscal 1952, Part 2, pp. 693, 800, 817.

4. The Subcommittee on Agricultural Appropriations of the House Committee on Agriculture caused a field study to be made of the operations of agricultural programs. 46 counties in 13 states were visited. Part of the report reads:

"In most of the States visited, the Extension Service, as a matter of policy, is strongly opposing not only the work being done by the Soil Conservation Service, but also is in active opposition to the formation of additional soil conservation districts. This policy was confirmed in conversation with the deans of the State colleges of agriculture and the directors of extension services. In one state, this bitter opposition has taken the form of Extension Service instigated suits in State courts to prevent the formation of . . . districts. . . . A typical propaganda handbill which was placed under the mail box of each farmer in one county on the night preceding a referendum [to determine whether farmers desired a district to be established] is as follows:

'FARMERS—FARM OWNERS
Stop—Look—Listen
'*Do you remember?*
"1. When Henry Wallace drowned all the little pigs?
"2. When Henry Wallace made us get permits to sell our wheat?
"He also got the pet idea about us using soil districts.
"What may a soil district bring to Perry County?
    "1. Two to five high-priced white collar men working in the county.
    "2. Higher taxes.
    "3. Centralized Washington control.
    "4. Dictatorship, bureaucratic control.
    "5. Strangle free enterprise:
        "(a) Force local contractors out of business.
        "(b) Kill individual initiative on the farm.
"The Perry County farmer has prospered on the basis of free enterprise. Our forefathers came to this country so that this freedom might be theirs. We had better be fearful for the future of our country if we expect the Government to take care of us. From 1936 to 1947 it cost the Government $237,752,000 developing plans on 364,479 farms. This number of farms

extension services have started out this way and changed their policies later. In some states, county agents have kept districts from forming in their counties, although state extension services have gone along with district establishment—Sangamon County, Illinois, is an example. In the Tennessee Valley, the controversy between SCS and the USDA versus TVA and the seven land-grant colleges has been complex; but for present purposes it is clear that the colleges, some state soil conservation committees, and the TVA have opposed the formation of districts in the valley. In Tennessee, however, the legislature established a number of districts in 1949. Mr. Dykes said in February, 1951, that plans were under way for the creation of 25 districts in Tennessee in fiscal 1951, the addition of 25 in fiscal 1952, and the establishment of districts everywhere in the state by 1953.[5]

Districts not only fail to coincide with "natural areas" and to appear through "spontaneous combustion"; they have not to

---

covered only 6 per cent of the farms in the United States. What would the cost have been if all farms had been covered?

"We are all for saving the soil. Let's not jeopardize our freedom. Let Perry County farmers manage their own farms.

"Vote 'No' Saturday, October 2, between 1 P.M. and 8 P.M.
                                                            "FARMERS COMMITTEE."

"The State director of extension admitted that the county extension agent in Perry County 'probably' participated in the authorship of this handbill and that members of the Extension Service sponsored State Conservation Contractors' Association 'probably' paid for its publication and were responsible for its distribution. In this same State, the secretary-treasurer of the State Conservation Contractors' Association is a full-time employee of the State extension service."
House *Hearings*, Agric. Approp., fiscal 1952, Part 2, pp. 688-89.

5. House *Hearings*, Agric. Approp., fiscal 1952, Part 2, pp. 799-800. See Norman Wengert, *TVA and Agriculture: A Study in Regional Decentralization*, to be published by the University of Tennessee Press. Cf. also Philip Selznick, *TVA and the Grass Roots*, University of California Press, 1948. The victory of SCS in Tennessee constitutes a defeat not only of TVA but also of the colleges of agriculture; for the colleges had praised the relationships in the TVA as a model to be imitated elsewhere in the United States. Within the Valley, there appears to have been tacit agreement among representatives of the seven colleges concerned and TVA to keep soil conservation districts out. But this agreement has been broken at the convenience of the colleges. Thus Alabama became the first state entirely organized in districts; this included northern Alabama, which is in the Tennessee Valley. The Alabama Extension Director said plaintively that SCS had promised that districts in the Tennessee watersheds would be given technical assistance through the colleges—but then had gone back on its promise!

date proven effective instruments of land-use regulation. Much was made of the standard act's provision empowering supervisors to promulgate land-use regulations. In light of Chief Bennett's views on the "coming technological revolution on the land," much is still made in official SCS circles of this coercive feature.[6] Until 1942, SCS, acting upon a perfectly legitimate interpretation of its basic legislation, the Soil Conservation Act of 1935, divided states into three categories according to the adequacy of state soil conservation district laws. Districts in the first category of states were eligible for complete SCS services, but these were reduced for the second category and denied to the third. The adequacy of land-use regulations was an important criterion in the decision where a state law fell. The late Professor John D. McGowen, of the University of Wyoming, prepared an article on the proposed Wyoming law for the *Rocky Mountain Law Review*. An SCS official read a draft of the article, objected to its critical appraisal of land-use regulations, and advised against publication; when McGowen was adamant, the official threatened to have him discharged from the university.[7]

Most land-use regulations have been employed in Colorado where 13 soil conservation districts have adopted ordinances.[8] In 1945, the Colorado legislature set aside all such ordinances except those repassed within 45 days by a 75 per cent majority of land owners affected. The Colorado ordinances have regu-

---

6. See below, chap. xiv, sec. 4. Edwin E. Ferguson says that SCS has ceased to press openly for enabling provisions in state laws to facilitate recourse to land-use regulations. "Nation-wide Erosion Control: Soil Conservation and the Power of Land-Use Regulations," 34 *Iowa Law Rev.*, 166, January, 1949. Nevertheless, there appears to be some tendency in SCS to work quietly toward the establishment of land-use regulations.

7. The article was published; cf. "Wyoming's Proposed Soil Conservation Act," 13 *Rocky Mountain Law Rev.* (February, 1941), pp. 115-26.

8. Many state laws either fail to provide for regulations or severely limit their application and enforcement. Although some 15 states have laws which facilitate the use of such regulations, only two districts outside of Colorado are known to have them. The Cedar District in North Dakota regulated grazing by issuing permits according to determination of the carrying capacity of land (since 1939). Such regulation may be more effective than that employed by grazing districts (notably in Montana) in which regulations apply only to members. The only other known example is the requirement in 1948 by the Warrington Dune District in Oregon that landowners control sand-drifting.

lated grazing, plowing up sod land, and the handling of land subject to wind erosion. Early grazing ordinances were held unconstitutional by the attorney general; later ones were not vigorously enforced and lapsed in 1945. "Blow-land" ordinances to check wind erosion have been popular and were made generally applicable in Colorado by the 1951 legislature; but they are now administered by county commissioners rather than district supervisors. Sod land ordinances caused controversy which directly stimulated the legislation of 1945. Objections in three southeastern districts apparently reflected poor administration. In other districts, similar ordinances were administered more acceptably and have sustained court tests which clarify somewhat the conditions under which such regulations may be held constitutional.[9] The courts looked favorably upon the practice of basing regulations upon objective physical determinations of erosion hazard (SCS land-use capability surveys) rather than upon the opinion of supervisors. Sod land ordinances have apparently checked the plowing up of such lands. Thus Colorado has been a useful laboratory; but the fact that only eight [10] of more than 2300 soil conservation districts currently enforce regulations indicates that the "coming technological revolution on the land" [11] is evolving very slowly.

Although the districts are hailed "as the most local of local institutions" and as the finest modern development in local rural democracy, the elected supervisor seems to have very little to do. As will be suggested in the following chapter, the SCS has developed its particular program as an orthodox and "highly scientific" approach to the soil. The approach discourages meddling by laymen. Thus Eugene A. Wilkening, discussing the Tri-Creek Soil Conservation District which includes four North Carolina counties, remarked that the supervisors have "few

---

9. The cases are discussed in a comprehensive study of "Land-Use Ordinances of Soil Conservation Districts in Colorado," by Stanley W. Voelker (mimeo., 1951: preliminary draft of a projected experiment station bulletin of the Colorado State College of Agriculture). Cf. Ferguson, *op. cit.*, and the discussion by James Patton, President of the National Farmers Union, in *Hearings*, H.R. 6054, 80th Cong., 2nd Sess., May, 1948, p. 57.

10. Six of these are in Colorado.

11. Ch. xiv, section 4, below.

duties outside of arranging for office space and assisting the conservationist in guiding his work in the county." [12]

A careful gleaning of the Hope and Aiken field hearings in 1947 as well as appropriate House and Senate hearings held in Washington during 1947–48 supports the interpretation that district supervisors generally have few important functions.[13] Thus Kent Leavitt appeared as President, National Association of Soil Conservation Districts. Leavitt argued that local democracy was achieved in the district program, yet maintained the need for unification (through the SCS) of a national program dealing with the soil. He opposed the Aiken bill because under it there would apparently appear 2000 different types of programs (in the 2000 soil conservation districts) rather than one

12. *Op. cit.*

13. Occasional brief references were of little value. Thus it was indicated that supervisors' activities in 13 Ohio districts consisted chiefly in maintaining good public relations, *Hearings*, H.R. 6054, 80th Cong., 2nd Sess., May, 1948, pp. 239-41. C. W. Huntley, a prominent figure in the Iowa Farm Bureau and a member of the Iowa State Soil Conservation Committee praised the districts and the SCS; but his testimony implied that district supervisors themselves had little to do. *Hearings*, S. Res. 147, 80th Cong., 2nd Sess., Part 2, pp. 907-908. George Welty, an Iowa Soil Conservation District Commissioner (as supervisors are called in that state), described how the board of his district had laid down a policy of putting conservation practices on the land most in need of them but added, "Later on, we hope that we can write a complete farm plan for each farmer." *Hearings*, H. of R., "Long Range Agricultural Policy," 80th Cong., 1st Sess., Part 12, pp. 1392-94. Lawrence McKinney, Secretary of the Indiana Association of Soil Conservation District Supervisors, said: ". . . As supervisors, our business is to coordinate the activity of the soil conservation work in the district or county, and we meet regularly and review the farm plans the soil conservation technician makes, and make recommendations and meet with groups on drainage projects." "Long Range Policy and Program," *Hearings*, Sub-committee of the Senate Committee on Agriculture and Forestry, 80th Cong., 1st Sess., Part 2, pp. 488-93. Frank Feser of South Dakota described how his district board conferred with the Forest Service and reached an understanding whereby the Brown-Marshall District obtained an agreement for a cooperative (and intensive) tree-planting campaign. It was the only example of its kind in the United States, according to the Forest Service, he declared. *Hearings*, H.R. 6054, 80th Cong., 2nd Sess., May, 1948, pp. 129-30. Since these references practically exhaust the 1947–48 hearings on the subject, it appears either that district boards were not very active at the time or, if they were, that the hearings failed to reflect this activity. Considering the direct bearing of the hearings upon the problem of administering soil conservation programs (a controversial subject then and since), one would expect the hearings fairly to reflect the actual situation.

unified program.[14] Yet no Senator asked the obvious question, namely, how local democracy is reconciled with a nationally-unified program.[15] Nor was any discussion elicited respecting what functions district supervisors actually perform. The paucity of information in thousands of pages of hearings on points such as this unfortunately—and, unnecessarily—diminishes the value of the hearings.

In general, the most exhaustive independent study of the subject agrees with these remarks about the failure of district supervisors to manage districts; yet the author finds increasingly hopeful signs:

"That district administration has not yet become supervisor administration is a commonly accepted fact. Supervisors generally are not yet fully carrying their governing responsibilities—either in determining policies or in the routine management work of the district. Even the stronger district boards, in their management activities, depend heavily upon the professional workers. Perhaps the most encouraging dimension in supervisor administration is that, within so brief a period as ten years, so much progress has been made in developing processes, organizational devices, and techniques for a productive operational merging of the skills of the conservation technician and the farmer supervisor. The resulting cross-fertilization of national and local experiences promises increasingly to produce a sounder and better proportioned approach to conservation activity than if either technicians or farmers were attempting to go it alone." [16]

14. *Hearings,* S. 2318, 80th Cong., 2nd Sess., p. 350.
15. This question W. R. Parks considerably illuminates, if he does not "answer."
16. Parks, *op. cit.,* p. 133. Supervisors have been influential in "marking out major emphases for district activity," e.g., drainage, irrigation, land-levelling, or stream bank control. Supervisor resistance has modified the fact, if not the form, of the SCS conception of the "complete farm plan." ". . . supervisor influence in modifying this policy is reflected in the frequency with which SCS farm planners 'boot-leg' on-site assistance to farmers who have no plan." Supervisor unwillingness to employ land-use regulations Parks considers as perhaps their "most important policy decision. . . ." After a discussion of the importance of establishing priority policies in districts, Parks says: "Today perhaps a half of the district governing bodies are giving at least formal routine approval to technicians' priority suggestions." But a much smaller number is actually reserving the right to decide such matters. In balancing various phases of conservation activity, supervisors have had some effect in modifying the SCS emphasis upon farm planning to include more application work. "Nevertheless, despite frequent examples of supervisors'

2. PROBLEMS AND POTENTIALITIES

If considerable mythology surrounds soil conservation districts, the same can frequently be said for agricultural cooperatives, labor unions, farm organizations, and other associations and agencies. It is misleading to conceive of the district as a new social invention which has spread across the country and affords a means for locally interested groups to organize their own programs of land improvement and soil and moisture conservation. The active interest of small organized groups often conveys an impression that "public" interest in particular programs is much more widespread than it is. Of course, much the same can often be said of farm organizations, e.g., the Farm Bureau. It is well to remember that SCS officials have a real professional and pecuniary interest in the establishment of districts, and that farmers with whom they work also have a strong interest in thus gaining valuable technical services for themselves, as well as other perquisites which have often been available.

Districts have to be voted in by farmers in special referenda, but the number of those voting is frequently very low. Again, the same is often true of elections for local PMA committeemen, or for township Farm Bureau presidents, or for local governmental offices—and all these phenomena reflect the "overburdened voter" in a country with approximately 900,000 elected public officers of one kind or another. But while the SCS has generally been the driving force behind the organization of districts, the example of Switzerland County, Indiana, indicates that many groups may press actively for the establishment of a

---

acting to put the technicians upon application work, the establishment of farm planning quotas for Service technicians has generally resulted in the Service's setting the balance." He stresses the rising supervisor activity in connection with equipment programs, but even here: "Not only have the SCS field employees had to take valuable time from 'operations field work' to perform such regularly assigned duties as equipment inspection, but they have largely carried the supervisors' work in the equipment field also." If the supervisors share little in preparing district programs and plans of work, they are increasingly active in preparing annual reports. Here, Parks finds that SCS policy has effectively stimulated supervisor activity. "The year 1943 marked the sharp turning point toward the writing of reports by supervisors." Cf. pp. 68-129.

district and also that large participation in referenda can be obtained.[17]

Districts have been important media of publicizing an important agricultural and social problem, the wastage of soil resources. State and national associations of district supervisors have effectively sought appropriations, chiefly in Washington, but increasingly from state legislatures. Further, another outlet for the energies of public-spirited farmers has been provided, as anyone who has talked with district supervisors, or attended one of their meetings, will testify. These men are rather substantial farmers, keenly interested in scientific farming, willing to spend their own time and money furthering the program, and commonly well-known in their areas. There is considerable overlapping, supervisors often being officers in farm organizations and having positions in the administration of other public programs. Attending a state-wide meeting of district supervisors in Urbana, Illinois (summer, 1947), the writer found a number of men who were currently serving as members of a state Farm Bureau committee to study public policy. Frank Feser of South Dakota is illustrative:

"I am familiar with every set of agricultural agencies out in the field. I am president of our local soil district and State board, chairman of the triple A county committee, member of the Farm Bureau

17. The Indiana State Soil Conservation District Law requires that 60 per cent of the eligible voters vote in the referendum on establishing the district; and, of these, 60 per cent must favor the district. In *Soil Conservation* (August, 1944), R. E. Babb, district conservationist, describes how Switzerland County, Indiana, brought out a vote of 74.3 per cent of eligible voters, 1357 voting for the district and 52 against it. The County Agent and the Home Demonstration Agent discussed the district in every group meeting in the county. A sponsoring committee and action committees were carefully selected, Babb does not say by whom, their principal function being to stir up interest, explain the district, carry petitions, and stimulate voting. The Vivay Kiwanis Club, town merchants, newspapers, theaters (through free advertising), the telephone company (through donating party line telephone calls), and two local banks which paid for newspaper advertisements—these supported the district. Local farm organizations actively helped. Cards explaining the district and the referendum were sent to every landowner. Receipts of absentee ballots were checked every three days, and each committeeman was notified about the situation in his township. Twelve days before the referendum, the organizing committee met to check votes and sentiment and to add more forces in townships where enthusiasm was lagging.

and the Farmers Union, and what-not and what-have-you. Any farmers' program." [18]

The needs of the districts, what are they? Assuming for the moment that the program continues to be one largely of physical erosion control and land development, districts are claimed to need more SCS technicians, nursery planting stock, and heavy machinery. As previously noted, districts cannot levy taxes, a circumstance which has caused some political scientists to deny that they are *bona fide* units of government. Districts must therefore seek resources from state legislatures, county boards, or the federal government (which so far has invariably meant through the SCS)—or through gifts.

Sometimes planting stock is very important. Trees, shrubs, and seeds of the kind not locally available are sometimes afforded. Kudzu, or Japanese porch vine, has proved one of the most important soil conserving crops in the Southeast. SCS had —and exploited—a monoply on kudzu crowns before World War II. The soil conservation districts have considerable machinery but need more.[19] Congressman Poage (D., Texas) attempted to get large transfers of government surplus machines transferred to SCS after the late war but without marked success. Other agencies (e.g., the Forest Service) had competing claims. Yet soil conservation districts owned $4,022,000 worth of machinery at the beginning of 1950.[20]

---

18. *Hearings*, H. R. 6054, 80th Cong., 2nd Sess., May, 1948, p. 124.

19. Thus a Vermont District was declared inadequately supplied although it had one 50 h.p. caterpillar tractor, two small graders, one 3/8 yard dragline excavator, another 3/4 yard, and one 5-ton dump truck and trailer. (*Soil Conservation*, April, 1944.) The needs of a Wisconsin District were listed as lime-grinding equipment, breaker plows, bulldozers, ditching machinery, dragline and scrapers, terracing equipment, trucks, cement mixers, sod cutters, small tools of various kinds, caterpillar tractors, and wire. (*Soil Conservation*, April, 1945.)

20. House *Hearings*, Agric. Approp., fiscal 1952, Part 2, pp. 793-94. Much of this was tied up in some 1500 pieces of heavy machinery, apparently. The Missouri Extension Service has advocated that farmers employ private contractors rather than machinery operated by soil conservation districts and subsidized by the public. Some private contractors have criticized government competition in this area. Contrarily, the district competition has been praised as forcing down custom rates. Actually, soil conservation districts have probably stimulated private contracting work. This is the opinion

In politics, a familiar statement is that "influence follows affluence." If counties are provided with SCS staffs including four or five technically-trained workers, and if the soil conservation districts acquire large amounts of heavy machinery and equipment available for farm use at cost of operation, what is the result? Much good erosion control work may be done. At the same time, local agricultural programs may become imbalanced in favor of physical work on the soil. The ability to direct these technicians and to control the machinery endows the SCS and its associated organizations with considerable political influence to use upon administrators and Congressmen whose task it is to weigh political demands for more physical erosion control against other demands that arise in rural areas.

Considering the independence of soil conservation districts and the base for political influence which they supply, it is understandable that the USDA has found cooperation with them to be difficult. True, the USDA declared its policy to be one of stimulating the creation of districts in February, 1951, and of collaborating with them in developing local conservation programs.[21] Yet, as recently as 1948, the Under-Secretary of the Department examined the problem of cooperating with locally-based soil conservation districts as against the practicability of operating agricultural programs through the state and local system of farm committees which the USDA was then advocating:

"There is, however, a very important distinction between soil-conservation districts and the farmer committees to which I have referred. Soil-conservation districts are agencies or instrumentalities of State governments with powers, of course, to obtain cooperation and assistance from various sources, including the Department of Agriculture. The Department, however, could not incorporate these districts into its administrative mechanism in the degree necessary to insure the proper execution of programs for which Congress holds the Department responsible.

of W. Robert Parks (*op. cit.*, p. 102), and H. H. Bennett declared that 32,000 pieces of major equipment were being operated in 1949 on the basis of soil conservation farm plans. House *Hearings*, Agric. Approp. for 1950, Part 2, p. 129. Heavy machinery manufacturers strongly support the SCS program. Thus several of them underwrote the soil conservation meeting in Urbana, Illinois, July, 1947.

21. See chap. xiii below.

"The proposed county USDA committees, on the other hand, would be elected by the farmers for the particular purpose of performing definite functions in the Department of Agriculture programs and thereby would become an integral part of the Federal Government's administrative machinery for that purpose. They would be subject to provisions of law laid down by the Congress and to regulations of the Department under those provisions of law. They would be representatives of the Federal Government, responsible to the farmers who would elect them for adaptation of the Federal programs to local requirements and conditions within the framework of law which would safeguard essential national objectives. Obviously, bodies such as soil conservation districts which are legal entities of State governments cannot fulfill all these essential requirements." [22]

Mr. Dodd's statement elicited the following critical exchange:

"Mr. Poage: . . . I never have heard you nor anybody else come down here and say, 'Well, the Extension Service is a State agency, therefore we cannot work through them.' Now, you tell us you cannot work through these soil-conservation districts because they are State agencies. I never have heard that complaint offered about the Extension Service. You do work through it. You do work through the Extension Service successfully."

"Mr. Cooley: Do you want to do anything to handicap the soil-conservation districts as they are now established?

"Mr. Dodd: No, sir.

"Mr. Cooley: Do you know of anybody else who wants to do that?

"Mr. Dodd: Not in the Department of Agriculture.

"Mr. Poage: Nothing except cutting their throats from one ear to the other; just cut their throats and let them lie there and bleed to death." [23]

A second question about the utility of soil conservation districts arises from the present SCS preoccupation with the discovery of local "natural leaders" who are believed to exist in small neighborhoods. Much imagination has been exhibited in the employment of sociological and social-psychological techniques to discover "natural leaders." The approach has much to commend it; yet it has some disturbing features. Thus, SCS

22. *Hearings,* H. R. 6054, 80th Cong., 2nd Sess., May, 1948, p. 14. The committee system which Mr. Dodd described was to be built upon the PMA committees described in chaps. vii and viii, below.

23. *Hearings,* H. R. 6054, 80th Cong., 2nd Sess., May, 1948, p. 40.

personnel are admonished not to manipulate natural leaders—not openly, at least; yet they are also advised to become "the power behind the throne." [24] As this search for natural leaders proceeds, where will soil conservation districts fit in? The rural neighborhoods are, of course, much smaller than the districts. Yet it will be into these neighborhoods that SCS ties for its real local control of the conservation program. The tendency to use natural leaders seems to be of a piece with the tendency noted in the previous chapter for SCS administration to reach farmers through local work units, which are not organized parallel to soil conservation districts. Both the employment of natural leaders and the form of SCS administration suggest that SCS expects districts to exercise political influence to defend and extend the program—but not actually to operate the local soil conservation programs, once established.

It might be possible to employ soil conservation districts somewhat as irrigation or drainage districts are used by farmers to meet rather specific problems that require group action.[25] The rationale of this conception is that the soil conservation problem is but one aspect of the complex problem of agricultural adjustment, the stimulation of agricultural production, and the improvement of farm family living. As W. Robert Parks has stated:

"It is well known that the conservation program is very much dependent upon proper arrangements in farm credit, size of farms, landlord-tenant relations, and so on. The district, of course, cannot be censured for not having corrected deep-rooted maladjustments in those arrangements."

Agreed. But the SCS approach does not appear sufficiently general if the conservation of private land is to be sought essentially as part of a broader program conceived in terms of the

---

24. The writer deals with the problem in "Natural Leaders and the Administration of Soil Conservation Programs," *Rural Sociology*, Sept., 1951.

25. The unusual effectiveness of Colorado districts may reflect the fact that they are typically smaller than counties and are really organized to meet one or two aggravated local problems. Voelker, *op. cit.*

objectives stated above, or some adaptation of them—nor does the typical current approach, at least, of soil conservation districts.[26]

26. Cf. Charles M. Hardin, "Land or People," in *Land Economics*, May, 1951, and chap. xiv below.

CHAPTER VI

The Soil Conservation Service in Politics

I. THE COMPULSION TO PLAY POLITICS

Many administrative agencies in the American government are under considerable compulsion to play politics.[1] The central government is a target for political interest groups many of which work through federal agencies. The agencies themselves are organizations interested in the fruits of the political struggle —increased appropriations and expanded grants of power. Ably led (and SCS leadership has been most able), agencies can become important political factors.

Hugh Hammond Bennett, Chief of SCS from its inception

---

1. Max Weber's distinction between the bureaucrat and the politician does not fit men like H. H. Bennett of the SCS. Such men are cast in Weber's political mold. Their function is to fight and to heap "scorn and derision" upon their opponents, following the manner of Weber's politicians. Cf. "Politics as Vocation," in Gerth and Mills, *op. cit.* A better characterization of administration in the United States is that of Paul Appleby: "the eighth political process." *Policy and Administration,* Univ. of Alabama Press (1949). Pendleton Herring declares: ". . . the politics of democracy cannot stop with the electoral and representative process. Nor can the task be surrendered to neutral administrators, however expert. Administration must carry on the representative and unifying process where the parties stop." *The Politics of Democracy,* Rinehart and Co., New York (1940), p. 421. Sometimes the "unifying" effects of agricultural administrative politics are less apparent than the splintering and divisive consequences; but it is a fact that such administration presents numerous channels through which organized group demands are pressed upon government.

to November 15, 1951, in view of the qualities of leadership
that he has exhibited in the last 25 years, must have chafed in
the Bureau of Soils (which he entered in 1903) and its successors in the USDA during the long years to 1929 in which
promotions were slow. Then came the erosion experiment station program, which Bennett had created almost single-handed,
but in which he served five masters! It is remarkable, even with
all the circumstances, that he could reach out so rapidly after
1933 in creating and extending the Soil Erosion Service. But
it is not remarkable that he should try to maintain an essential
autonomy in SCS after it "came home" to the USDA in 1935.
Even then the fight was only begun. Our system of government
rewards tangible accomplishments. Appropriations rear annually
from the ashes of the old funds—if these are properly consumed.
A big appropriation is *prima facie* evidence of its need. The
game is to double the stakes, but stakes are not doubled by faint
hearts. Humility respecting accomplishments of one's program
is not a well-rewarded virtue on Capitol Hill. The upward trend
in SCS appropriations has evidenced great political acumen.

Meanwhile, SCS has promoted the passage of state soil conservation district laws—sometimes over strenuous opposition of
colleges of agriculture. SCS also strove to get some early laws
amended in accordance with the principles of the standard act—
as well as with the "code" or bundle of concepts which SCS
developed, the political significance of which is considered later.
The agency stimulated the organization of soil conservation districts, sometimes over considerable opposition. Farmers had to
be signed up for conservation plans. Chief Bennett remarked
that "in the beginning, we had to go around and argue with
people and beg them to take better care of their land." [2]

According to its lights, SCS also had to keep from being decentralized to the states and also from being combined with
other programs, or made subject to other programs, at the national level. In the late 1930's arrangements had been made
through the Assistant Secretary of Agriculture, Harry Brown,
to decentralize SCS operations to the colleges of agriculture.

---

2. House *Hearings*, Agric. Approp., fiscal 1952, Part 2, p. 784.

This move was stopped by dramatic appeals of ranking SCS officials and allies to Secretary Wallace, and the Assistant Secretary resigned. Thus also SCS seems to have systematically disregarded secretarial memoranda or directives "requiring" coordinated administration with other agencies—memoranda based upon an Inter-bureau Coordinating Committee Report of 1939. Further, SCS fought the State and Local Land-Use Planning Program, based on the Mount Weather Agreement in 1938, which Congress liquidated in 1942.[3] SCS also chafed at the double harness during its brief union with AAA in the Agricultural Conservation and Adjustment Administration (1941–42). In 1945, Secretary Anderson's reorganization committee created the Production and Marketing Administration but was unable to unify conservation administration; whenever the committee discussed combination of SCS with other agencies, it was flooded at once with protesting communications from the field. Faced with a Congressional reorganization not to its liking in 1947 (the Cooley Bill), SCS apparently inspired the Jensen Bill as a counter-irritant. In 1948 it repeated its maneuver by promoting the Hope Bill in answer to Title I of the Aiken Bill. In 1950, SCS apparently helped kill President Truman's Reorganization Plan for the USDA in the Senate. In 1951, however, it was forced to bow to the reorganization of February 16; but it could insure considerable recognition of its interests in the matter.[4]

Rather continually, therefore, SCS has had to fight to keep and enlarge appropriations, to press its program in the States where it often met unfriendly rival agencies, to avoid being decentralized to the states, and to prevent what seemed to it undue "coordination" with other agencies in the USDA.

---

3. Cf. the writer's "The Bureau of Agricultural Economics Under Fire, . . ." *JFE*, August, 1946.

4. The Cooley, Jensen, Hope, and Aiken Bills, are discussed in the writer's "Current Proposals . . . ," *JFE*, November, 1948. For 1950 and 1951 developments, see chaps. xiii-xiv below, and the writer's articles, "Land or People," *Land Economics*, May, 1951, and "The Politics of Conservation: an Illustration," *Journal of Politics*, August, 1951.

2. POLITICAL STRATEGY AND TECHNIQUES

Making friends with strategically located Congressmen, especially chairmen and members of important committees. The value of this strategy can hardly be exaggerated. SCS is in position to do favors for Congressmen, although the only striking example that appears well-verified was the purchasing and landscaping of the acres that provide a prominent Congressman's front-porch view.[5] Nothing reprehensible is implied in this illustration nor in examples of lesser appeals to the legislative sense of prestige. At any rate, SCS has developed important Congressional friendships. The Jensen Bill in the first session of the 80th Congress, for example, was developed to counter the Cooley Bill which SCS considered unfriendly. In the second session of that Congress, the Hope Bill favored the SCS whereas the Aiken Bill would have advanced the interests of the colleges of agriculture. Just as staff workers from colleges of agriculture were prominent in drafting Title I of the Aiken Bill, so, reportedly, SCS technicians helped frame the Hope and Jensen Bills.[6] Earlier, Congressman Terry of Arkansas, a member of the Appropriation Subcommittee for Agriculture, strongly criticized the BAE-Land-Grant College state and local planning program, which SCS considered a rival. BAE was accused of trying to take credit for what SCS had done. Again in 1949, Congressman Whitten, chairman of the Subcommittee on Agricultural Appropriations, upheld the SCS position in favor of flood control surveys as against the Secretary of Agriculture's position favoring a comprehensive agricultural survey for the Missouri Valley.[7] Congressman Poage of Texas, an influential member of the House Committee on Agriculture, has also been a stout champion of SCS.[8]

SCS has cultivated powerful Congressmen more effectively than any other agricultural agency known to the writer. SCS

---

5. An SCS nursery was thus established.
6. Internal evidence also testifies to the origins of these measures; cf. "Current Proposals . . . ," *JFE, op. cit.*
7. House *Hearings,* Agric. Approp., fiscal 1950, Part 2, pp. 3-35.
8. Chap. v, sec. 2, above.

appears to have concentrated especially upon members of the
agricultural appropriations subcommittee in the House. Its success helps explain the long period of near autonomy of SCS in
the USDA. That is, bureau autonomy is directly proportionate
to the bureau's ability to maintain its appropriations independ-
ently from the budget-making process in the department.

SCS *has stimulated the formation of soil conservation districts.*
Thereupon, SCS can appeal to Congress for additional funds to
serve farmers thus organized. This method has proved the most
efficient ratchet for jacking up the SCS budget.

SCS *has developed associated organizations as political allies.*
While these include the Soil Conservation Society of America
(an organization of professionals) and Friends of the Land
(which might not unfairly be characterized as the Back Bay,
Park Avenue, North Shore devotees of the soil), by all odds the
most important is the National Association of Soil Conservation Districts (NASCD). The NASCD has been most active
in supporting SCS before Congress since its organization in
1946. Vice-President George F. Heidrich of the NASCD told
the House Agricultural Appropriation Subcommittee, respecting
Secretary Brannan's reorganization of February 16, 1951: "We
think that the memorandum is very sound. Our group worked
with the Department on it from the very beginning." [9]

Soon after state district laws were passed and districts began
to be created, state organizations of district supervisors appeared.
A number were active before World War II, but efforts to form
a national organization were unsuccessful until 1946. The first
president, E. C. MacArthur of North Carolina, was killed in an
automobile accident. Subsequently, the NASCD enjoyed the
vigorous leadership of Kent Leavitt of New York (September,
1947 to February, 1950). The organization elects a president, a
national vice-president, and a vice-president for each of seven
regions (which coincide with the administrative regions into
which SCS divides the country). Annual conventions are held;
the Oklahoma City Convention in February, 1951, drew 1296
delegates from 46 states. A number of committees are maintained, including Finance, Education, Publicity, District Opera-

9. House *Hearings,* Agric. Approp., fiscal 1952, Part 2, p. 1279.

tions, Legislation, and Public Lands. The national and state associations are active before Congress and state legislatures in securing appropriations for the SCS and soil conservation districts. The NASCD publishes the *American Soil Conservation District News,* a quarterly. It is financed by contributions from soil conservation districts ($5 per year), affiliate memberships (each district being asked to get one at $25 per year), and contributions from other sources. In 1949 Kent Leavitt reported an annual budget of only $7,000 which compares very unfavorably with the budgets of general farm organizations. But efforts are being made to stimulate the payment of individual dues to soil conservation districts, part of which would be given to the NASCD (as the American Farm Bureau, for example, now receives 75 cents for each dues-paying member in state farm bureaus). If this method of financing can be established, it will add greatly to the financial strength of NASCD; moreover, it will give that organization a clearer title to "speak for farmers." [10]

Another technique might be phrased as follows: "Who is ready to move with concrete programs when the time is ripe, to him will the appropriations fall." On the eve of World War II, SCS was rapidly developing a backlog of projects useful either for natural resource conservation or make-work policies. These projects were summarized by SCS administrative districts, areas, and regions, with outlays shown for each area of organization. In the post-war period, a similar device was used in the Missouri Valley wherein the SCS fought hard to make the USDA plan essentially one of erosion control and physical development rather than the "comprehensive agricultural plan" which Secretary Brannan favored.[11]

A closely related technique is the time-table of conservation operations which SCS vigorously advocates. The first step

10. The best source of information on the NASCD is found in its publications, especially the *Information Letters,* published monthly during Mr. Leavitt's presidency, and the quarterly currently being published. See also Mr. Leavitt's testimony in *Hearings,* S. Res. 147, 80th Cong., 1st Sess. (1948), p. 1112.

11. After several postponements, the Secretary was successful—in reporting the comprehensive plan, at least. See "The Missouri River Agricultural Program," House Doc. No. 373, 81st Cong., 2nd Sess. (1949).

would be a survey to classify all agricultural lands according to their suitability for cultivation, forestry, grazing, etc. Conservation practices would be identified for each classification. The Secretary would then present a time-table to Congress for carrying out these practices. If SCS can get the time-table enacted into law, it will have scored a major victory, for it will have established a schedule which will be a powerful argument for appropriation increases. So far, Congress has not accepted the proposal.[12]

SCS strives to make soil conservation the primary end of agricultural policy. If successful, SCS may emerge as the paramount agricultural agency in all matters dealing with land-use and even production problems of farmers. The establishment of conservation policy as paramount in agriculture was a cardinal feature of the Hope Bill; it represents the reach of SCS imperialism, but a reach which, to date, has exceeded the grasp.[13]

SCS has secured friendly appointments in, or rendered friendly services to, various influential organizations. SCS has prepared brochures, e.g., for the American Bankers Association. A considered policy seems to have been the placement of SCS "alumni" in strategic positions. A man on the editorial staff of an influential newspaper can be very useful. So can a faithful friend in the Bureau of the Budget or in an agency like the Office of Land-Use Coordination (a staff and coordinating agency of the Secretary of Agriculture from 1937 to 1944). An

---

12. See the thoughtful remarks of Congressman Whitten in his colloquy with H. H. Bennett on the "long-range conservation plan," House *Hearings,* Agric. Approp., fiscal 1952, pp. 784-85. The time-table espoused by SCS for a number of years was laid out in "Soil and Water Conservation Needs Estimates for the United States," SCS, USDA (1945) (revision). The Hope Bill of 1948 employed the survey and time-table and it is notable that both were added to the Aiken Bill by amendment. See "Current Proposals . . ." *JFE,* November, 1948.

13. Since the Hope Bill has been frequently cited, it should be said that the writer's interpretation is that Congressman Hope introduced his bill primarily as a diametrically-opposed counter-measure to Title I of the Aiken Bill. He acted, it appears, largely for two reasons: (a) to get before the country (or, more precisely, before the various "publics" involved) the entire range of possible proposals for the organization of conservation administration, and (b) to postpone action which he believed was not yet ripe. Cf. "Current Proposals . . ." *JFE,* November, 1948.

interesting example is a former SCS employee hired by a private power company as a soil conservationist, a move enthusiastically described as "private power's answer to the TVA." Good relationships between SCS and chambers of commerce as well as the manufacturers of machinery useful in conservation engineering are notable.

SCS has followed the election returns. Many early New Deal agricultural programs had their strongest initial development in the South; and SCS was one. But during the war, the political temper seemed to many to suggest a return to Republicanism. SCS promptly discovered that the major problem of control of erosion and depletion was emerging in the corn belt. This discovery was paralleled by an apparent desire to slough off, or at least to depreciate in importance, the land-utilization program that smacked of the New Deal approach. The soil conservation conference in Lincoln, Nebraska, May 7-8, 1948, seemed to be an overture to the Republicans.[14]

This section on the political techniques of SCS can be concluded by referring to an amusing accident. The occasion was an SCS meeting in Columbia, Missouri, during 1947 when the Cooley Bill, which SCS disliked, and the Jensen Bill, which it favored, were pending in Congress. Mr. William H. Coleman, an SCS employee, attended the meeting and took notes in a booklet with the words *United States Department of Agriculture* on the cover. He then lost the notebook, which was found and turned over to Congressman Albert L. Reeves, Jr., who printed much of it in the *Congressional Record* (Appendix) for June 19, 1948.

Mr. Coleman took full notes from the discussion of his Assistant State Conservationist on the art of exercising political influence. *One object was to create a favorable public opinion.* ("Three letters to editor of Post-Dispatch by farmers next week." "Two letters to Globe for October 3, editorial. Stress what Soil Conservation Service has done in my district." "Publicity to 35 to 40 southwest newspapers.") *Soil conservation districts were to be mobilized.* ("Each bill should be discussed with supervisors' board meeting. Have members ask questions.") *The aid*

14. See the *Hearings,* H. R. 6054, 80th Cong., 2nd Sess., p. 455.

of other organizations was to be sought. ("Resolutions from Cape and Pemiscot Farm Bureau." "Letters from priests at Jackson, Portageville, Leopold, and Wintergarten to Congress." "Mrs. Wilson to write or see Mrs. Jackson (garden clubs for resolution.)" "Talk to Rotary Clubs in Southeast Missouri." "Cape Federated Club through Goodwin.") *Influential people were to be cultivated.* ("Know State and National key people." "Know key editors.") *Congressmen were to be lined up.* ("Get every Congressman in soil district. Have him invited to meetings." "Two or three farmers to see Congressman.") *It was important to know how to approach some Congressmen.* ("Banta [Congressman in the 8th District, Missouri] obligated to Hall. (This is Len Hall, St. Louis columnist.) Len will see him this week." "J. R. Byrd, Cape County, influence with Zimmerman (the late Congressman Zimmerman.)" *Arguments were suggested in favor of the Jensen Bill and against the Cooley Bill. Finally, advice on the art of writing letters to Congressmen was spelled out in some detail:*

"Supervisors and others should be encouraged to write their Congressmen for a copy of the Jensen bill and study it. A request for a bill is usually construed as a vote for it. (In view of that fact, it will be well if many of those writing for the Cooley bill indicate that they have heard about it and don't like it and want a copy so that they can study it. But don't stimulate a flood of the latter letters. We do not want that at this stage of the game.)

"Prepare for final action. Lay the groundwork for a direct line of letters and other communications from the people back home expressing their wishes, to their Congressmen when either or both bills come before the Congress. We may not need that action but the people should be prepared.

"The type of letters needed now are a few good ones going in to Senators and Representatives from local people or groups to let Congressmen know what is going on in the way of soil conservation progress; what a farmer thinks of his plan, and the fact that SCS helped him do it; a progress report from supervisors to their Senators and Representatives. If these are bona fide letters written by the individuals (or groups), they mean more going in during the fall and winter than a flood of letters when the bills are before Congress. In other words, people should let Congress know they are interested in soil conservation, in districts, and in the SCS all the time." [15]

3. THE IDEOLOGY OF SCS

Examination of the politics of conservation soon convinces one that analysis of political techniques in terms of the organization and strategic application of power and influence is not enough. As Rousseau declared, "The strongest is never strong enough to be always the master, unless he transforms strength into right, and obedience into duty." [16] The myth in politics—the ideas that surpass experience but that are accepted as explaining the ways of the state to man—are vital political phenomena. These occur on the grand scale to help maintain the state itself—or to create the "proper" state. One is reminded of Plato's "golden lie," of Cicero's compelling myth to induce obedience to the powers that be. "True law is right reason." The law is a silent magistrate. The magistrate is speaking law.[17] The social contract in various forms represented myths; so did Rousseau's general will. Marxism is full of myths—economic determinism, the surplus labor theory of value, the great and wonderful change in man that will occur under the dictatorship of the proletariat and will lead to the withering away of the state. Mussolini advanced his myth in the "Doctrine of Fascism." Hitler and Rosenberg expounded the racial myth which is fundamental to Nazism. Herring suggests a myth for democracy:

"Government, whether by party, president, or bureaucracy, must have a basis in some combination of group interests. These interests can be rationalized in various ideologies. I would defend the myth of the public interest because by its very vagueness it permits the freest interplay of group interests." [18]

---

15. 94 *Cong. Record*, A4520-22; cf. Hearings, H. R. 4150, etc., 80th Cong., 2nd Sess., pp. 73-103.
16. *Social Contract*, Everyman's ed., Book I, chap. iii.
17. C. H. McIlwain, *The Growth of Political Thought in the West* (1932), pp. 106, 114.
18. *The Politics of Democracy, op. cit.*, pp. 424-25.

Our concern, however, is with myths or ideas on a lesser scale. Chester Barnard [19] has emphasized the function of the business executive to define, elaborate, and communicate the "code" of his organization in order to create authority. His analysis applies to governmental executives as well. Any agricultural administrator is well-advised to define his agency's purposes, to spell out appropriate doctrines, and to clarify the principles that lend authority to his hierarchy. These actions create the network of understandings and common values so that representative statements may be made with all the weight of common statements—as though the agency had spoken with one voice. The SCS has accomplished this task admirably.

The writer attempted to characterize the SCS code in 1948:

"Soil erosion is a national menace. We must save the topsoil. We must develop a technology to achieve this end and an organization to apply the technology. Since the problem is national, a nation-wide organization is called for; since the benefits will be diffuse, a public program is indicated. The technology is sufficiently generalizable, moreover, that national administration appears to follow. For purposes of applying the technology, local contacts are necessary. In order to protect the integrity of the technology, adequate organization and procedures need to be developed. To this end, the land use capability tables provide a common method of action and the complete farm plan provides the standard of application in the final analyses. The achievement of organization to fulfill the possibilities of technology requires a high order of technical analysis at the farm level with the technical criticism and control at higher levels. Yet conservation is not altogether an individual farm matter; it may be a watershed or a regional problem; but common action in the U. S. requires consent and even spontaneity. Moreover, individual soil conservation activities are undertaken in the presence of economic criteria—'How much conservation can I afford on my farm?' And our economic beliefs emphasize the importance of the farmer's individual decisions. Now, how to (a) protect the scientist's integrity, (b) bow to democratic concepts to the degree that conservation is a common problem or a social problem, and (c) admit entrepreneurial self-determination? The code allows for all these things. The soil conservation district is to approach the problem in communal fashion; the

19. *The Function of the Executive,* Harvard University Press (1938).

farmer is to remain his own entrepreneur, adapting technical soil conservation if he wishes and incorporating *from other* agencies what he needs and can get to round out his farm management according to economic criteria. But SCS protects its integrity (subjectively viewed, that is) by defining the manner in which it will cooperate— i.e., the complete farm plan, etc." [20]

Numerous examples of the SCS code are encountered in the course of interviews and conversations; others occur in the literature. Thus Mr. Fred Sherman, appearing in 1947 in the New Hampshire hearings of the House Committee on Agriculture, set forth an argument which embraced point after point of the SCS code.[21] Each of his paragraphs ended by a summary, invariably introduced by the words: "a point to remember." For example, regarding soil conservation districts, he concluded: "A point to remember; soil conservation districts are farmer organizations, represented by soil conservation district supervisors or directors." The contrast in style between his first three paragraphs, which were extemporaneous, and the rest of his remarks, is strong evidence of the presence of an SCS ghost-writer.[22]

---

20. "Reflections on Agricultural Policy Formation in the United States," *APSR*, October, 1948.

21. "Long-Range Agricultural Policy," 80th Cong., 1st Sess., Part 6, pp. 733-37. A recent statement of much of the SCS code is contained in six proposals, which SCS has asked all soil conservation districts to consider. Cf. *American Soil Conservation District News*, June 1, 1951.

22. The preparation of material for others to use is, of course, a common activity of governmental agencies. It is not unknown for an agency staff analyst to prepare an attack upon his program for a Congressman or Senator to give—and then to prepare a speech in defense of the program for another Congressman or Senator to use in reply. An amusing example occurred in 1949 when a speech was prepared in the first person to be delivered by Senator Thomas (D., Okla.) in an analysis of the Commodity Credit Corporation's program. The speech contained an attack upon the Bureau of the Budget. But the Senator failed the agency by merely rising to request the publication in the Congressional Record of the statement of the United States Department of Agriculture! 95 *Cong. Record*, 5079-85, April 25, 1949 (Daily Ed.).

Another amusing illustration occurred in 1948 when President Kent Leavitt of the National Association of Soil Conservation Districts, Senator Wherry, and others suddenly employed very similar arguments, with comparable illustrations, to urge retention of SCS regional offices. All urged that large business organizations operate through such offices for efficiency; the same businesses were cited. Cf. 94 *Cong. Record*, 8863, June 17, 1948 (Daily Ed.).

This business of fashioning and communicating the agency code is so important that further analysis is justified. SCS has had magnificent leadership. All SCS personnel appear to exult in Hugh Hammond Bennett, a truly "charismatic" leader in Max Weber's term.[23] Dr. Bennett has made the SCS program a crusade; its members are dedicated. Only SCS of all controversial federal agricultural agencies of the 1930's has had stability of leadership. The "Chief's" legendary attraction has to be felt to be appreciated. Lacking this shared feeling, the writer is as much at loss as William James was in examining the *Varieties of Religious Experience*. James could only know such experience vicariously, hence (as Lawrence Hyde in his devastating *Learned Knife* points out) could never really comprehend religious ecstasy. The point is that SCS has not merely a staff; it has a corps and an *esprit de corps*, a goal, a body of dogma—indeed it has fired the imagination of a number of followers with that trilogy of "authority, mystery, and miracles" celebrated by Dostoyevsky's Grand Inquisitor in *The Brothers Karamazov*.

The soil carries magical properties, only one being streptomycin; classical mythology knew another and immortalized it in Anataeus who, thrown to the ground, the earth, the soil, rose again twice renewed—and again, and again. In the elegant program of SCS, the soil is the source of life, the bastion, the substructure of civilizations. Why this should be is inscrutable (the element of mystery); yet it is so, but it is precariously so, for men can ruin their priceless heritage. However, by a combination of dedication and science some men are competent to be custodians of this precarious balance which keeps the famous six inches of topsoil where it should be. In due time they will be recognized through grants of authority (authority!) to prescribe soil management. Then, with the "coming technological

---

23. See, e.g., the discussion of charismatic leadership in Talcott Parsons, *The Structure of Social Action*, McGraw-Hill, New York (1937), "Charisma," index. Compare the biography of Bennett by Wellington Link, *Big Hugh*, Macmillan, New York, 1950—a book which may well seem idolatrous to those who have not fallen under the charm of "the chief" but which will probably be accepted in full by SCS personnel.

revolution on the land," comes the miracle (the miracle!) when man achieves peace with nature and with himself.[24]

Already the shape of technological perfection is at hand: the "complete farm plan" and the "land-use capability tables." Land-use capabilities are found by conservation surveys which go much farther (it is said) than the old soil surveys, "taking samples right and left." "You can't show the slope and the degree of erosion in the laboratory." Land-use capability tables are translated through conservation surveys into farm maps which classify the land according to its capabilities. Class I will not erode even if farmed with present practices; class II can also be farmed intensively, but simple practices are called for—stripcropping, perhaps, and contour tillage. Class III calls for intensive practices, and so on to class VII, which is to be kept permanently in woodland. Thus every acre gets the treatment which it requires. There is an exact measure of good works which induces salvation.

This is an intensive approach, and it is held forth as absolutely the only path to grace. Roads that seem shorter are blind alleys, and any civilization which persists in following them will come upon evil days. "The lone and level sands stretch far away." Mark the elegance. If this *is* the true gospel, then

---

24. While numerous examples of the paramount role of soil conservation in the maintenance of civilization could be cited, one will suffice: H. H. Bennett, "Development of Natural Resources: The Coming Technological Revolution on the Land," in *Science,* January, 1947; cf. chap. xiv, sec. 4, below. The same source will also indicate the employment of authority. The miracle to come is colorfully suggested by the following:

"Fair is the land that rims the Tuscarawas, the Conotton, and the McGuire. Quiet, cool, are the dawdling streams. Green, happy, are the cradling slopes. Gentle is the rule of order and discipline. A canoe slices like a whisper across a shaded pool, and a drinking doe mothers her fawn to the protective cover of the brush. Nature smiles the old-young smile of memory and hope.

"Here, where calm waters pile back in a twelve-mile lake from the breast of a man-made dam, a new faith stands to cheer the rising sun. A noble and intelligible faith that moves within a widely-drawn periphery. Here, vigorous and clean as morning dew—and as welcome to the aging throat of civilization—lies upon every leaf and stem a concept of an Earth at peace with itself. Here, Science and Youth move in comradeship with that which is on, and of, the soil." Wellington Link, *Soil Conservation,* September, 1944, p. 51.

it is equally valid in Nevada and New Hampshire; hence, a *national* program is required. But, since climate, topography, and other variables obtain—and since forty-eight field offices could not do justice to the twin requirements of orthodoxy and adaptation, regional establishments are needed—seven of them (down from the original ten). Contrarily, elaborate state offices are unnecessary (or were in the beginning, although SCS has bowed more and more to the federal-state system in delegating responsibility to state offices); the real work must be carried to farmers on their own farms.

In evaluating the SCS myth, it will not do to forget the role of prestige and the drive for security. If one is to understand the motivations of many SCS personnel as part of the general analysis of the policy forming and administering process in agriculture, he must remember that SCS got its start precariously in the early 1930's when unemployment often shrouded the professional man's future. That the Great Depression, blown up to gigantic proportions in the minds of men, broods over many issues of public policy is obvious if we consider controversy over the level of agricultural support prices. The same is true with respect to such programs as SCS. In and after the 30's Soil Conservation Service personnel have been exhorted by their leaders to fight for their jobs. It is all too easy for people sitting in relatively safe positions to condemn such exhortations and subsequent actions as morally reprehensible.

To round out the analysis of SCS employment of ideology, it may be said that the agency (with characteristic diligence and imagination) leaves no stone unturned. It is not for nothing that SCS currently spends $364,000 annually for information and education! [25] Many items in the foregoing section are relevant here; for example, the development and display of statistics respecting erosion, of the conservation time-table, etc. In addition, symbols of nationalism are heavily employed. Jefferson is reputed to have said, "He is the best patriot who stops the most gullies." Much research has been done to suggest that the SCS stems from some of the best thoughts of the founding

---

25. It should be added, of course, that all members of SCS are expected assiduously to cultivate the public in the interests of the program at all times.

fathers. During a considerable period of the war the magazine *Soil Conservation* employed a flag motif on the cover consistently and also devised pictures, the usual ones of the beautifully strip-cropped fields with the terraces gracefully flung around the contours, but with the unusual touch of bombers flying overhead. Finally, a stroke of genius created a composite picture in which the flag of the United States was represented, the stars by shocks of grain, and the stripes by strip-cropped fields, with bombers flying over these and the dramatic words *mene, mene, tekel, upharsin* inscribed underneath! [26]

The religious motif is vigorously used. A brochure written by Morris E. Fonda is entitled *"The Lord's Land."* The only other words that appear on the cover are "U. S. Soil Conservation Service." This brochure was published by Sears-Roebuck Foundation, Chicago, and is prepared in cooperation with and distributed by the Foundation, Friends of the Land, soil conservation districts, and national and sectional religious organizations. The author associates soil building and depleting with man's and civilization's physical and spiritual growth and decay. The SCS program and the work of districts are described. A positive correlation is found between the quality of soil, the size of church congregations, the amount of contributions to churches, and the amplitude of the pastor's salary. Some quotations are, "The soil on this Wisconsin farm is being used with the reverence due 'The Lord's Land.' There is little opportunity here for erosion of either the soul or the soil." "People living on land properly taken care of are more healthy in their religious attitudes." A clergyman is quoted: "It ought to humble us and fill us with gratitude and inspire us to a genuine stewardship to remember that *ours is a heritage of soil, not of achievement*. God's goodness is there in soil, minerals, plants and animals." (Italics supplied.)

4. INTERPRETATIONS

The foregoing pages have provided an example of the politics of administration in the United States. The techniques and

---

26. See *Soil Conservation* during 1942–43.

strategy employed, the development of powerful friends, the interlocking with an organization (the National Association of Soil Conservation Districts) which is growing in significance—all have rather obvious meanings for the improved understanding of the American political system. In addition, a few points may be made.

First, SCS in politics is not to be understood merely through an examination of the struggle for power, with attention to the alliances, counter-alliances, and in-fighting that goes with it. Political action is conditioned and illuminated by ideals. It is notable that SCS has developed an ideology which fires the imagination of many men not on the payroll. This ideology gains in significance when one turns to an examination of possible modifications of the SCS program or alternatives to its approach.[27]

Second, the significance of SCS within the USDA needs reemphasizing. Clearly, an agency of this sort gains a degree of autonomy which makes it extremely difficult to coordinate. Further, the actual method of playing politics which SCS has adopted seems to have internal dynamics which impel the agency toward imperialism. That is, the SCS is forced to distinguish its program in order to repel critics who proclaim that it duplicates and overlaps the Extension Service. But in this process of self-distinguishing, SCS has perfected more and more a comprehensive approach to land-use. Then, in order to achieve the purposes set by this comprehensive approach ("each acre used according to its capability"), the SCS goals have to be made into the major premise of much agricultural policy. We are indebted to the Hope Bill for illuminating the potentialities of SCS for expansion.

Third, in the process of elaborating its code and spelling out its ideology into concrete intentions, SCS has developed the compelling idea of a conservation time-table. This is a device of considerable general political significance. The time-table assumes a degree of knowledge about the extent, causes, and cures of soil erosion that many informed people would con-

27. Chap. xiv, below; cf. the writer's "Land or People," and "The Politics of Conservation: An Illustration," *op. cit.*

test.[28] But let us pass that and comment upon the political aspects.

Why not have similar time-tables for (a) wiping out malnutrition, (b) removing inequalities in education, (c) doing away with major health hazards, and eliminating the chief diseases, (d) eliminating monopoly, (e) achieving adequate housing, (f) replanning cities, (g) adjusting man-resource ratios, and finally, (h) resolving intergroup and interracial hatreds? These and other purposes may be among those of a democratically organized society, but their very statement invokes disagreement about the content of social goals, the speed and method of their attainment, and priorities among them. It is the problem of any political society to decide upon which of these or other purposes it wants to achieve. The purposes have to be measured against each other. And while confusion may arise from insisting upon consideration of too many purposes at once, the multiple purposes which emerge in a democratic society demand some kind of recognition. The situation is distorted by the erection of one or two such purposes into paramount social goals. Reflection upon these aspects of the democratic process makes one appreciate the reluctance of Congress to accept the SCS invitation to enact the conservation time-table into law. To do so would be to surrender unduly to one interest. However important it may be, soil conservation remains only one of the numerous social interests which have to be continuously reconciled and adjusted in the on-going process of democracy.

Fourth, it is somewhat paradoxical in view of the tendencies toward expansion in the SCS approach to note that it fails to acknowledge many factors which are closely associated with mismanagement of farm land. The criticism is that the engineering approach of SCS treats the symptoms of erosion instead of the disease.[29] Economic instability of farming, unfavorable man-land ratios, educational disadvantages, rural poverty, insufficient amounts of the right kinds of credit, unfortunate tenurial arrangements, and a culture which tends to reinforce

---

28. See the contrast between the Kellogg and Bennett interpretations of the extent of the erosion problem, Ch. i, section 3.

29. For elaboration, cf. the writer's "Land or People," *op. cit.*

the establishment and maintenance of these conditions and of the farming practices and customs that go with it—these are the kinds of things alone and in combination, which are often reflected in eroded land. Now this concentration on engineering without attention to the social maladjustments that may be the real strategic points to attack in a soil conservation program makes the SCS attractive to many people. These people are anxious to identify themselves with a noble cause, but preferably one without "radical" connotations. SCS can be supported without risking the social displeasure of the respectable. *There is no damned nonsense about the plight of the sharecropper or of migratory labor in the area of policy with which SCS deals.*

This emphasis of SCS, and the corresponding lack of focus upon social maladjustments, does not invite the indictment of the agency on grounds of indifference to these profound social problems. What it does is to suggest another reason for concluding that, if these problems need to be dealt with as part of a well-rounded program for agriculture, neither SCS nor the soil conservation districts are adequate agencies for the purpose.[30]

---

30. Cf. the conclusions of the preceding chapter.

CHAPTER VII

The Union of Conservation and Parity

I. THE PRODUCTION AND MARKETING ADMINISTRATION

The Production and Marketing Administration (PMA) is a direct descendant of the Agricultural Adjustment Administration (AAA). No serious study of farm politics can ignore this agency. As C. J. Friedrich has stated:

"Out of a justifiable pride in later developments, constitutionalism and democracy, the myth has grown up that the origins of modern government in Britain and America were different, that constitutionalism came first and the administrative services afterwards. Such a view is not only contrary to the facts, but it obstructs a real understanding of the strength of constitutionalism itself. Constitutionalism comes as a restraining, civilizing improvement; there must first be government . . . before it can be constitutionalized. That is why we suggest the study of administrative government, of bureaucracy, as the necessary preliminary of the full grasp of constitutional government." [1]

The thrust of government into economic regulation requires the re-examination of constitutionalism. The question is not only one of efficient administration; it embraces the effect of administration on the organization and control of political power. What is the meaning of PMA in this respect?

---

1. *Constitutional Government and Democracy*, Little, Brown, and Co., Boston, 1941, p. 37.

The AAA-PMA is loaded with ideological meaning. It is charged to achieve parity for farmers. Parity is much more than a ratio of prices received to prices paid—it is "simple economic justice." It is an economic right turned into a political obligation upon government.

PMA is not only government of and for farmers—it is government by farmers. Its regulatory programs (marketing quotas and orders) rest upon favorable referenda among producers concerned. It is essentially administered by farmers. Elected PMA county and community committees cover rural America; from these committees appointments and promotions are made up the line—on occasion even including the Secretary of Agriculture.

The AAA-PMA program has consolidated the bulk of the enormous financial power developed by government for agriculture in the United States. In 1940 the total ordinary expenditures of the USDA were $1,444,700,000. Of this sum nearly 60 per cent was spent upon the AAA program—agricultural conservation and adjustment payments, the sugar act, parity payments, etc. In 1950, the comparable total USDA expenditure was $1,385,800,000; of this approximately 46 per cent was spent by PMA.[2] In addition the Commodity Credit Corporation, the financial engine of the price support, stock-piling, storage, and purchase programs, was administered by AAA in 1940 and by the PMA in 1950; the CCC remains identified with AAA-PMA in the minds of farmers. In 1940, the CCC had a capital of $100,000,000 and the authority to borrow and lend up to $1,400,000,000 on the credit of the United States. In 1950, with the same capital, the borrowing and lending authority of CCC had been increased to $6,750,000,000.[3] These figures underscore the significance of AAA and its successor, the PMA, in the Department.

AAA-PMA has posed a constant challenge to the Secretary of Agriculture. Secretary Wallace summarily dismissed Howard R. Tolley from the head of AAA in 1938, shifting him to the head

2. House *Hearings*, Agric. Approp., fiscal 1952, Part 1, Table on pp. 64-65.
3. House *Hearings*, Agric. Approp., fiscal 1942, Part 1, p. 1075; *ibid.*, fiscal 1952, Part 1, p. 101.

of the Bureau of Agricultural Economics. In 1951, Secretary Brannan summarily shifted Ralph S. Trigg and Frank K. Woolley out of their jobs as administrator and deputy administrator of PMA. Thus Secretaries of Agriculture have felt a perennial challenge from subordinates whose very position tends to make them outrank the Secretary in the eyes of farmers. In the reorganization which created PMA in 1945, a proposal was made to create two separate agencies, one for marketing, one for production. But this was vetoed by the vigorous objections of a member of the reorganization committee with long experience in helping administer the Department. He said that it would place the Secretary in an impossible position to force him to mediate between two such powerful administrators! But the alternative seems to be to consolidate so much power in PMA that its administrator is perennially forced into the position (or the appearance of the position: it does not really matter) of challenging the prestige and authority of the Secretary himself.

These remarks help set the problem. The conservation program of PMA is subject to analysis not only respecting its intrinsic merits and disadvantages but also in its relationship to the PMA generally and, therefore, to the problem of organizing and controlling the power of government itself. For much of PMA's activity, the farmer committee system is a prime source of political strength. But the committees have to perform accepted functions to continue to operate. Since 1936, a significant function of the committees has been administration of the conservation program. *During 1945-1949 conservation administration became virtually the sole function of the PMA committees in most of the country.*

2. HOW PMA IS ORGANIZED

In addition to the Agricultural Conservation Program (ACP), this agency administers production and marketing programs—price supports, subsidies, loans, purchase, storage and disposal of farm commodities and products, marketing quotas, school lunch and direct distribution, inspection, standardization, the administration of grades, and the administration of regulatory laws.

Headed by an administrator and deputy, PMA has assistant administrators for production, marketing, commodity operations, and management. The administrator is president of the Commodity Credit Corporation and a member of its board; his deputy and four assistants are all vice presidents of the CCC. There are nine commodity branches and twelve functional and staff branches.[4]

The Agricultural Conservation Programs Branch reports to the Assistant Administrator for Production. His office contains program coordinators and field representatives. The coordinators have charge of the production aspects of two or more branches—one is responsible for ACP but also for rice, tobacco, flood control, and river basin development. The nine field representatives divide the United States and share the responsibility of being the "eyes and ears" of PMA.

The ACP branch is the route through which the PMA state, county, and community committee system operates. The U. S. Government Organization Manual for 1950-51 states:

"PMA state and county committees are the key units in PMA's field organization. Through the farmer-elected county committees PMA obtains recommendations and advice in the formulation of policies and program plans. State and county offices are also responsible for local administration of such national programs as agricultural conservation; production adjustments; price support and stabilization, surplus removal, and related programs as assigned; Sugar Act payments; and other programs requiring direct dealings with farmers and other agricultural interests." [5]

---

4. The commodity branches include cotton, dairy, fats and oils, fruit and vegetable, grain, livestock, poultry, sugar, and tobacco. Functional or program branches include: agricultural conservation, food distribution programs, fiscal, information, marketing and facilities research, price support and foreign supply, and transporting and warehousing. There are offices of: audit, administrative services, budget, compliance and investigation, and personnel services. Nine commodity offices are distributed over the country; and several of the PMA branches maintain field offices.

5. P. 232.

3. THE PMA VARIETY OF CONSERVATION

The ACP program dates from 1936. That year the Supreme
Court invalidated most of the AAA of 1933 in the decision,
United States v. *Butler*.[6] Farm leaders, agricultural administrators, and Congressmen anxious for a substitute, hit upon the
combination of price support-production control with conservation. The Soil Conservation and Domestic Allotment Act
authorized annual appropriations of $500,000,000 to reimburse
farmers for soil conserving practices.[7] It was clearly understood,
however, that the primary practice involved would be the reduction of soil-depleting crops, which also happened to be the
crops in "surplus" production.

Thus a farmer who cooperated with ACP by agreeing to
limit his soil-depleting crops became eligible not only for conservation payments, but also for parity payments, and for non-
recourse loans from the Commodity Credit Corporation (or
from local banks which could then rediscount with the CCC).
In 1938 Congress passed legislation establishing acreage allotments and marketing quotas for the so-called "basic" crops,
initially, cotton, corn, wheat, rice, and tobacco.[8] Acreage allotments were proclaimed by the Secretary of Agriculture on the
basis of formulae provided in the Act; marketing quotas were
similarly proclaimed, but only after their original announcement
and a favorable referendum thereon by the producers concerned. Allotments bear no penalty except that a farmer loses
his eligibility for the maximum loans from the CCC and any
other perquisites of the program that happen to obtain; quotas,
however, can be exceeded only at the expense of paying rather
heavy penalties. All these programs—conservation payments,
parity payments, CCC loans, acreage allotments, and marketing

6. 297 U. S. 1 (1936).
7. Act of February 29, 1936, ch. 104, sec. 1, 49 Stat. 1148, as amended.
This Act itself was an amendment to the Soil Conservation Act of 1935
which established the SCS in the USDA. In turn, the 1936 Act was incorporated into the Agricultural Adjustment Act of 1938, as amended. For
one discussion of the passage of the Act, see O. M. Kile, *The Farm Bureau
Through Three Decades, op. cit.*
8. Ch. 30, U.S.C. sec. 1281, *et seq.*

quotas have been administered by the same agency as part of a package. Clearly, this is *prima facie* evidence that agricultural conservation is inextricably involved in price and production control policy.

To return to ACP. In 1940, when it reached some 4,329,327 participating farms or ranches including 80 per cent of the Nation's cropland, payments were divided between Class I, earned merely by staying within acreage allotments of soil-depleting crops, and Class II, earned by performing positive practices (terracing, seeding cover crops, etc.). In those years, Class I payments were regularly used up, but Class II were used much less extensively, except in New England. Class I payments were criticized as bribery, as grossly uneven in their distribution (20 per cent of the farmers got about 60 per cent of the payments, a proportion that still holds), and as not involving any positive conservation action by farmers. Class II payments were criticized as paying for things that farmers would do anyway.

Considerable recent changes have been made. Beginning in 1942, with the disappearance of acreage allotments and therefore of the "total soil depleting base," requirements have been added. With Class I discontinued, all payments have had to be earned by positive practices. Meanwhile, participation decreased. As farm prices rose above support levels, there was less incentive to sign up with ACP to be eligible for supports. As farm incomes rose, the extra money from ACP became less attractive, especially as it had to be earned through positive practices and farm labor had become scarcer and more expensive. Yet 2,729,794 participating farms with 63.5 per cent of the nation's cropland were still reached in 1947. Meanwhile, limitations upon individual payments under ACP, placed at $10,000 in the 1938 Act, had been reduced to $750 by 1949 (for fiscal 1950 this maximum was raised to $2,500); yet the decline in cooperation had been chiefly among farmers earning smaller payments.[9] But the disproportionate benefits of the program

---

9. Average assistance per payee in 1940 was $73.67; by 1947 it was $80.71. More than four-fifths of the payees in 1940 received payments of less than $100; this proportion rose to nearly 85 per cent in 1943 but

continued, with a minority of the farmers still drawing down the
bulk of the payments.

Originally, programs were prepared in Washington, but after
a process of conferences "from the grass roots up." Since 1945,
the procedure has been to decentralize the program formulation
to states, in each of which a technical committee (particularly
scientists from the land-grant colleges) assist in drawing specifications. Subsequently, some decentralization to counties has
been achieved, the last two states joining in fiscal 1949. And in
New York, for the first time anywhere, some delegation to
communities of discretion respecting the ACP was reported.

Estimates of the success of decentralization vary. Program
planning division officials report considerable stimulation of interest within states. Some counties resisted assumption of authority, demanding that farmer field men, working out from
state officers, tell them what to do; some say this resistance is
disappearing; others are doubtful. Most would agree that county
and community committeemen are incomparably better informed now than they were ten or fifteen years ago, even though
the program is much more involved.[10]

Discretion permits counties to add one practice to the approved list in the state bulletin. ACP hoped that some flexibility
would thus be introduced, but PMA officially criticized the
locally-adopted practices in 1951 as providing payments for what
farmers are doing already.[11] The program remains heavily rou-
tinized, with emphasis upon a few practices. The statistical summary of the program for 1947 shows that 151 practices were
approved and used in the United States and territories. But one
practice, the application of limestone, accounted for 22.26 per

---

declined to less than 77 per cent in 1947. The biggest decline was in payments of less than $20—from 27.47 per cent of the payees in 1940 to
18.32 in 1947.

10. One says that in 1933 farmer administrators "had a hell of a time to
understand the program. I've seen them break out in sweat in school house
meetings; I've got them out to run around the building, then back for another hour. Now I can get most of a much more complicated program across
in thirty minutes." Another says that the chairman of a present state PMA
committee was doing such things in 1933 as running a bicycle wheel around
fields to measure the acreage.

11. *Hearings*, Agric. Approp., fiscal 1952, Part 1, p. 554.

cent of the payments. Another, application of superphosphate, accounted for 14.46. Five other practices totaled 22.12 per cent. So seven practices accounted for nearly 60 per cent of the payments that year. At the same time, only 2.38 per cent of the payments were made for "local practices," although 1947 is too early a year by which to judge the potential share of the latter.[12]

Not until 1947 did ACP establish a program planning division with a small technical staff charged to keep abreast of research and to develop policies to improve the quality of the program. That the division has a difficult assignment is indicated by the following. In Alabama, the ACP program has contributed to an expansion of winter cover crops on about one million acres—yet an estimated 3,000,000 are needed. The program planning division found that farmers planting about 25 per cent of the one million acres had planted for five years continuously in 1947; at the other end, about half the million acres was attributed to farmers who had not planted cover crops continuously, but had planted once or twice. But again, about half the farmers in Alabama appeared not to be planting such cover crops at all. So, how to withdraw aid from farmers who have the practice well-established, maintain aid for those who have begun but not established the practice, and reach the farmers who have not yet begun the practice? Further, can ACP combine this kind of differentiation among farmers with the principle that ACP makes an "open offer" to all farmers? It might seem easy enough to provide that farmers who had thoroughly established the practice were no longer eligible for this particular payment (although few would envy the task of the local committeeman who had to explain this principle to a farmer no longer eligible); but the real problem would be in

---

12. These figures hide variations by regions and states. Inorganic materials constitute a group of practices for which payments are made. They account for 82.14 per cent of the total payments in the North Atlantic states as against 50.69 per cent in the North Central (1947). Within these states, the ranges are from nearly 95 per cent in New Hampshire to less than one per cent in the Dakotas. Many variations can be explained by varying soil requirements; yet analysis of the program would doubtless disclose considerable unevenness.

deciding how long to extend payments to farmers who were making some progress toward establishing the practice. An arbitrary figure, two or three years, for example, would be easy to administer but might be ineffective in getting the practice established. On the other hand, complete discretion in the hands of the local committee would pose a severe problem of relationships of the committee to its clientele. Finally, it must be remembered that ACP can assist in financing only one million acres of winter cover crops in Alabama.

The ACP, along with numerous other administrative agencies in the USDA, needs a continuing analysis of the manner in which its programs are received. At one time the program surveys division of the Bureau of Agricultural Economics was available for this kind of inquiry. But that division has been renamed, reduced in size, and redirected (and narrowed) in its focus. Only an improved Congressional understanding of the needs of such agencies as ACP for services of this kind could pave the way for effectively reconstituting the program surveys division.[13]

4. ACP AND SCS: CONTRASTS AND RECRIMINATIONS

Like SCS, then, ACP operates with individual farmers on private land and by agreement. Beyond this, the programs differ. ACP is extensive, dealing with some 2,700,000 farms in 1947, for example. ACP has not had the services of technically trained personnel to offer farmers, as SCS has; [14] but it has been able to make cash payments of grants-in-aid of conservation materials, as SCS has not. Farmers are eligible for payments in an amount proportionate to their cropland, generally speaking, although Congress has modified this provision in favor of smaller farms.[15] Payments are for particular practices which are authorized for the county in which the farmer is situated. Payments

---

13. Cf. Charles M. Hardin, "The Bureau of Agricultural Economics under Fire . . . ," *JFE*, Aug., 1946.

14. Reportedly, however, PMA has provided some technical services in the Great Plains area.

15. Congress has provided a formula for scaling up payments smaller than $200.

are conditioned on specific performance—e.g., the application of a stated amount of limestone per acre or the construction of terraces according to specification. The payments are designed so that the government pays about one-half the cost of production.[16] The program has frequently been criticized as providing essentially for annual practices. In contrast, the SCS operates generally on the theory of establishing "complete farm plans."

AAA's field personnel, chiefly some 9,000 county and 97,000 community farmer committeemen, plus 1,811 in state and 1,231 in Washington,[17] are not trained natural scientists. SCS personnel, 315 in Washington, about 1,000 in regional offices, 450 in state offices, 1,000 in district offices, and 10,000 in work unit offices (except for clerical, administrative, and fiscal employees) are professional soil conservationists, with training chiefly as engineers or agronomists, or sub-professional conservation aides.[18]

This contrast of farmer-administration of one conservation program based on payments to encourage individual farm practices against technically-trained conservation farm planning and "on-site" technical assistance (e.g., in running terrace lines) as furnished by SCS is productive of disagreement. SCS claims that only its approach is scientific as being based upon the whole farm plan. ACP argues that its own goal, progressively better achieved, is to fit the practices which it supports into the general operations of farmers and adds that it could do better if SCS did not monopolize technical personnel. The question then arises, Can SCS help train farmer committeemen to improve their performance as conservation planners? Schools have been held in several states (Georgia, Pennsylvania, Alabama, Iowa) for this purpose, cooperatively between SCS, ACP, and Extension Services. In commenting on this experience, both ACP and SCS agree that Extension cooperation was only nominal. But SCS claims that its genuine effort to train ACP committee-

---

16. In 1951 it was reported that the average rate of assistance for all practices in the ACP program is less than one-half the cost of performing them. House *Hearings,* Agric. Approp., fiscal 1952, Part 1, p. 539.

17. Generally true, although it appears that ACP has employed some technical personnel in the Great Plains.

18. House *Hearings,* Agric. Approp., fiscal 1948, p. 1244, SCS figures from same source, p. 1003, *passim.*

men produced only inconsequential results. ACP argues that the experience so far has been inconclusive and wonders why SCS can train sub-professional conservation aides but not farmer committeemen. In the appropriation bill for fiscal 1950, SCS supporters got the House to agree that up to 10 per cent of ACP funds available in any county could be used to defray expenses of technical assistance by SCS personnel respecting the ACP program. The Senate struck this provision. The conference restored some of it, but reduced the figure to 5 per cent and added that the SCS services should be specific performances according to the requirements of the ACP committee.[19]

Two other charges and counter-charges are pertinent, SCS argues that its program is more democratic, being carried out through local units of government, directed by locally-elected supervisors who are not paid federal per diems. ACP counters that the soil conservation district program is very little in the hands of locally-elected supervisors—that the district is merely a means for carrying out SCS farm-planning techniques. SCS considers the ACP program as inflexible and superficial because of its association with a price-support and production-control program which requires great uniformity of application. ACP answers that its coverage is much greater than that of SCS; that its program is really an open offer available to farmers generally, whereas the SCS serves only the favored few; and that, in reporting the success of its program, SCS is prone to take credit for work which has been done by ACP, without any acknowledgment of the same.[20]

---

19. In 1951 there was criticism of the failure to announce a program after Congress had authorized that each county could use up to 5 per cent of its ACP funds to assign to the SCS for payment of technicians. PMA Administrator Ralph Trigg explained that this was because SCS and PMA were slow to work out an agreement. House *Hearings*, Agric. Approp., fiscal 1952, Part 1, pp. 545-46.

20. ACP officials considered reports of accomplishments in 23 soil conservation districts (*Soil Conservation*, Dec., 1948) as unfairly ignoring contributions to twenty of these from ACP. House *Hearings*, Agricultural Appropriation Bill, 1950, Vol. II, p. 353.

CHAPTER VIII

Farmer Administration

I. THE FARMER'S OWN SHOW

How did farmer administration come about? [1] The first AAA (1933) signed up individual farmers who promised to reduce their acreage in return for government payments. The law authorized the Secretary of Agriculture to establish state and local associations of producers to help in administration. But how to call them into being? It was natural to look to the Extension Service and especially to the county agents. But from the federal Director down, Extension leaders were reluctant to take responsibility for action programs—until the apparent threat of a rival national administration reaching to the grass roots prompted Extension to participate.[2] Once this decision was made, Extension worked whole-heartedly; without the unstinting labors of state and county Extension staffs, the program would have been foredoomed.

But a vast amount of help was needed to sign up millions of farmers, inspect their fields, and certify them for payments. In the South, county agents appointed farmer committees to assist

1. The best sources on original development of AAA administration are E. G. Nourse, J. S. Davis, and John D. Black, *Three Years of the AAA*, Brookings, (1937) and the several monographs prepared in the same Brookings series.
2. Southern Extension Services cooperated vigorously with the program from its inception.

in local administration. In the Midwest, producers' control associations were formed from committeemen elected by farmers.
Elections spread, and in 1936 the Congress directed the Secretary to employ local and state committees to administer the
program.[3]

A network of state, county, and community committees of
farmers was thus created by law to administer *the* farm program.
There is little doubt that AAA-PMA dwarfs all other governmental programs for agriculture in the farmers' eyes. The program and the men who administer it are the bulwark against
repetition of the disasters of 1930-1933. The committee system
has survived many reorganizations [4] and has been adapted to
the performance of remarkably different kinds of services.[5] Re-

3. The first AAA provided that the "Secretary of Agriculture is authorized
to establish . . . State and local committees, or associations of producers . . ."
to facilitate administration (May 12, 1933, Ch. 25, Section 10(b), 48 Stat.
37). But in 1936 Congress took note of the trend toward elected committeemen and declared that in administering the Soil Conservation and Domestic
Allotment Act in continental United States, "the Secretary is directed to
utilize the services of local and State committees selected as hereinafter provided." The law then provides for the designation of "local administrative
areas" in which cooperating farmers are to elect annually not more than
three committeemen plus one delegate to a county convention for the purpose of electing a county committee. The county agent might serve as secretary to the county committee (of which he is designated an *ex officio* member, but without a vote.) The state committee (three to five farmers) is to be
selected by the Secretary of Agriculture; the State Extension Director is
designated an *ex officio* member. (Feb. 29, 1936, Ch. 104, Sec. 1, 49 Stat.
1149.)

4. The committee system remained as the AAA (Agricultural Adjustment
Administration) through some ten reorganizations from 1933 to the creation
of the PMA in 1945. The letters AAA were probably dropped in 1945 in
order to deprive the agency of an important symbol and thus to diminish its
political influence. When PMA was first created, the committees became the
Field Service Branch; in 1946, the name was changed with some travail to
the ACP Branch.

5. During World War II, the committee function shifted from price support and production control to the stimulation and guidance of production.
Committees also were the nucleus of state and county war boards which performed considerable services in the rationing, special payment, and incentive
payment programs. In 1951, the committees became the nucleus of the mobilization committees in agriculture (Secretary Brannan's memorandum 1280
of Feb. 16, 1951) and were also charged to carry out the controversial
Family Farm Policy Review. During the period 1945–1949, however, the war
programs disappeared and the pre-war production control programs were not

currently since the "farmers' march" on Washington in 1935,[6] the committee system has been controversial. Nevertheless, men in high places and of different political faiths strongly believe that the committees must be maintained at all costs. In 1948, E. T. Winter of the Mississippi Valley Association and a staunch friend of SCS recommended that SCS appropriations be increased and that ACP funds be abolished. Congressman H. Carl Anderson (R., Minn.) declared:

"I think there is a lot of merit in your proposal that we seriously consider discarding the individual payments to farmers; but . . . we have to be careful . . . also to maintain that structure of county committees which has to do, and will have charge, naturally, of the ceiling programs, which of course is the main thing, in my opinion, to the farmers of America; that is, the maintenance of an adequate floor price. That comes ahead of anything. I say that as a farmer myself." [7]

In 1951 when the USDA again built a mobilization program around the committees, Secretary Brannan declared:

"In our preparedness program, how do we organize a production program? How do we translate decisions at the administrative level into action in the field? How do we make sure our farmers are getting the labor and supplies and materials necessary to do the job we are expecting them to do?

---

re-introduced, except in tobacco. Consequently, the conservation program assumed great importance, if the committees were to have a demonstrable usefulness.

6. "By 1934 . . . officials of the Department of Agriculture began to receive reports of a growing movement for federation of these county AAA committees into state and national organizations. . . . Early in 1935 occurred the 'farmers' march' on Washington. . . . The climax was an address by the President from the South portico of the White House. Following the speech, the AAA committeemen who made up the bulk of the marching farmers selected a committee for the purpose . . . of discussing national organization. To their credit, leaders of the American Farm Bureau Federation opposed the proposal, and many in the United States Department of Agriculture let their fears be known. Ultimately the idea . . . came to naught." H. R. Tolley, *The Farmer Citizen at War*, Macmillan (New York), 1943, p. 121. The Farm Bureau was probably motivated in part by a keen regard for its organizational interests.

7. House *Hearings*, Agric. Approp., fiscal 1948, p. 2067. Cf. Senate *Hearings*, Agric. Approp., fiscal 1948, p. 10 for Secretary Clinton Anderson's views and p. 486 for those of Undersecretary N. E. Dodd.

"We learned during World War II that the use of farmer committees was the most practical and most efficient method. Fortunately, we now have available an effective Nation-wide farmer committee system, already functioning and familiar with such important responsibilities." [8]

2. THE MEN AT THE GRASS ROOTS

County and community committeemen are paid per diems. Their money was to be deductible from funds available for conservation payments to farmers—the policy was designed to check committee expenditures on the assumption that farmers would scrutinize their accounts. Actually, Congress began earmarking funds for committee administration. In fiscal 1943, over $40,-000,000 were so earmarked. $65,000,000 were requested for fiscal 1944. But the AAA had been fighting the Farm Bureau and the Extension Service in the corn belt, and Congress cut the committees to some $30,000,000. The lowest annual expenditure of the committees was $18,000,000 in fiscal 1948; after that, the trend turned upward. The committees had survived the threat of the economy drive in the 80th Congress led by Congressman Dirksen. In 1951 they also survived the attack of the American Farm Bureau Federation.[9]

Payment of committeemen remains a subject of controversy.[10] Some SCS personnel and SCS supporters contrast paid ACP

---

8. House *Hearings*, Agric. Approp., fiscal 1952, Part 1, p. 8.

9. The Bureau of the Budget had recommended $285,000,000 for conservation payments, which the committees administer, for 1952. The AFBF asked a reduction to $150,000,000 but lost in the Senate by 41 to 36. AFBF *Official News Letter*, July 30, 1951. If production control is reintroduced, committee functions and expenditures will be considerably increased. In 1949, county committees worked slightly more than 200,000 man-days and community committeemen a somewhat larger number of days. But in anticipation of wheat and cotton marketing quotas in 1950, it was estimated that county committeemen would work 270,000 man-days and community committeemen 850,000. $46,500,000 were needed for committee administrative expenditures. The fact that wheat quotas were not imposed changed these anticipations, but the figures indicate what may be anticipated if controls are widely reintroduced. *Hearings*, Agric. Approp., H. of R., fiscal 1950, Part 1, pp. 76-77. The 1949 average per diem for county committeemen was $7.06; for community committeemen, $6.86.

10. Cf. Chap. xii, below.

personnel with the gratis services of soil conservation district supervisors to the advantage of the latter. Others suggest that district supervisors, some of whom get certain travel expenses under state laws, are not wholly comparable in their services to ACP committeemen, who have a broad range of administrative responsibilities. Considerable duplication exists between district supervisors and ACP committee personnel, although no figures are available. Again, some assert that impecunious farmers have sought ACP jobs to collect their salaries while others claim that farmers have actually served on such committees at a financial loss. Support for almost any statement about committeemen and their per diems can be adduced, but the available evidence permits nothing conclusive to be said on any of these claims and counter-claims.

What kind of men served as farmer committeemen? Ernst Kneisel reports that in 1945, 213 county committeemen in Wisconsin owned farms averaging 191 acres and had an average of 19 milk cows per farm (the state average of milk cows per farm being 12 in 1943). These men ranged from 30 to 76 years old, averaging 53. Two hundred of them owned their own farms; 177 had finished the eighth grade, 168 had gone to high school, and 58 had gone to college. Bertha Whitson, reporting in Iowa for 1945, found that Triple A committeemen exceeded the average Iowa farmer in formal education, size of farms operated, number of organizations belonged to, and number of soil building practices of the Triple A program used.[11] Internal, unpublished studies, made in east central and southern divisions of AAA before the war, indicated that county committeemen tended to be farm owners more than average farmers, to operate larger acreages, to have more education, and to have joined more farm organizations; on nearly all points, county committeemen rather sharply outranked community committeemen. One general impression from observations over the country, as well as reading the field hearings of the Hope and Aiken committees (1947), suggests that AAA committeemen tend to be rather able and vigorous men.

11. Cf. Ernst Kneisel, "Administrative Politics and the AAA," Unpublished honors thesis, Harvard University, 1947, pp. 86, 127.

The rural life and rural organization studies, jointly between BAE and various land-grant colleges, shed little light upon the background and position of committeemen. This may indicate that the present chapter exaggerates the importance of the committee system; or it may suggest that penetrating studies of the committee system are ordinarily too controversial for scholars on the public payroll to undertake.

True, the study of Irwin community, Shelby County, Iowa, made in 1939,[12] finds that the leadership of the new farm programs constitutes "to a considerable extent a new group." This is in contrast to leaders in church, school, fraternal orders, and village and township government—"the same group that have been active for a long time." In the early AAA, traditional leadership staffed the committees. "Recently, men who are not so active in local organizations have been increasingly called into positions of leadership."

In the most penetrating study so far made of PMA-AAA committeemen, Robin M. Williams [13] found a wide differential in size of acreage operated between committeemen interviewed (averaging 220 acres) and non-committeemen interviewed (averaging 119 acres). In view of the frequent charge that AAA tends to freeze agricultural production by areas and on farms within areas, Williams' finding that committeemen were mark-

12. Edward C. Moe and Carl C. Taylor, "Culture of a Contemporary Rural Community," *Rural Life Studies:* 5, USDA, BAE, 1942. For all these studies, see the sixth, Waller Wynne, "Culture of a Contemporary Rural Community," Harmony, Georgia, USDA, BAE, 1943. Other studies of rural social organization are being issued by the USDA or the states; cf. Frank D. Alexander and Lowry Nelson, Goodhue County (Minn.), Agric. Expt. Sta. Bul., U. of Minn., 401, Feb. 1949. See Eugene A. Wilkening, *A Socio-Psychological Analysis of Certain Agricultural Programs and Practices in a Piedmont Community of North Carolina,* Unpublished Ph.D. thesis, University of Chicago, 1949, chap. ii, for a resume of the literature on the subject.

Considerable opinion holds that the quality of PMA-AAA committeemen has deteriorated. By this is meant that such men no longer have an economic and social standing in their communities equivalent to the earlier committeemen. The writer depreciates these opinions as impressionistic and as possibly representing biases against the committee system.

13. *Sociological Aspects of Farmers Responses to AAA Programs: Selected Kentucky Areas, 1938–1940,* Unpublished Ph.D. thesis, Harvard University, 1943; cf. pp. 61-62, 117, 129, 285 ff.

edly more aggressive or, at least, more successful in increasing their own holdings is interesting; as he notes, this may merely reflect more financial resources in the families of committee-men.

Williams closely observed the tendencies among interviewees, committeemen and others, for official positions in social organizations, both governmental and other, to be held in few hands. He found committee members much more involved in office-holding generally than non-members; for both groups, he found that "office holding is pyramided upon a very small proportion of the total population"—a striking contrast to the findings in Irwin, Iowa, already noted, but a confirmation of what Chapter XI (below) suggests. Williams further states: "The farmer-administrators of AAA programs are concentrated in a relatively small 'class' of the farm population, and there is a high degree of duplication of leaders in various public agricultural programs."

Perhaps the most important conclusion of Williams is that the committees constitute buffers for the program. "The evidence is unequivocal that, at least in these specific areas studied, *the hostilities created by the operation of the AAA program were directed primarily against the local committeemen*." Interviewees, generally, imputed restrictions of the program to the committees. Interviewees who were committee members felt that their service had hurt their standing in their communities. Williams suggests that the AAA is visible and identifiable in the persons of elected committeemen. His analysis trenchantly illuminates both the need for comprehensive educational work in the field of public policy and the need for much of the content of that work to have to do with illuminating the processes of government. For, as he suggests, farmers will only rarely see a complex of causes, economic discontent, the activities of pressure groups, the legislative process, partisan politics, the role of the administration generally and of the AAA in particular, etc.—in short, the entire complex and apparatus by which their tobacco acreages are cut. What the farmer sees is his neighbor, an AAA committeeman, who tells him to cut his acreage.

No doubt many committeemen have felt local antagonisms

and have expressed regrets about their administrative assign-
ments. But it appears to be appropriate for officials in the United
States—from the highest to the lowest—to emphasize the self
sacrifice involved in public service. On the other hand, the PMA
committee system offers a new prestige ladder as an alternative
to those already existing. The committee system and the soil
conservation district boards furnish opportunities for emergent
leadership to rise and challenge established leadership—e.g., in
the Farm Bureau. Thus John Taylor, long prominent in AAA-
PMA circles in Illinois, is said to have been the one man who
succeeded in changing a resolution of the Illinois Agricultural
Association (the Farm Bureau) against the wishes of President
Earl C. Smith.

3. AN ADMINISTRATIVE CAREER LADDER—
WITH POLITICAL IMPLICATIONS

In the Western and North Central divisions particularly, the
AAA farmer-administrators became part of a career service.[14]

___
14. In the Western, North Central, and (to some degree) the Northeastern AAA regions, which existed from 1936 to 1945, the county committees of farmers took over active administration of the local programs and
the state committees moved into the state offices and took charge as full-time
governmental employees. The first state committees in these and other regions
were appointed by the Secretary of Agriculture upon recommendation of the
state Extension Directors. Beginning about 1938, the divisional (regional)
directors of AAA in Washington began to nominate replacements to state
committees. This event illustrated the tendencies to form a strong and responsible line administration from Washington to the grass roots—but it also
marked a shift in the location of power.
    The Southern division (South Carolina to Florida, to Texas, to Oklahoma,
and back to South Carolina) was somewhat different. Here, state administrative officers were the permanent operating officials, and some of them
gained real power. State AAA committees acted as policy making and appeals
boards. Where the North Central division had farmer field men, the Southern
state offices employed men with professional backgrounds. Where county
committees actively administered the North Central program, Southern county
committees acted as boards of directors and boards of appeals while county
administrative officers ran the local AAA offices.
    The East Central division (Tennessee, Kentucky, West Virginia, Virginia,
Delaware, Maryland, and North Carolina) was something of a hybrid between the North Central and Southern forms of organization. But in the
early 1940's, state administrators (professionals) were pushed out of state
offices in the East Central, and state committeemen took full charge of the

County committeemen were typically appointed, perhaps promoted, to become farmer field men, or to be members of state committees. State committeemen were frequently drawn into the divisional, i.e., regional, offices of the AAA in Washington. In the North Central divisional Washington office in 1940, probably a score of important administrative posts were held by farmers from the middle west. Claude Wickard emerged from this career service as Secretary of Agriculture. N. E. Dodd, beginning as a county committeeman in Oregon, eventually became Under-Secretary of Agriculture; Fred Wallace came up from the Nebraska administration to head the entire AAA.

The trend has continued. An example is afforded by the career of Albert J. Loveland who was first elected as a community committeeman in Iowa. In 1936 he became a county committeeman and in 1939 was appointed a farmer field man. He was made a member of the Iowa AAA state committee in 1941. In 1947 he headed the ACP branch of PMA. In 1948 he was made Under-Secretary of Agriculture, a position he resigned to run for the Senate in Iowa. He won the Democratic nomination but was defeated by Mr. Hickenlooper in the election of 1950.

Consider the Commodity Credit Corporation. It was made theoretically distinct from the PMA by an act of Congress in 1948.[15] But its manager, Mr. Elmer F. Kruse, had come out of the farmer committee system in Ohio much as Mr. Loveland

---

program. This was an example of perennial efforts to strengthen the roles of committeemen in order to capitalize on the power inherent in an authentic farmer bureaucracy—especially a bureaucracy resting upon local elections.

15. Paul Appleby in *Big Democracy* argues for a distinct administration of the CCC from that of the AAA on grounds that it is advisable for the different criteria which each employs thus to be institutionalized sufficiently independent of each other so that emergent policies may not be made on one point of view alone. The AAA is essentially interested in promoting farmers' prosperity through support prices; the CCC is, of course, likewise interested but it also shares a duty to maintain the financial soundness of the general government. For a considerable time, these two agencies, though closely collaborating, were sufficiently distinct so that internal USDA policy respecting the "farm program" had to be in part the product of the association between the AAA and the CCC. After the reorganization of 1945 creating the PMA, these two agencies became identical. This was especially notable after J. B. Hutson retired from the Department.

had in Iowa. Ralph S. Trigg, then PMA administrator, continued to refer to Mr. Kruse as his assistant administrator for the CCC, in spite of the separation. On the five-man board of directors for the CCC under the Act of 1948 were Secretary Brannan, Mr. Trigg, Mr. Loveland, and two former members of state PMA committees—Mr. Glenn R. Harris and Mr. L. Carl Fry.

The following situation existed in the summer of 1949: W. B. Crawley, assistant administrator for production, PMA, had been brought up from the Alabama state committee. Six of the nine administrator's field representatives attached to Mr. Crawley's office had come up from the committee system, and the other three were old AAA men. In the Grain Branch, L. K. Smith, Director, had been a state committeeman in Nebraska; and six of the ten high-ranking personnel in his office were formerly committeemen. C. D. Walker, Director of the Cotton Branch, had been a state committeeman in Oklahoma.

The trend appeared to be continuing in 1951. On March 30, Secretary Brannan [16] suddenly removed Administrator Ralph S. Trigg and his Deputy, Frank K. Woolley, from the PMA; both were assigned positions in the Secretary's office as "special assistants to the Secretary for CCC affairs." Neither was a product of the committee system; but both their successors, Gus F. Geissler and Harold K. Hill, had climbed to their posts on the ladder provided by AAA-PMA committees.

Development of the career ladder in AAA-PMA has many implications, some of which are discussed in the following chapter.[17] There is a tendency to elevate the "hard-headed,

---

16. It is said that PMA had its candidate for the Secretaryship when Mr. Brannan was appointed in 1948.

17. Not all the influential persons in PMA are or have been former farmer committeemen. What is called "the old AAA crowd" includes some career administrators, e.g., some of the state administrative officers in the South. Nor should one infer that AAA-PMA is a phalanx. Considerable internal friction has occurred, much of it between divisions or regions. But some friction has existed between PMA branches since the regions were abolished in 1945. Again, there is considerable autonomy in some PMA branches. Most activities of the fruit and vegetable branch have been carried on with little or no relationship to the committee system or to the farmer-administrator career service. The same is true of the dairy branch.

practical man" above the scientist. There is an inclination to consider experience in management of one's farm to be qualification for virtually any administrative job in the USDA. About 1938, a planned move reportedly occurred to replace the AAA personnel who had come up from the Extension Service with farmer committeemen. A decade later, there were numerous reports of vigorous efforts to vest all possible functions and authority in the committee system—whether or not such authority and functions were concerned with purchase, storage, transportation, and marketing problems for which experience as a farmer represented little qualification.

Farmer-administration has its defenders. It has been supported as providing a necessary counterweight to representatives of the "trade" (processors, handlers, etc.) who figured importantly in the War Food Administration during the war. By mid-1949, however, the consensus was that few representatives of the trade remained in PMA employ; further, some heretics believed that the interests of farmers were upheld better by professionally trained men than by career farmer-administrators.

The retention of farming interests by PMA administrators may give them a considerable degree of independence. One observer remarked, "These fellows are big farmers. They can't be convinced easily by appeals to administrative authority. They are supported in their positions by the knowledge that they have their farm businesses as continuous and profitable alternatives. But I am not a big farmer, and I need to keep this job, so don't quote me!" Many would name numerous climbers of the farmer-administrator ladder who have proven excellent administrators, citing such men as N. E. Dodd, former Under-Secretary of Agriculture, and, since 1949, Director General of the Food and Agriculture Organization of the United Nations; Claude R. Wickard, Secretary of Agriculture (1940–1945), and Administrator, Rural Electrification Administration since 1945; Elmer F. Kruse, formerly manager of the CCC, currently (1951) assistant administrator for commodity operations of PMA; and Gus F. Geissler, formerly manager of the Federal Crop Insurance Corporation, currently (1951) administrator of the PMA.

4. A CONTRAST WITH SCS

SCS has enjoyed great continuity in its leadership. Dr. H. H. Bennett was Chief from its inception until November 15, 1951.[18] Jefferson C. Dykes has been assistant chief since 1942; earlier he was assistant regional conservator in Fort Worth. A. E. Jones, head of the operation division since 1942, was formerly assistant regional conservator in Lincoln. Men like Thomas L. Gaston, Jr., assistant to the chief, and Mark L. Nichols, head of research, have had long professional careers in SCS. Of the regional conservators, five held the same positions when the writer was visiting regional offices in 1941.[19]

PMA and its antecedent organizations have had no such continuous top leadership. Beginning with George Peek, at least thirteen men have held positions as head of AAA, WFA, or PMA, before the present administrator, Gus Geissler. Two of the thirteen are deceased, and only one of the survivors is with the USDA in mid-1951. The old AAA regions or divisions are gone, and all but one of the men who were regional administrators in 1941 are no longer with PMA.

At the same time, a large proportion of the present state PMA committeemen were state AAA committeemen in 1938. On the basis of those who were honored for ten years' service at the St. Louis conference in 1948, the writer estimated that between 10 and 15 per cent had held their positions for a decade or more. In view of those who had died, retired, or moved into Washington, this constituted considerable continuity.

In contrast to SCS, where continuity of top-level personnel in Washington and regional offices is marked, and where this kind of continuity contributes to the establishment and maintenance of the agency line or "code" elsewhere discussed, PMA

18. On October 29, 1951, Secretary Brannan appointed Dr. Bennett as a special assistant to the Secretary in charge of conservation and resource matters. Dr. R. M. Salter, Chief of the Bureau of Plant Industry, Soils, and Agricultural Engineering in the USDA, became Chief of SCS.

19. The 10 original regional offices were reduced to seven. In the subsequent consolidation, two regional conservators left SCS, five remained in similar positions, and three had important roles in the administration of remaining regions (1949).

is somewhat different. Here, the chief nucleus of continuity seems to be at the state level. The result may be to create a considerable decentralization in the center of influence in PMA. The independence manifested by a good many state committeemen in their open letter to the Secretary in 1946 (mentioned below) is in point.[20] To students of government, the possible strength of state officers, presumably line officers in a national administration, suggests an important consequence for administrative organizations and procedures of our system of federally-divided political power. Specifically, even a "line organization" like PMA may exhibit an actual decentralization of power and influence into its state offices so that the ordinary concepts of hierarchy are modified in their application.

This leads one to comment that the federal system in the old AAA organization, in which divisional offices were in general charge of the program for groups of states, worked toward establishing regional autonomy. It was probably the fact that regions were based on states, with state offices and state committees, that strengthened the hands of AAA regional directors. The present functional organization of PMA finds the regions gone, but the political phenomenon of federalism still manifests itself in a rather continuous bid for power and influence within PMA —which means within a vital part of government-in-agriculture —on the part of the PMA state committeemen. Again, the contrast to SCS is rather pointed, for state SCS offices have never attained great influence.

5. THE COMMITTEE SYSTEM AS A FARM ORGANIZATION

At the Colorado Springs conference of PMA in 1947, Jesse B. Gilmer, Administrator, said "I think this is the most representative group of farm program administrators which has ever been called into conference." Pointing out that PMA represents a consolidation of some 14 previously independent agencies or offices of the Department, he remarked that this was the first

---

20. Cf. the following chapter. The position of the state committeemen on this occasion may have been considerably influenced by the divisional offices in Washington, however.

conference in which all these had been brought together into a national meeting. He recognized the breadth of the agency and its functions and expressed a belief that this was but the first of a series of conferences which will bring "farmer representatives and Government officials together each year, and that these meetings will become *the* occasion when sound national planning is done in the interest of both producers and consumers." He then added:

"This is a sobering thought. Recognizing the scope of our agency, and the influence it can bring to bear on the welfare of agriculture, we are faced with the challenge of responsibility."

In a resolution unanimously adopted by the PMA national conference at St. Louis, Missouri, on December 9, 1948, the conference was referred to as "This Working Organization of United States Farmers, united in the effort to guarantee stability and prosperity to this whole nation and all its people . . ." The previous year's conference at Colorado Springs was referred to as follows: "Out of that conference came the greatest advance in sound planning for American agriculture and the most valuable broadening of vision for farm leaders that has ever occurred in the history of American agriculture." The St. Louis conference had 400 delegates from all the states and the insular possessions, as well as from Washington, D. C. They represent the field offices of the basic marketing services of the Department and the 100,000 elected farmer committeemen. The conference considered itself as "representatives of the working farmers of this greatest nation on earth . . ."

Thus PMA, as AAA before it, continuously bears the aspect of being not only an administrative agency but also an organization of farmers. To the extent that it becomes a farm organization, PMA represents a development of the relationship of government to economic life that must be carefully weighed. It is one thing to have an administrative organization carrying out programs to implement policies hammered out in the traditional political processes in which farm organizations have considerable influence. It is another thing to develop an agency whose members are paid from federal appropriations yet which threatens to become a farm organization.

CHAPTER IX

The AAA-PMA in Politics

I. POLITICAL CHARACTERISTICS OF PMA

"Not all politics is party politics," Paul Appleby observes. There are farm, labor, business, medical, military, and other politics as well.[1] Public agencies and pressure groups jostle for power in agriculture. But ideological differences are also involved; some of them cut very deeply. Again the AAA-PMA has emerged as the administrator, caretaker, defender, and extender of "the farm program." So the alleged efforts of PMA to influence Congress must be examined. The question needs raising whether administrative agencies can be prevented by law from attempting to influence legislation. Finally the relations of AAA-PMA to partisan politics cannot be overlooked.

Throughout the discussion the unique characteristics of PMA should be kept in mind—its size and significance in the USDA, its obligation to administer "the farm program," and its farmer administration, resting eventually on elected community and county committeemen. Agricultural agencies muster political strength in different ways; but there are fairly common characteristics. The development of a program, its statement and communication in a manner to elicit the loyal and enthusiastic support of its employees—this is apparently common to most if not

---

1. *Big Democracy, op. cit.,* pp. 132-33.

all agencies, including the PMA. But PMA is significantly different from its sister agencies.

Take the matter of alliances with other groups. The oldest and historically most important of these alliances has been between the colleges of agriculture and particularly the agricultural extension services and the Farm Bureau.[2] The alliance between SCS and the National Association of Soil Conservation Districts has been discussed, but SCS has also been supported by such special purpose groups as the Mississippi Valley Association,[3] as well as a general farm organization, the Grange. The Rural Electrification Administration has been assisted by the National Association of Rural Electrical Cooperatives; the Bureau of Reclamation, U. S. Department of the Interior, by the National Reclamation Association.[4] The Forest Service has had the support, at times, of the American Forestry Association and the Izaak Walton League; but the Forest Service [5] appears to be somewhat unique among agencies in the personal appearances of Congressmen in support of parts of its program.

The AAA and the PMA have pretty well "gone it alone" in the last ten or twelve years, at least. The PMA incorporates its own farm organization in its committee system. Furthermore, the PMA is so large and powerful that any organization other than the Farm Bureau would have to accept the role of the junior partner in a permanent alliance.

Some agricultural agencies appear to seek support of a few strategically-located Congressmen. Such friends can be very potent allies. Congressional prestige and influence is largely measured by seniority, and rural Congressmen have often been returned for many consecutive successions. The strategy of SCS in secur-

---

2. See chap. iii, above.

3. *Hearings,* H. R. 4150, *et al.,* 80th Cong., 2nd Sess., 1948, p. 142.

4. The National Reclamation Association apparently was formed at the request of Dr. Elwood Mead, then Commissioner of the Bureau of Reclamation, at a meeting called in 1932; the object was to provide protection for the Bureau. "Irrigation and Reclamation," *Hearings,* Subcommittee of the Committee on Public Lands, H. of R., 80th Cong., 1st Sess., February, 1947, pp. 85-86.

5. For example, 73 Congressmen appeared in support of various Forest Service appropriations in 1947; cf. House *Hearings,* Agric. Approp., fiscal 1948, Part 2, pp. 229 ff.

ing Congressional friendships has been suggested; and an examination of other agencies would reveal similar action. But
PMA would probably not be among these. Its general coverage
of the United States, the number of farmers reached, and the
significance of its program—all combine to place the PMA in a
different relationship to Congress. PMA's support must be in
the "farm bloc" rather than in a few strategically-located Congressmen.

Just as the PMA has "gone it alone" it has also "taken on all
comers." More fundamentally and more consistently than most
agencies, it has apparently challenged the authority of the Secretary of Agriculture. At the same time it has proved to be the
most formidable antagonist of the powerful American Farm
Bureau Federation.

AAA-PMA has apparently been subject to more than usual
degrees of internal friction.[6] Being like the Farm Bureau both
in scope and in primary concern with economic programs, PMA
has some of the same problems of internal compromise. On the
other hand, PMA has been united in favor of high level support prices, an issue that threatened to split the Farm Bureau
in 1948 and that might have repeated the threat had not the
Korean War begun in 1950.

2. JOSTLING AGENCIES AND PRESSURE GROUPS

The writer's introduction to the politics of agriculture was the
word in 1941 that "the AAA and the Farm Security Administration hate each other." The Farm Security Administration
(FSA: it was succeeded by the Farmers Home Administration
in 1946) was the New Deal agency established to help low income farmers, especially through rural rehabilitation loans. The
original Agricultural Adjustment Act stimulated owners in the
South to make wage-hands out of their share-croppers and thus

---

6. Cotton provides the best recent example. It appeared necessary to cut
back from 27,000,000 acres in 1949 to 21,000,000. How was the cut to be
distributed among counties, states, and regions? This question was too sharp
for one agency to handle; rather, Congressmen, the Cotton Council, the
PMA, the Farm Bureau, and others met in a series of conferences which
culminated in the Memphis Agreement (1949).

acquire the croppers' share of the benefit payments. Controversy over administration of the law led to the "purge of the liberals" in AAA during 1935.[7]

Congress attempted to favor tenants and small farmers in the law,[8] but AAA's obligation to bolster farm prices meant that its program must favor commercial farmers. The FSA, on the other hand, was designed to help low income farmers, and the bulk of its clients were among tenants and share-croppers of the South. To characterize the resultant situation as conflict between the conservative AAA and the radical FSA overgeneralizes a complex relationship; yet there is considerable truth in this characterization. The sharpest ideological cleavage in agriculture was involved. And it must be added that on this issue the southern Farm Bureaus and colleges of agriculture were generally aligned against the FSA—although this did not necessarily make them full partners of the AAA.

More germane to the present inquiry are the controversies between AAA-PMA and the Extension Services and Farm Bureaus. The early AAA had to reach millions of farmers in a hurry. For a time in 1933 it was questionable whether checks could be distributed to farmers quickly enough to exceed the amount of money which the government was taking in the processing taxes—if this could not be done, the program would have had a deflationary effect! The pride with which AAA announced early in 1934 that it was now able to write a million checks a month is understandable.

The only organization capable of reaching farmers quickly

---

7. Cf. Russell Lord, *The Wallaces of Iowa,* Houghton Mifflin Company, Boston, 1947, Ch. xi, sec. 3.

8. In the Soil Conservation and Domestic Allotment Act of 1936, Congress required a division of conservation payments among landlords, tenants, and sharecroppers in proportion as they "are entitled to share in the proceeds of the commodity with respect to which the payments are made. . . ." Congress declared that a reduction in the average number of tenants or sharecroppers should not operate to increase the landlord's share of the payments, unless the local committee found the reduction justified, subject to appeal to the state committee. Act of Feb. 29, 1936, Ch. 104, sec. 1, 49 Stat. 1149, as amended. Congress also established minimum acreage allotments to help small farmers. The best—and worst—example is burley tobacco. Cf. "The Tobacco Program: Exception or Portent?" *JFE,* Nov., 1946.

was the Extension Service; even it had to be supplemented by some 700 emergency county agents (paid by AAA money to replace county agents discharged during the depression by economy-minded county boards). Generally, the Extension Service fell to with a will. Yet there was friction inherent in the situation. Extension had always developed programs co-operatively and with great decentralization, but to discharge national programs involving the strict accounting of large sums distributed to farmers in return for specific performance on the farmers' part was another matter. In 1934 the Kerr Tobacco and Bankhead Cotton bills were passed; and AAA began to ad-minister penalties against farmers. Extension, with its educa-tional tradition, found itself in an increasingly uncomfortable position. With the Butler decision and the passage of the 1936 Soil Conservation and Domestic Allotment Act, it seemed that the emphasis upon conservation would stimulate programs more in line with Extension's traditional approach. Indeed, this legis-lation was initially designed to be administered by colleges of agriculture under state enabling laws. Yet it was obvious that the conservation provisions of the 1936 Act were really aimed at income support and production control. At this time the AAA divorced itself from the agricultural Extension Services outside the South, developed its regional (or divisional) offices, in Washington, and initiated line administration through the com-mittee system. Furthermore, the annual AAA conferences were begun to develop the conservation program; these conferences were held in the counties, were then generalized in state con-ferences, and eventually produced regional and national pro-grams.[9]

In 1938, new AAA legislation again changed the emphasis of the program. Now, the sanctions rested not merely on the farmer's eligibility for ACP payments but much more than this on his eligibility for Commodity Credit Corporation loans and for parity payments; moreover, on those crops where market-ing quotas were established, penalties for non-cooperation were

---

9. Charles M. Hardin, "The Food Production Programs of the USDA," in John D. Black, ed., *Nutrition and the Food Supply: the War and After, The Annals*, Vol. 223, Jan., 1943. See Appendix.

provided. There also occurred a change in leadership in the
AAA. Howard Tolley was shifted to the BAE and R. M. Evans
placed in charge of the AAA. Afterwards, some say immediately, some say after 1942, divisional or regional directors of the
AAA became increasingly powerful. The career-ladder for farmer
committeemen became more and more manifest. AAA employees
with Extension backgrounds were squeezed out. The state Extension Services found themselves pushed further and further
from AAA conferences. When Chester Davis became War
Food Administrator in 1943 he called a conference of Extension
Directors. One told the writer the following week: "This is
the first time in five years that Extension Directors have for-
mally been consulted on the farm program."

Meanwhile, other action agencies in agriculture, operating
direct to the farmer, had multiplied the challenge to the Extension Service. Federal-state relationships became an increasingly pressing subject in extension and land-grant college meetings. Finally, in 1938 at Mount Weather, Virginia, an agreement
was reached between the land-grant colleges and the USDA
which proposed a division of responsibility, the colleges taking
essentially the research and educational functions of agricultural
programs the USDA agencies to handle the "action" aspects. A
state and local land-use planning program (later called the
agricultural planning program) was undertaken jointly between
the Bureau of Agricultural Economics and the colleges of agriculture.

Elsewhere the writer has commented on the fate of this
program.[10] Both the SCS and the AAA would have been coordinated by it, and both helped kill it. The Farm Bureau was
also inimical to it; and the colleges of agriculture were, on the
whole, indifferent to its demise. The land-use planning program had an opportunity, perhaps, of important development
in 1941. Secretary Wickard felt that the defense emergency
called for more integrated administration in the field. Washington conferences in June of various agencies, including the
AAA and the Extension Service, were followed in July by the

10. "The Bureau of Agricultural Economics Under Fire," *JFE*, August,
1946.

surprise announcement of the creation of the agricultural defense boards, later the war boards. It was clear that these boards were to center around the AAA organization. Remembering its own service to the country in World War I, as well as in the emergency period of the New Deal, the Extension Service felt insulted over this lack of recognition.

At this point, the colleges might have united to press for administration of the defense program through the state and local land-use planning system, including the committees that had been set up in some 1800 counties. But the AAA systematically fed a story into the field that Howard Tolley (who as chief of the BAE was the primary federal official in the cooperative program) had declared that with the land-use planning committees in full swing, farmers would find no need for the Farm Bureau. This story (made out of whole cloth) seems to have spiked any joint effort of the colleges to rally around the only effective method of counter administration to the Secretary's defense boards. Many Extension Directors seem to have resented a reported attack on the farm organization with which they were associated, without critically evaluating the story.

This incident invites consideration of AAA-Farm Bureau relationships. The American Farm Bureau Federation (AFBF) had a prominent part in the passage of the AAA of 1933, and it profited greatly from administration of the program in its early years. In the Depression its membership had fallen to 163,-246; by 1937 it had climbed to 409,766.[11] This gain reflected not only improved farm incomes but also the systematic cooperation between early AAA administration (in which state Extension Services were prominent) and the Farm Bureau. One device was for the county agent to solicit Farm Bureau memberships at the same time that he distributed AAA checks.

Soon, however, the Farm Bureau was disturbed by the development of the committee system and, indeed, by the progressive tendency for New Deal action agencies to join hands with farmers organized as FSA committees, in soil conservation districts, or otherwise. The "farmers' march on Washington" in 1935 was reportedly inspired by the AAA and deplored by the

11. Gladys Baker, *op. cit.*, p. 23.

Farm Bureau.[12] In 1940, the Farm Bureau launched a broad attack against "duplication and overlapping" in agricultural administration. Its real goal was to stop the tendency for new agencies to stimulate new farm organizations. The original attack of the AFBF was leveled at the BAE state and local planning program, the FSA, and the SCS. These were probably attacked in what seemed to be the order of their vulnerability. But the ultimate goal of the Farm Bureau was probably to cut the committee system of the AAA down to size.

In 1942–43, the fight between AAA and the Farm Bureau and state Extension Services came into the open, especially (but not exclusively) in the corn belt. In December, Joe Storm resigned from the USDA information office to publish *Spade* magazine. Mr. Storm had been in AAA information work which Secretary Wickard, who came from AAA, transferred to his office in 1941.[13] *Spade* might be described as a house organ, once removed, of the AAA. In its pages the Farm Bureau was roundly attacked, and the link between the Farm Bureau and state Extension Services criticized.[14]

---

12. H. R. Tolley, *The Farmer Citizen at War*, Macmillan and Company, New York (1943), p. 121.

13. Mr. Storm, then in the Amarillo office, explained his new role to the Great Plains Conference Meeting at Estes Park, Colorado, in July, 1941. Information men were to be the eyes, ears, and voice of the Secretary. "We have had many gospels [he said in effect]. There is the gospel according to Saint Hugh, the gospel according to St. Beany, and I have been giving out the gospel according to St. Spike. But from now on, gentlemen, there is going to be just one gospel—according to St. Claude." Reference was to Hugh H. Bennett of SCS, "Beany" Baldwin of FSA, R.M. (Spike) Evans of AAA, and Secretary Claude Wickard.

14. E.g., *Spade* for May 20, 1944. The practice of southern farmers to enroll their tenants was criticized; so were the business memberships in the Farm Bureau. Thus the *Montgomery* (Ala.) *Advertiser* for March 26, 1943, was quoted. The county extension agent for Montgomery County had commended the landlords in the Farm Bureau membership drive. 400 farmers had bought memberships for tenants. One had bought 81 memberships; another, 50 memberships. The First National Bank of Montgomery paid $50 for 25 memberships, etc. The *Arkansas Central Leader* (McCrory) was quoted to show the leadership of the county agent in the Farm Bureau membership drive (Feb. 19, 1943, edition). The Memphis *Commercial Appeal* for April 4, 1943 was cited as quoting W. C. Mimms, a state Extension Service official. Mimms said that the Extension Service was 100 per cent behind the Farm Bureau and "we are going just as far as we can without getting the pink slip."

The Farm Bureau's side of the controversy is shown by the following letter:

"Hassil Schenck
President, Indiana Farm Bureau
Indianapolis, Indiana

"This is to call your attention to a condition existing in Indiana agriculture which threatens to destroy the attempts of the farmers to contribute their utmost to the food-production program. Harry Jackson, district farmer field man of the Agricultural Adjustment Agency, held a meeting with the Agricultural Adjustment Agency committeemen of Harrison County in Coryden today. Mr. Jackson stated that this is one of a series of such county meetings with Agricultural Adjustment Agency committeemen. He said the time has come when 'I am going to call names. I am speaking about organizations at the State and National level. Plainly Ed O'Neal of the American Farm Bureau Federation, and the Extension Service are trying to throw the Agricultural Adjustment Agency out the window. They are working with some rats in Congress and there are too many rats there. Ed O'Neal don't represent the Farm Bureau members' opinions. They are trying to take the farm program out of the hands of we farmers.' Mr. Jackson read at length to the committeemen from a paper called the Spade, which he said came to him from Washington, but he didn't know who published it, in which the Farm Bureau and Extension Service were criticized at length. Mr. Jackson said that the Farm Bureau wishes to place the Agricultural Adjustment Agency program in the hands of the Extension Service through the State colleges. He said, 'We are bringing this information out to you so you can see your neighbors and get them to write to their Congressmen.' In the discussion period which followed, Mrs. William Enlow of New Amsterdam, farmer field woman for the Agricultural Adjustment Agency in Harrison County, stated as follows: 'I have just returned from a farmer field women's conference at the Claypool Hotel in Indianapolis, where Mr. Schooler, regional Agricultural Adjustment Agency director of the North Central Agricultural Adjustment Agency region said: "When I left Washington Mr. Wickard (Secretary of Agriculture Claude Wickard) said the fight is on. Strike below the belt, above the belt, or anywhere you can. Tell the people to join the Farmers' Union (Congress of Industrial Organizations), read the Spade, and write their Congressmen! . . ." ' Mr. Schenck, I urge you to take immediate action State-wide and nationally to save our farmers from the programs which will be handed down from Washington if this Agricultural Adjustment Agency organization is successful in gaining the power they seek. This organized gangster program in the Agricultural Adjustment Agency is being carried out at Government expense. The statements that I have given you, as coming from the meeting here today, are facts brought to me by Farm Bureau members who were there, and they have been verified.

> Herschel O. LaHue,
> Chairman, Harrison County
> Farm Bureau

"P.S.—Dr. Cannon, chairman of the Floyd County Agricultural Adjustment Agency, spread this poison stuff over station WGRC today, but luckily this is a small station so probably only a few farmers heard it.

> H. O. LaHue." [15]

In 1943 Chester Davis became War Food Administrator; and in his brief administration moved to discharge Harry Schooler and otherwise break up the AAA pressure group particularly in the north central region. Wayne Darrow, who had been effective in the AAA as a collaborator with Mr. Schooler, soon left the Department and joined the staff of *Spade*, later replaced by *Farm Letter*, which continues as an informed newsletter on matters relating to agriculture. Secretary Wickard had to repudiate the activities of the AAA in pressuring Congress. Congressman Clarence Cannon sent investigators into middlewestern states to inquire into the activities of the AAA to influence legislation. The Farm Bureau attacked the AAA at this time very strongly. The appropriation bill for 1944 forbade the AAA to carry information to farmers,[16] and the appropriation for administration in the AAA was sharply cut.[17]

The sequel to the above demonstrates that behind the 1943 fight lay a deeper issue, namely, Who is going to control the power structure in agriculture? Thus in 1946, both the Farm Bureau and the National Farmers Union supported the AAA

---

15. Agricultural Appropriation *Hearings*, House, fiscal 1944, at pp. 1506-7.
16. A prohibition removed only in the 1950 Appropriation Act and then only for County PMA offices.
17. Cf. chap. viii, sec. 2.

state committeemen (now PMA state chairmen) against Secretary Clinton Anderson.

The background is as follows. The War Food Administration involved a redirection of agricultural policy. Prices and subsidies were used to influence agricultural production. So were purchase, storage, transportation, and disposal programs. Production items were rationed to farmers. In all this, the AAA (as nucleus of the war boards) played a large role. Meanwhile, acreage controls were virtually eliminated, but the conservation payment program was maintained.

Then the Production and Marketing Administration was created in 1945. State AAA chairmen [18] became the majordomos for all agricultural action programs, except FSA, SCS, and the Rural Electrification Administration. The state PMA chairmen were in position to consolidate their collective power in a manner that would both increase their independence from USDA control and also enhance their significance in making agricultural policy. Thus Secretary Anderson's second major reorganization (1946) was designed to perfect line administration so that PMA state chairmen could be held responsible for the execution of those programs with which they were charged.

The reorganization order attempting to centralize the PMA was issued September 30, 1946. Immediately the AFBF and the NFU attacked it bitterly. The Farm Bureau denounced "professional planners" and "bureaucratic control." President O'Neal declared that the reorganization would:

"1. Wreck the Triple-A programs as established by Congress. It divided among several branches of PMA the jobs originally assigned AAA . . . Triple-A itself was nearly wiped out and replaced by the Field Service Branch in the earlier reorganization of PMA. This new order finishes the job, for under it Field Service Branch becomes a glorified errand boy without responsibility for formulating programs.

"Also, planning and direction of the soil conservation program is taken from AAA and handed over to the 'conservation' branch (of PMA). Responsibility for acreage adjustment programs and marketing quotas for cotton, corn, wheat, and tobacco (when such programs are needed) also are taken from AAA and assigned to various commodity branches." AFBF *Official News Letter*, Oct. 16, 1946.

18. In the South, read "state administrative officer."

The National Farmers Union lambasted what it considered the surrender of agricultural policy to the "food trades people," whom it found prominent in the higher councils of the PMA.

At this time the state chairmen of PMA were in Washington at the annual outlook conferences. Climaxing a series of developments, most of these men signed a letter of protest to the Secretary of Agriculture. They requested the revocation of the reorganization order, the acceptance of the resignation of the then administrator of PMA (Robert H. Shields), and the temporary appointment of Under-Secretary N. E. Dodd as head of PMA "Until the confusion caused by the PMA reorganization can be straightened out, and a permanent PMA administrator with a similarly well-established record of public service to agriculture can be selected. . . ." [19]

Secretary Anderson did hold up the reorganization temporarily. But he refused to be cowed. Shields' resignation went through, but Jesse Gilmer, one of the crack USDA administrators, was appointed acting head of PMA. In an address to the National Grange,[20] he declared:

"Farm organizations also have a definite interest in program formulation and administration because they naturally want the government to use the most effective means for carrying out existing policy. But ultimate responsibility for farm program formulation and administration [in terms, of course, of Congressional grants of power] must necessarily lie with the Secretary of Agriculture. He must not be charged with administrative responsibility and at the same time have his hands tied so he cannot move."

Speaking of the current reorganization of the Department, he cited his search for competent advice.

"I wanted responsibility placed firmly and squarely on definite positions all down the line. I wanted to make certain that I could account fully and currently for the Department's use of every cent of the public money available to it."

Secretary Anderson said that his reorganization attempted to meet the need for continuous two-way consultation between

19. *The National Union Farmer,* Nov. 1, 1946.
20. Portland, Oregon, Nov. 15, 1946.

the USDA and farmers as well as those engaged in the distribution, etc., of agricultural commodities. The second reorganization was being held up until he could make it clear to leaders in Congress and in farm organizations that agricultural policy was not involved. "This . . . is clearly a matter of administrative organization rather than a matter of policy."

All will agree that the Secretary was faced with a real problem in maintaining responsible government. Nevertheless, it was no mere matter of administrative organization. *The kind of major administrative organization we have is a matter of high policy since it cannot be considered except in conjunction with an analysis of the organization and distribution of political power in this country.* The perennial fight over control of the "farm program," here lightly sketched, illustrates this fact. It is interesting to note that of the ten north central state PMA chairmen whose letter of protest to the Secretary has been described, seven were state AAA chairmen in 1941! Many of them must have participated in the AAA-AFBF-Extension battle in 1942–1943. Secretary Anderson also declared at Portland:

"The goblins said I was going to fire great numbers of State PMA directors, one publication listing twelve of them. A United States Senator was so disturbed that he wired, 'Hope you will not approve discharge of State directors without detailed consideration and hearing of individuals affected.' The truth was and is that no discharges were contemplated by any responsible official and none has happened. It was a complete lie."

Striking testimony, indeed, to the fact that state chairmen have become factors in the (not merely partisan) political situation in agriculture! [21]

It is against this background that the struggles between and among PMA, Extension, and Farm Bureau must be understood

---

21. This is true even though the then regional directors may have strongly influenced the stand of the state committeemen—as seems to be indicated by the uniformity with which committeemen signed the letter of protest throughout the midwest and in some other sections. It was important that regional directors had to appeal to state committeemen for support. Further, although regional directors are gone, the problem of coordinating state PMA organizations and of their role in the general functioning of PMA remains.

as they impinge on the controversy over the administration of soil conservation programs. During 1947 and part of 1948 the issue seemed to many in the PMA as one of preserving the farm committee system. In consequence, there was reason to stave off any assault by the Soil Conservation Service and its allies. In 1947 the annual conference of the PMA was strongly involved with the question of conservation administration. Although the 1948 conference of the PMA gave considerable attention to the conservation issue, the much larger questions of the level of support prices for agricultural products and of controls of farm production were paramount.

The issue in 1948 and after appeared rather clear between the PMA and Farm Bureau in midwestern states. This issue is whether the PMA or the Farm Bureau more correctly represents farmer attitudes toward the support price program. PMA appeared to be in a stronger position than seemed possible after the debacle of 1943. In at least two midwestern states, powerful PMA influence in state Farm Bureau conventions was reported in 1948—with respect to resolutions on the level of price supports and on controls. Spokesmen in two other states declared that PMA represents farmer opinion better than the Farm Bureau. Meanwhile, the 1948 election strengthened PMA's position, but the 1950 election weakened it—and so it goes.

3. PMA INFLUENCE UPON POLICY

The last section examined the administrative politics of PMA in maintaining and expanding its role among agricultural agencies. The influence of PMA upon the content of farm legislation has been noticed, but the chief emphasis was upon *who* is to administer. The discussion now turns to emphasize *what* is to be administered. When the AFBF came out for flexible price supports in 1947, the lines were drawn on this issue particularly in the middle west between PMA and the Farm Bureau. The struggle for power turned on the issue of what the content of agricultural legislation should be. Further, the level of support prices became a partisan political issue in 1949; and so is germane to the next section.

Although a legal issue is present, the primary questions concern political behavior and the nature of political opinion formation and its operation within and upon government. The writer has little doubt that the PMA committee system engenders a common point of view upon policy issues or that this common viewpoint is able to make itself known in Washington. Farmer administrators charged with carrying out a given program are natural supporters of that program if it is challenged. In 1948 the writer listened to a southern state PMA chairman describe a series of district meetings which had been attended by several hundred county committeemen. All but one such committeeman vigorously favored a controlled agriculture. In 1950, the writer attended a midwestern state meeting of county and some community committeemen who listened to an analysis of the Agricultural Act of 1949. The analyst, an agricultural college economist, was strongly critical of the high level of support prices in that law. He declared his belief that, in the absence of support prices, corn would not fall below ninety cents a bushel. The roar of disagreement from his audience was immediate, loud, and apparently universal. The PMA line then held that corn would have fallen to about 60 cents in the free market! The unanimity with which this political opinion (for it was that) seemed to be held by this group was impressive.

In this midwestern state, the Farm Bureau, with some 150,-000 members, was currently sponsoring a flexible price support program. The PMA, with at least as many farm cooperators, was sponsoring a uniformly high price support program. Both purported to speak for the same farm public. Which was the authentic voice? Was either the Farm Bureau or the AAA "superior" to the other in eliciting "grass roots" sentiment and formulating it in political demands? Or were both formulating programs at state and national levels and then attempting to sell the same to farmers?

At any rate, politicians who frame legislation for agriculture can hardly disregard opinions of the committee system on matters of primary concern to the PMA. The political nature of the problem can be further demonstrated by examining its *legal* aspects.

In 1919, Congress enacted legislation to penalize lobbying by federal officials.[22] But Congress has also authorized and directed numerous governmental agencies to disseminate useful information on a variety of subjects. If the consequence is pressure upon Congress for legislation, can the chain of events be proved in court to show exactly who was influenced, and by what? Moreover, if the agency is obeying a Congressional directive, who is the guilty party? This is not to deny that "big government" multiplies the pressures upon Congress or that a problem of control emerges. But—let the lawyers squirm as they may—it is essentially a *political* problem. On some occasions, power can only be checked by power. Two illustrations from the PMA's experience are in point.

In 1948, allegations were made that the PMA committee system was being used to influence Congress. The Committee on Expenditures in the Executive Departments, House of Representatives, investigated charges. It was found that actions by the PMA to inform personnel of the impending cut were proper —how else administrators could learn that they might not spend money which they did not have one cannot understand. But the committee also found that in Nebraska a state meeting of the PMA to analyze the effects of the impending cut was fol-

---

22. "No part of the money appropriated by any Act shall, in the absence of express authorization by Congress, be used directly or indirectly to pay for any personal service, advertisement, telegram, telephone, letter, printed or written matter, or other device, intended or designed to influence in any manner a Member of Congress, to favor or oppose, by vote or otherwise, any legislation or appropriation by Congress, whether before or after the introduction of any bill or resolution proposing such legislation or appropriation; *but this shall not prevent officers or employees of the United States from communicating to Members of Congress on the request of any Member or to Congress, through the proper official channels, requests for legislation or appropriations which they deem necessary for the efficient conduct of the public business."* Violations are punishable by removal from office and also constitute a misdemeanor. Conviction carries a fine (maximum $500) or imprisonment (maximum one year) or both. 18 U.S.C. Sec. 201, italics added.

The italicized words, however, can be used to legitimatize nearly any action by officials. Mr. Frank H. Weitzel, Assistant to the Comptroller General, said: "Concrete evidence of irregular methods on part of Federal personnel, involving either direct or indirect attempts to influence congressional action, is quite elusive." "Legislative Activities of Executive Agencies," *Hearings,* House Select Committee on Lobbying Activities, 81st Cong., 2nd Sess., Part 10, p. 33, and *passim.*

lowed by Congressional receipt of letters from many county Triple-A organizations. Examining letters from 25 county organizations, the committee found that not all the letters were identical, yet all contained considerable identical language. The committee concluded that the letters prepared at the state headquarters became the basis of letters demanding reversal of Congressional action written to Congress by the county organizations. The committee considered this action a violation of the Act of 1919 (cited above). The report (signed by fourteen Republicans and two Democrats) spoke warmly of the "farm members of the AAA committees, elected by their friends and neighbors . . ."; but it found that USDA employees had used the farmer committeemen to bring pressure upon Congress. The Congressional committee held that its duty was to lay the facts before the proper authorities for action. The Department of Agriculture had been apprised of the situation in June, 1947; but no action had been taken by February, 1948.

The minority report of Carter Manasco and other Democrats shows how hard it is to discipline the PMA by law on such matters. Congressman Manasco charged the majority with attempting to absolve the county and local committees while saddling the blame on PMA employees at state and national levels.

He stressed the non-political character of the local committees. "It would go hard with anyone who tried to regiment their thinking." Then he asked who the employees were that the majority charged with violating the law. They, too (he declared), are part of the farmer committee system.

"They are themselves all farmers, drawn from the ranks of the previously elected local committeemen. They are in no sense 'career employees,' or 'bureaucrats.' It would not be surprising if some of them failed to have the detailed understanding of government regulations expected of career employees."

Rather than attempting to place the onus on the Secretary of Agriculture, the majority (in Manasco's opinion) should have called for the indictment of farmer committeemen. Only after such men were indicted, tried, and found in violation of federal law could the Secretary withhold their salaries. But Manasco did not believe that the majority desired such action.

"I do not believe we representatives from farm areas would want snoopers and detectives from the Department going around all over our local communities in an effort to dig up charges to convict our own neighbors and constituents."

It is not surprising that the committee's investigation and report was without effect.[23]

The second illustration occurred in 1950.[24] On April 11, Senator Aiken addressed the Senate in criticism of a state PMA meeting in Minnesota on April 3-4.[25] Senator Aiken was not critical of the meeting of county PMA committeemen to formulate the 1951 conservation program, but he objected to invitations to 5000 community committeemen to hear political speeches, chiefly by Secretary Brannan and Senator Humphrey. He quoted the letter to community committeemen from state PMA Chairman Charles W. Stickney, which included the following:

"The decline in farm prices has placed even greater emphasis on the price-support program which we in PMA are administering. We know you realize how controversial this subject has become. We feel it is extremely important for you community committeemen who represent agriculture at the grass roots to have this chance to hear your Secretary who is making a terrific fight to maintain some measure of economic stability for farmers."

Senator Aiken "searched diligently" Secretary Brannan's speech without finding "any reference to the subject matter for which the conference of county committeemen was called, namely, the formulation and administration of agricultural programs as authorized by law." He quoted, among other things, an article by Alfred D. Stedman in the St. Paul *Pioneer Press* for April 5:

" 'Before a record-breaking crowd of 8,000 farmers in St. Paul Auditorium, the Truman administration's campaign for the Brannan farm plan was opened Tuesday afternoon and headed straight for the national elections of 1950 and 1952.' "

---

23. Committee on Expenditures in the Executive Departments, H. of R., 8th Intermediate Report, 80th Cong., 2nd Sess. (1948).

24. See Part 10 of the House Selective Committee on Lobbying Activities (cited in n. 22, above), pp. 59-306.

25. *Ibid.*, pp. 277 ff.

Secretary Brannan's answer was contained in a letter to Comptroller General Lindsay C. Warren, June 1, 1950.

"This was an ordinary staff meeting of the same type and purpose as many others held by this agency and other agencies and bureaus of the Department . . . for many years, and, I am confident, held by many other agencies of Government from time to time." [26]

Some 2,322 PMA committeemen were present, including some 2,077 community committeemen, according to the Secretary. Construing Secretary Aiken's objection as being only to the presence of community committeemen, the Secretary noted that both county and community committeemen "do identical types of work." He noted the provision in the law for electing committeemen and for paying them per diems and travel expenditures; he pointed out that there was just so much money for community committeemen who, therefore, could receive nothing extra for attendance at this meeting. Furthermore:

"The implication that representative American farmers could be bribed or induced to attend a meeting by the offer of $8 per day plus 5 cents a mile for travel is unthinkable, unwarranted, and unjust to American farmers."

In addition to training and instruction at such meetings, the Secretary declared experience to show that

". . . a very useful purpose can be served by providing committeemen with the opportunity to hear first hand the views of some of the leading agriculturalists of the country."

He pointed out that Senator Aiken had addressed the 1950 Vermont PMA conference.

In his speech at St. Paul, the Secretary had carefully noted that he was acceding to Congress' request in formulating a farm program.[27] In his letter to Mr. Warren, he declared that

"No reference was made to a political party or to a political candidate . . . The listeners were not exhorted to vote in one fashion or another . . ."

---

26. *Ibid.*, pp. 77 ff.
27. *Ibid.*, p. 66.

And finally:

". . . the fact that Senator Humphrey addressed this meeting in political terms cannot be charged to those who organized the meeting or to the Secretary of Agriculture. Senator Thye, a member of the opposite party, was invited and could have spoken as vehemently on the other side of the same issues if he had chosen to do so."

After a lengthy hearing and the accumulation of a considerable set of documents on the matter, the House Select Committee on Lobbying Activities vindicated the administration.[28]

This chapter might end here with a summary which emphasized the following:

1. The politics of conservation clearly involves issues respecting other agricultural policies, especially price supports.

2. Administrative organization and procedures may be of obvious political significance, through their effects upon the organization of power and influence. At the same time agencies charged with carrying out large public programs, such as providing price supports, require a degree of authority and discretion which makes the *legal* control of their political actions all but impossible.

3. The AAA-PMA committee system is not only a powerful arm of government but also a pressure group. Because of its base in local elections, because of the moral connotations of economic justice for the farmers involved in its program, and because of its demonstrated ability to survive, the committee system appears to be almost beyond challenge politically.

4. In the struggle for control in agriculture, power analysis is not enough; the conflict is among organizations but also among ideas or ideals.

5. Centralization versus decentralization—action agencies versus state Extension Services—is a continuous issue in agricultural politics; but it is an issue confused by (a) the propensity for action agencies to become autonomous to a degree which challenges the ability of either Congress or the President to control them; and (b) the interrelationships between Extension

---

28. Washington *Post*, July 20 and August 1, 1950.

and the Farm Bureau which, if it is not exactly centralized, still has a very powerful national organization in the AFBF.

6. Finally, in view of the tremendous growth of the American Farm Bureau Federation, with some 1,500,000 family memberships, the only effective challenge in agriculture to its monopolization of influence respecting major agricultural policies, at least, may be in the PMA committee system.

There is some supporting material for each of these points in the foregoing; but most of them would require a degree of elaboration and qualification outside the scope of this book. Listing them indicates that the politics of soil conservation needs to be analyzed in a very broad context. But even this canvass is not broad enough. For AAA-PMA has also become involved in partisan politics.

4. AAA-PMA AND PARTISAN POLITICS

Allegations have been made to the writer that the AAA was systematically strengthening the Democratic Party organization in some midwestern states as early as 1934. In 1935 Chester C. Davis retired from the administration of the AAA.

"He later declared that some members of a Washington group, in disregard of the position of the Land-Grant Colleges, were building a powerful centralized agency which they might seek to use for political purposes." [29]

In 1940 partisan considerations were said to play a role in promotions up the line from the county committees. One story which could probably be authenticated has it that a Washington AAA official attempted to use the committee system to collect Democratic campaign contributions about 1942—the assembled committeemen were given a choice "between the hatchet and the Hatch Act." *Spade* magazine for October 5, 1944 praised the Democratic Party:

"With all its faults it has done more for farmers than any other administration in history. Above all else it has established the policy of protecting farm income.

---
29. Cf. the writer's "Programmatic Research and Agricultural Policy," *JFE,* May, 1947, at p. 375.

"Here are valid Democratic claims: price supports, including commodity loans, parity payments, surplus purchase and distribution; ever-normal granary; solid conservation programs; rehabilitation and tenant purchase programs for small farmers; rural electrification; and inflation control." [30]

In some PMA meetings after the election of 1948, there was a disposition to claim credit for a share in President Truman's victory.

In 1949 the Democratic Party initiated a series of regional conferences. A 16-state rally was held in Des Moines on June 13-14. J. S. Russell wrote:

"Brannan gave two speeches, answered questions, . . . and in general provided party workers and the farm program—PMA and AAA—groups with some ammunition for carrying the program to the rank and file of farmers and consumers."

And also:

"A crowd of 2,500 persons was in KRNT theater. It was a tribute to Brannan's popularity, and also to the organization of the county AAA committeemen who turned out a crowd to hear the chief of the department of agriculture.

"Several of the state production and marketing administration leaders were here from the middlewest—such men as Charlie Stickney from Minnesota and Walter Katterhenry, Wisconsin State PMA chairmen, and Fred Wallace of Nebraska, former chief of the AAA in Washington." [31]

But Marr McGaffin reported that Secretary Brannan denied the truth of Republican charges that department field men and county committee chairmen had been instructed to bring eight or ten farmers with them to the Des Moines meeting.

" 'That is not true,' he said. 'More than that, I have issued orders to all department employees not to try to sell the program to anyone.' " [32]

Secretary Brannan consistently maintained that departmental employees were under no obligation to support his plan, although he naturally expressed a desire that departmental em-

---

30. *Spade*, it will be recalled, was published by former AAA employees as a kind of unofficial AAA house organ. Its subscribers were probably very largely AAA committeemen.

31. Des Moines *Register*, June 13, 1949.

32. *Ibid.*, June 14, 1949.

ployees should understand the proposals and be able to explain them. But this disclaimer has not silenced the critics.[33]

Whatever its efforts, the PMA organization has certainly not been a major factor in elections. The 1948 election has been variously interpreted. Louis Bean and Professor A. N. Holcombe are inclined to stress the role of the midwestern farm vote in the election of President Truman. Samuel J. Eldersveld has emphasized the significance of large metropolitan areas in this and other recent presidential elections. The writer suggests that the midwestern farmers contributed to Mr. Truman's election but were by no means decisive.[34] Respecting Congress, the balance of power in 1948 did not lie in the midwestern farm districts. From Ohio and Michigan west to the Dakotas and thence south through Kansas there were 48 Congressional seats which appeared to be more than 50 per cent rural on the basis of the 1940 census.[35] Republicans held all these seats after 1946; in 1948 the Democrats won only ten of them, four being in Missouri. Had the Democrats made no midwestern farm gains, they would still have enjoyed a majority of 72 in the 81st Congress. If PMA influence was brought to bear in campaigns, it is most difficult to discern any effect upon election returns.

It will be recalled that the Hatch Acts of 1939 and 1940, listing and penalizing "pernicious political activities," were efforts to control partisan activity of federal employees, excepting, of course, political officials, such as heads of departments, their assistants, and officials, appointed by the President and confirmed by the Senate, who are active in determining either foreign or nation-wide domestic policy. All other employees are

---

33. Cf. the controversy raised by the PMA Minnesota meeting in 1950, previous section.

34. Cf. Bean, "Forecasting the 1950 Elections," *Harper's* Magazine, April, 1950; A. N. Holcombe, *Our More Perfect Union,* Harvard University Press (1950); Eldersveld, "The Influence of Metropolitan Party Pluralities in Presidential Elections since 1920," *APSR,* Dec., 1949. An analysis of the 1944 and 1948 votes in Iowa by Henry J. Krueger of the research department, *Des Moines Register and Tribune,* indicates that the shift toward the Democrats in counties with *less* than 25 per cent of their income from agriculture was of greater significance in Mr. Truman's victory than the shift toward the Democrats in counties with *more* than 50 per cent of their income from agriculture.

35. Ralph Goldman, "Some Dimensions of Rural and Urban Representation in Congress," Unpublished M.A. thesis, University of Chicago, 1948.

prohibited (among other things) from using their "official authority or influence for the purpose of interfering with an election or affecting the result thereof." The 1940 amendment made the prohibitions of the act applicable to employees of state and local government "in connection with any activity which is financed in whole or in part by loans or grants made by the United States . . ." But in 1942, Congress thoughtfully exempted employees of "educational or research institutions" supported in part by state or local governments.[36]

These proscriptions apply to state PMA offices but are not strictly applicable to committeemen, locally elected. Nevertheless, the Secretary of Agriculture has published strict administrative regulations for the PMA local committees, embodying substantially the same proscriptions as contained in the Hatch Acts.[37] If political analysis fails to disclose concrete evidence of effective influence by PMA upon elections, research has found no examples of PMA officials found guilty of violations of the Hatch Act or of departmental regulations.[38]

But politics cannot be fully understood by legal analysis even when supplemented by quantitative examinations of election returns. Politics always will remain an elusive, compelling, and frustrating study. Politics concerns human interrelationships which bear upon the organization, distribution, and control of power—usually, but not necessarily, power organized in governments. How do people act politically? Whom do they define as political enemies? With whom do they ally? What techniques do they use to get and keep power? How do they appraise political situations? These are important political questions. In

---

36. 18 U.S.C. Sec. 61.

37. *Federal Register*, September 29, 1949; cf. *Hearings*, House Select Committee on Lobbying Activities, *op. cit.*, Part 10, pp. 163 ff.

38. The Civil Service Commission's 1950 *Report* notes that between August 2, 1939 and June 30, 1950, removals were ordered in 172 political-activity cases processed by the Commission. (p. 79.) The Commission does not designate agencies involved; efforts by the writer in 1949 conclusively to ascertain whether any PMA personnel had been involved in "political-activity" action under the Hatch Acts were inconclusive in their result. Nevertheless, since only 172 cases were reported in an 11-year period it is reasonable to conclude that few if any actions involved the PMA. The Iowa Federal Crop Insurance Director was suspended for activity in the 1950 campaign. AFBF *Official News Letter*, Jan. 7, 1952.

agricultural politics, it is significant that many Farm Bureau officials, agricultural college personnel, and Republican leaders appraise the PMA as a politically active arm of the Democratic Party.

It is equally significant that many people on the Democratic side are convinced that state Extension Services (outside the South) often play Republican politics. Allegations of Extension political activity are much more general and less specific than those of AAA-PMA partisanship. But the well-known ties between Extension and the Farm Bureau are cited, and Farm Bureau action in support of Republican candidates is pointed out.[39] On this basis, critics assert that Extension can hardly be neutral.

What are "the facts"? They are most difficult to ascertain. But the "milieu theory" of electoral behavior is suggestive. Wilfred E. Binkley poses the "paramount question" for political leaders: "What motivates the voter in making his decisions how to vote?"

"The answer is perhaps as complex and varied as human nature itself. By and large the decision is reached by non-logical processes. If there is any one determining factor it is probably the climate of opinion in which the voter has lived, and this was originally provided for him by his family. Hence no one need be astonished to learn that three out of every four voters have the same political affiliations as their fathers, according to an estimate of Charles E. Merriam." [40]

---

39. The AFBF carefully eschews partisan endorsements. O. M. Kile, *The Farm Bureau Through Three Decades, op. cit.,* p. 188. The writer believes that allegations of President Kline's active support of Governor Dewey in 1948 were based upon misinterpretations of the facts—especially upon an understandable tendency of persons in the Governor's entourage to claim a valuable support which actually they did not have but only hoped to get. Officials of the American Farm Bureau, with membership almost equally divided, Republican and Democrat, can hardly take official and formal partisan positions. On the other hand, numerous examples exist of state Farm Bureau's actively working in electoral campaigns. Thus the Minnesota Farm Bureau worked unsuccessfully to defeat Mr. Humphrey in 1948. Frank H. Jonas has shown that the Utah Farm Bureau opposed Senator Elbert Thomas (along with other Democrats) in the 1950 campaign. "The 1950 Elections in Utah," *Western Political Quarterly,* March, 1951. In both Utah and Minnesota, Extension and the Farm Bureau are very close.

40. *American Political Parties, Their Natural History,* Knopf, New York (1943), p. vi.

The careful study of the 1940 election in Erie County, Ohio, bears out this thesis. "Social characteristics determine political preference," say authors Lazarsfeld, Berelson, and Gaudet; and

"If a person's vote intention is to a great degree a symbol of the social group to which he or she belongs, then we should not be surprised that people iron out inconsistencies in their thinking in such a way as to conform to the group with which they live from day to day. In a way, the content of this chapter can be summarized by saying that people vote, not only *with* their social group, but also *for* it." [41]

Finally, while the sample used was too small to make a study of specific associations feasible, the authors concluded that active membership in formal associations (of which the Farm Bureau might be one) tends to strengthen the political predispositions which the voter already has.

The *milieu* theory of electoral behavior has been demonstrated in Illinois. Earl C. Smith, when President of the Illinois Agricultural Association, would plead with his members to forget their rock-ribbed Republicanism in order to enjoy the leverage they might have if they would shift their allegiance between candidates of both parties. His audience listened with deference —but voted no differently. The same theory was demonstrated in North Dakota when the Farmers Union officially backed Democratic candidates in 1950. The NDFU could not even elect its personable, well-known, and able candidate for Governor, Obed Wyum; indeed, the principal consequence was to disaffect some of its own members.

Colleges of agriculture, their experiment station staffs, and their extension organizations, including county agents, are part of the *milieu*—and they are associated in many states with strong and conservative farm organizations, the Farm Bureaus. It is difficult, if not impossible, for northeastern, midwestern, and western colleges of agriculture to keep from reinforcing in a thousand subtle ways the network of common understandings,

---

41. Paul F. Lazarsfeld, Bernard Berelson, and Hazel Gaudet, *The People's Choice*, Columbia University Press (1948), pp. 27, 145-47, 149.

Cf. Charles E. Merriam and H. F. Gosnell, *The American Party System*, Macmillan (New York) 3rd ed., 1940, p. 107, and V. O. Key, Jr., *Politics, Parties, and Pressure Groups*, Thos. Y. Crowell (New York, 1942), pp. 616 ff.

expectations, and customary ways of acting that form the culture of which it is a part. Part of this culture has been a traditional Republican orientation.

It would be asking a great deal of the college of agriculture, under such circumstances, to mount a critical examination of the institutions, traditions, customs, etc., by which its *milieu* is characterized. Similarly, it is asking a great deal of policy makers in the USDA to refrain from considering that the colleges, in their very acquiescence, are playing the Republican game. Remember that USDA top policy makers got there by the legitimate and necessary partisan political processes; remember that they consider themselves as political representatives of the farmer and also as in position to make political appeals to the farmer. Remember that "the farmer" in question is the same commercial farmer who, in the midwest, has been traditionally identified with Republicanism, and is often a staunch supporter of his land-grant college. The upshot appears to be as follows:

If the milieu *theory of electoral behavior is generally valid, midwestern college and Farm Bureau personnel, merely by carrying on their accustomed activities, have a share—wittingly or not, it does not matter—in reinforcing customary political behavior. If the PMA is to make a dent in this situation, it must do so in the same area by active, overt campaigning, thus incurring the disapprobation of those who equate politics with evil—without ever realizing that they themselves are inevitably immersed to their ears in the continuous flow of politics.*[42]

---

42. The writer anticipates vehement denials from both sides. For example, the late Dave Davidson's address on Conservation to the 1947 PMA conference contained these remarks:

"Another question they asked was, 'Do you make these payments as a means of engaging in political activities, in other words, are these checks just high class political propaganda?' Again, this question didn't bother me and the reason it didn't is because our program is handled by the farmers themselves through their elected community and county farmer committees. A person doesn't have to be a Democrat to be eligible to vote for these committees nor does the question of political affiliation come up in regard to membership on these committees. I don't know, and I don't believe anyone else knows, what percentage of committeemen are Democrats and how many are Republicans. I would not be surprised if there are more Republican than Democratic committeemen. In some areas I know there are. In any event, there has been no justified accusation of politics and I am extremely proud of that."

PART TWO

THE PROCESS OF
POLICY FORMATION

CHAPTER X

The Politics of Administration in the United States Department of Agriculture

I. THE PERSPECTIVE: THE STRATEGIC ROLE OF APPROPRIATIONS

The first part of this book has defined the issues in soil conservation policy, has shown the organized interests and agencies, has described and analyzed the antagonisms and alliances among these various interests, and has attempted to relate these analyses to other issues of agricultural policy as well as to broader political issues of the organization and distribution of power. The next four chapters shift the focus somewhat by centering upon efforts to redefine soil conservation policy and to reorganize its administration—efforts, therefore, to change the configuration of political power and influence in agriculture.[1]

Thus the present chapter describes the USDA's actions in beating off attacks of the Farm Bureau and in attempting single-handedly to reorganize its programs. Chapter XI deals with field hearings held by the Senate and the House during the Repub-

---

1. The Division between parts I and II is somewhat arbitrary. The characterization of the organized interests has required some examination of attempts by some participant agencies to change the scope and functions of others. One example is the effort by the colleges of agriculture to secure transfer of soil conservation administration to the states in 1938. Another is the joint endeavor of the USDA and the colleges to coordinate programs and administration through land-use planning, 1938–1942. Both failed (cf. chap. ix, sec. 2). What distinguishes part II, therefore, is its emphasis.

lican-dominated 80th Congress.[2] This is followed by an analysis of the Hoover Task Force and Commission recommendations in 1949 and their aftermath, the failure of President Truman's reorganization plan for agriculture in 1950 (Chapter XII). Part II concludes with an examination of the reorganization of conservation and related administration in February, 1951 (Chapter XIII).[3]

2. The field hearings have been examined exhaustively because they throw light on the problem of Congress in securing and analyzing information at the "grass roots." The effort was to go beyond the organizations which appear in Washington and to reach farmers *qua* farmers. But what Congress actually reached was the same organized interests which appear in Washington, although the organization was tapped at a somewhat different level. Those familiar with A. F. Bentley's classic work, *The Process of Government* (University of Chicago Press: 1908) might have predicted the result. See also David B. Truman, *The Governmental Process, op. cit.*

3. The writer intended to include an analysis of the Hope and Aiken Bills in the 80th Congress; but since such an analysis has been published, it is omitted here to conserve space. (Charles M. Hardin, "Current Proposals . . ." *Journal of Farm Economics,* Nov., 1948.) This analysis, however, is an integral part of the story, since it demonstrates (a) the reflection of group interests in proposed legislation and (b) the difficulties of securing legislation even in a Congress controlled by one party with considerable stake in reorganization, if the Congressional leaders differ both in their ideas about the content of policy and in their interpretations of political strategy. Thus the reorganization proposals of the Aiken Bill reflected the interests of colleges of agriculture and the Farm Bureau. Proposals of the Hope Bill advanced the interests of the SCS which were strongly supported, among others, by the National Grange. While the Hope and Aiken Bills were active, it was declared to the writer that a gap across which virtually no communication took place existed between the Committee of Agriculture and Forestry in the Senate and the Committee of Agriculture in the House. Observations also bore out this interpretation.

It was also intended to include an analysis of the National Soil Fertility Bill of 1947, prepared by Dr. Norman Wengert. This bill represented the interests of the Farm Bureau, the TVA, and colleges of agriculture; it was written by the American Farm Bureau Federation in consultation with TVA. It proposed to re-define soil conservation and related policies according to the TVA model, which would be established as a national pattern. Also to be included were a characterization of TVA's agricultural program by Dr. Wengert and an analysis of relationships between TVA and the USDA by the writer. Since the national soil fertility bill is no longer a live issue and since the TVA-USDA controversy has been resolved essentially in favor of the USDA, these chapters have been omitted to conserve space. Their inclusion, however, would provide a more rounded treatment as would the inclusion of the relationship of the comprehensive agricultural plan to the development of the Missouri Valley.

See Norman Wengert, "The Land—TVA—and the Fertilizer Industry,"

What emerges from a review of the various efforts to change the form and content of conservation policy is a considerable respect for the power inherent in the appropriation process. The failure and demise of the land-use planning program has been noted. Again, in the fluid situation created by Pearl Harbor, Secretary Wickard consolidated the SCS and the AAA in the Agricultural Conservation and Adjustment Administration; but the union was never consummated and the two were divorced within a year. Other efforts have been marked by a succession of failures to achieve as much as an initial reorganization.[4]

Reorganization was accomplished, nevertheless, in 1951 through a combination of the sustained and courageous efforts of Secretary Brannan and the vigorous persistence of the House Committee on Appropriations (and especially of its subcommittee on agriculture). It is too early to estimate the effectiveness of the 1951 reorganization. As noted later, the precise meaning of the reorganization is difficult to interpret; in the words of Congressman Whitten: "We are not trying to put any of these agencies on top of the other." Indeed, the immediate upshot of the "consolidation" of SCS and ACP may depend

---

25 *Land Economics*, 11 (1949), and his forthcoming book, *TVA and Agriculture: A Study in Regional Decentralization*, to be published by the Bureau of Public Administration, University of Tennessee. See also John D. Black, *Federal-State-Local Relations in Agriculture*, National Planning Association (1949); Philip Selznick, *TVA and the Grass Roots*, University of California Press (1948); and the review by R. G. Tugwell and E. C. Banfield, "Grass Roots Democracy—Myth or Reality?" in 10 *PAR*, 47 (1950); Charles McKinley, "The Valley Authority and Its Alternatives," 44 *APSR*, 607 (1950); the symposium on conservation in the *Journal of Politics*, August, 1951; Henry C. Hart, "Valley Development and Valley Administration in the Missouri Basin," 8 *PAR*, 1 (Winter, 1948); and M. S. McDougal, ed., "A Symposium on Regional Planning," 32 *Iowa Law Review* (January, 1947); Ross R. Rice is preparing a Ph.D. thesis at the University of Chicago on the political aspects of the Missouri Valley development.

4. The colleges did not succeed in taking over SCS in 1938. The Farm Bureau tried to cause reorganization in 1941 but failed—and failed again in 1947 with the national soil fertility bill, in which it had the backing of the TVA and many colleges of agriculture. The USDA proved unable to reorganize these activities in 1945 and again in 1947–48. In the 80th Congress, committees in both houses offered plans of reorganization and succeeded in frustrating each other. The efforts of the Hoover Commission in 1948–49 were no more successful than that of the President in 1950.

upon the relative proficiency of the personnel of each as in-fighters. Nevertheless, to accomplish the reorganization at all is something. It could hardly have been done without the willing cooperation of the Secretary; yet on the evidence of recent history, the Secretary would have been unable to act without the backing and insistence of the House Appropriations Committee members.

It will not do, of course, to overlook the possible cumulative effects of the numerous efforts to change soil conservation policy and administration over the last decade; yet one may tentatively conclude that another example has been offered of the great importance of Congressional appropriations in shaping policy and administration—and, through these actions, in affecting the organization and distribution of political power and influence. Full dress inquiry into general agricultural policy by the subject matter committees on agriculture is a relatively rare event. Ten years separated the consideration of the bill that eventuated in the Agricultural Adjustment Act of 1938 from the deliberations that resulted in the Agricultural Acts of 1948 and 1949. The extremely important consideration of Commodity Credit Corporation legislation has been under the jurisdiction of the Banking and Currency Committees. Meanwhile, the Appropriations Committees of both Houses give broad consideration to matters of agricultural policy each year.

The influence of the appropriations process upon agricultural policy remains to be fully examined,[5] but it has been considerable. The Tarver amendment, which limited the Farm Security Administration's purchase of farms for tenants, is a notable example of substantive policy in an appropriation bill.[6] Another was provided by the death sentence for the agricultural planning program in 1942.[7] Others occur in the history of develop-

---

5. David Knapp is preparing a Ph.D. thesis upon the relationship of the appropriations process to a number of AAA and PMA policies during the 1940's. For a general discussion, see A. W. Macmahon, "Congressional Oversight of Administration: The Power of the Purse," 58 *Political Science Quarterly*, 160-90; 380-414 (1943).

6. Cf. House *Hearings*, Agric. Approp., fiscal 1943, Part 2, p. 187.

7. Cf. the writer's article, "The Bureau of Agricultural Economics Under Fire . . ." *JFE*, August, 1946.

ment of conservation and related policies and administration. Thus it was through appropriations action that the AAA was forbidden to carry on information activities in 1943. It was in the annual rounds before the appropriations committee that SCS built up its appropriations from less than $28,000,000 in 1940 to approximately $55,000,000 in 1951.

Finally, a significant limitation upon the ability to change the ACP appropriations lies in the manner in which the appropriations process operates. Funds are appropriated for fiscal years, but the program employs the calendar year which corresponds more nearly with farm operations. During any given calendar year, the ACP is approving specific plans, providing grants of conservation materials, checking compliance by examining conservation practices actually carried out, and making payments; but it is also making up the program for the following year and accepting preliminary agreements with farmers concerning their intentions of participating with the coming program. Thus the annual budget appropriation act does two things: it *makes appropriations* for ACP which were authorized in the previous session, and it *authorizes appropriations* to be made in the following session for the same program. Thus the 1951 appropriation act carried an advance authorization of $285,000,000 for the 1951 crop year. The 1952 appropriation bill appropriates this sum and also authorizes a similar sum for the crop year 1952.

This means that any serious reduction in the ACP program has to be made a year in advance; any given session of Congress is apparently estopped from reducing the appropriations which it is not merely authorized but apparently morally bound to make. All it can do is to reduce the authorization for the coming year. Perhaps with some clairvoyance about the possible outcome of the 1946 elections, Congressman Tarver (D., Ga.) made an interpretation on the floor of Congress in March, 1946, that the acceptance by Congress of the advance authorization constituted a moral commitment to the farmers of the United States. This pledge was recalled in 1947 when an economy-minded Congress sought to reduce the ACP appropriations.

Why is it much more difficult to reduce ACP appropriations

"in two bites" (as it were) rather than one? The answer may be that it is difficult enough to engineer one economy drive in Congress, but that it is almost impossible to engineer two such drives in succession. For, if one session reduces the authorization for the following session, there is nothing to prevent that authorization from being raised the next year in the sum actually appropriated. The moral commitment is only against lowering the appropriation. Meanwhile the PMA has had an additional year to marshal its forces to save the appropriation. In any event, the manner of handling ACP appropriations in the Congress adds further evidence to support the position that the appropriations process is extremely influential in shaping agricultural policy.[8]

2. POLICY AS AN "ORGANIZATION PRODUCT"

Preceding chapters show how administrative cross-purposes result from semi-independent bureaus in the Department of Agriculture. This chapter will demonstrate the consequent difficulties for departmental coordination and integration. An example was the short-lived Agricultural Conservation and Adjustment Administration, the ineffective, post-Pearl Harbor union of AAA and SCS. Another example occurs in the default of Secretary Anderson's 1945 committee, which struggled with the problem of integrating conservation administration but never made recommendations upon it.[9]

---

8. Cf. House *Hearings*, Agric. Approp., fiscal 1948, pp. 1281-82; Senate *Hearings*, Agric. Approp., fiscal 1948, p. 1004.

In 1951 the issue was examined at some length. Ralph S. Roberts, Director of Finance and Budget Officer, USDA, told the committee that some consideration had been given to the possibility of changing the appropriation method in 1943 or 1944, but that nothing resulted. House *Hearings*, Agric. Approp., fiscal 1952, Part 1, pp. 540-44; cf. p. 31.

9. Congressman Pace emphasized one aspect of the difficulty. Any proposal for liquidation, consolidation, or transfer of agencies (he said) evokes a host of complaints from farmers, stockmen, and others. Such complaints are inspired by employees, fearful for their jobs. "I still insist that whenever you try to consolidate an agency in this government the most terrific fight you have is the personnel problem." *Hearings*, National Land Policy, Committee on Agriculture, H. of R., 80th Cong., 2nd Sess., May, 1948, pp. 76-77.

This situation in the USDA stimulated Paul Appleby's analysis in *Big Democracy*, which declares that policy should be an
"organizational product." This position is based upon the inter-
action of one policy upon another and of the consequent need
for general agricultural policies to be synthesized out of the
incisive analyses which come not only from separate bureaus
and their divisions but also from the proposals of farm organizations and out of the strategic needs of political parties. Appleby
enjoins officials to learn to "operate on their proper level." This
means as much that top officials learn to delegate and then to
respect discretion in their subordinates as it does that these
subordinates should temper their efforts to shape departmental
or general policy in the light of their agencies' needs. Appleby's
analysis constitutes a model or an ideal type, useful both in its
delineation of aspirations, and also in its criteria for considering
the administrative system as it exists and operates. What follows
often supports the validity of his analysis as well as suggests the
difficulty of attaining his goals.

3. THE USDA REPLIES TO THE FARM BUREAU

In its 1940 convention at Baltimore, the American Farm Bureau Federation made sweeping proposals for reorganization of
the USDA.[10] It recommended creation of an independent,
five-man, non-partisan administrative board, appointed by the
President and confirmed by the Senate. Among other programs,
this board would administer the AAA, the SCS, the Commodity
Credit Corporation, and the planning activities in the Bureau
of Agricultural Economics. It was apparently designed that
membership of the board would be drawn from leading farm
organizations.

Regional offices of USDA action agencies were to be eliminated. Such offices have always been thorns in the flesh of both
the Farm Bureau and the colleges of agriculture. The Farm
Bureau is organized nationally and by states but is not well

10. See House *Hearings*, Agric. Approp., Fiscal 1942, Part 2, pp. 396-546.
AFBF presentation, pp. 407-18, 468-522, chart showing proposals 546; USDA
answer, pp. 522-45.

adapted to dealing with regional offices. State boards were to be created to administer the AAA and related programs; their members were to be appointed by the national board from lists proposed by state Extension Directors (who would consult with farm organizations before making nominations). The Extension Service was to administer the SCS program and the farm planning work of the Farm Security Administration as well as the state and local planning programs then cooperating with the Bureau of Agricultural Economics. Farm Security would be combined with the Farm Credit Administration, and both were to be administered nationally by a board which was to be placed outside the USDA. No change was to be made in local AAA administration.

In its reply, the Department of Agriculture declared the following to be "the crux of the matter":

"The issues crystallized by the proposal, then, are: (a) Shall the unified national farm program be broken down into 48 State programs? (b) Shall any of these separate State programs be dominated in any State by a farm organization? (c) Shall a State official have sole authority to nominate the members of any Federal board? (d) Shall we experiment with a discredited form of board administration now of all times in a period calling for sensitive reactions to world forces? (e) Shall we sacrifice the specialized zeal of the Farm Security Administration? Of the AAA? Of the SCS? (f) Does the Congress wish to establish a new principle in Federal-State relations under which states, though not required to match or even furnish any of the funds, are given responsibility for the execution of federally financed programs?"

The Farm Bureau had declared as evidence of duplication that four agencies were engaging in soil conservation, etc., seven agencies in land-use planning, four agencies in demonstrating farming methods, five agencies helping farmers to carry out grazing improvement programs, seven agencies having contact with farmer committees, etc. The USDA answered each Farm Bureau charge separately and in detail. Regarding the four agencies in soil conservation and similar work (Extension, the AAA, SCS, and FSA), the USDA said that actually more were so engaged. It is suggested that conservation was not the responsibility of any one agency but one of the major responsibilities of all branches and levels of government. It analyzed the complementary nature of the work of various programs. The only way this so-called duplication could be avoided would be, for example, to direct lending agencies to stop requiring conservation practices of their borrowers. Respecting the Farm Bureau charge that numerous agencies were contacting farmer committees, the Department rejoined that under the law several agencies did function through local groups. Congress had sanctioned work through local committees to guarantee that the program should be in close touch with and responsive to farmer opinion.

A number of counties had been investigated by departmental officials to canvass what conflicts existed. Two such counties were cited. In one, it was argued that the conflict was nonexistent; rather, an example of cooperation was given. In the other, a North Dakota county, it was admitted that the programs "do not fit too well." While the programs did not conflict, the agricultural adjustment needed was so radical that present programs were insufficient; among other things, state legislation would be required to effect desirable changes. The Department suggested that the AAA, the SCS, and the FSA were not duplicating each other greatly in light of their different coverages. AAA reached nearly all farmers; SCS, contrarily, annually reached no more than 10 per cent of the farmers in soil conservation districts; and the Rehabilitation and Tenancy programs of FSA reached only 8 to 10 per cent of the farmers. The Department also argued that if these three programs were put in a single bureau, that bureau would require divisions corresponding to the present program.

Pointing out that the "organizational history of the Department for the past twenty years shows that there has never been a year in which major changes have not been made," the Department argued that the Farm Bureau's proposal would lead to duplication and conflict. The Farm Bureau proposal to create three heads of agricultural programs in Washington rather than one (the Secretary of Agriculture) would invite dissension! The USDA foresaw conflicts between state farmer committees and directors of state Extension Services and further queried whether differing attitudes among state Extension Directors would not lead to administrative disagreement. The Department then argued that AAA was more efficient in 1941 than it had been in its earliest period, 1933–35. The AAA was reaching 40 per cent more farmers than in 1936—was reaching, indeed, more then 6,000,000 farmers. Moreover, the AAA was outstripping earlier operations. For example, in 1941, the AAA was furnishing six and two-thirds million tons of liming material to farmers; in 1936 it furnished none. In 1941 some 650,000 tons of 20 per cent super-phosphate and 190,000 tons of triple super-phosphate were furnished the farmers; in 1936 none had been furnished. The USDA's reply also analyzed departmental efforts to coordinate agricultural administration through development of the state and local planning program and creation of the Office of Land-Use Coordination.

The Farm Bureau's efforts to reorganize the Department represented a full-scale attack. Testimony was carefully prepared, and representatives of a dozen state Farm Bureaus appeared in the House Appropriations Hearings. If the Farm Bureau was frustrated in its main effort to secure administrative control of the adjustment and conservation programs, it succeeded in setting the pattern for many subsequent critics of USDA field administration by emphasizing duplication, overlapping, and conflict. Yet everyone immediately concerned understood that real stakes of political power were involved in the control of the field organization.

The USDA made an interesting and often convincing answer to the Farm Bureau. The assertion of inter-agency harmony, however, is at odds with subsequent findings of the Hoover Task Force (1948–49) and of the House Appropriations Committee investigators in 1950. In 1941 the writer worked extensively in regional, state, and local offices of the USDA in company with Dr. John D. Black of Harvard, and E. L. Haff now of the University of California. Our experience disclosed considerable conflict at all levels. It is frequently argued that conflict is sharpened as one ascends the hierarchy, but our findings did not bear this out. We soon learned that to interview a number of local agency representatives together was to secure a picture of harmonious relationships; but if the same local representatives were contacted separately, the differences and conflicts tended to come to the surface rather sharply.

It is also interesting that the examples of coordination which the USDA offered were soon to pass out of existence. Congress put a stop to the state and local planning program in 1942, and the Office of Land-Use Coordination was liquidated by the Secretary on January 1, 1944. Despite its categorical denials of the Farm Bureau's 1941 charges, the USDA has continued to struggle with the organizational problem throughout the years. The next major effort which is fairly well-reported was in 1947.

4. FAILURE OF SINGLE-HANDED REORGANIZATION BY THE USDA IN 1947

Several committees of the USDA worked many months during 1947 to analyze agricultural policy and administration.[11] On October 6-8, the findings were given before a rare joint meeting of the Agricultural Committees of both Houses. Discussion here will be confined to the general administrative recommendations and to the efforts of the technical committee on conservation to find some common approach to the problem at the farm level.

USDA views on administrative reorganization were consistently expressed by four ranking officials;[12] most references will

11. The House Committee on Agriculture printed the *Hearings* and the USDA collected its tables and statements: "USDA Testimony Proposing Long Range Agricultural Policy and Programs . . .," April 21, October 6-8, 1947 (mimeo.). The inquiry into the technical problem of combining intensive SCS and extensive ACP approaches by the committee chaired by O. V. Wells should be high on the list of reading for those who are responsible for making the February 1951 reorganization work.

12. Secretary Anderson testified in the joint *Hearings*, October 6, 1947, and again with W. A. Minor, Assistant to the Secretary, April 12, 1948, in *Hearings*, S. 2318 80th Congress, 2nd Sess.; Under-Secretary Dodd testified May 4, 1948, *Hearings*, H. R. 6054, 80th Cong., 2nd Sess.; Mr. Brannan's testimony, March 1, 1948, is in *Hearings*, H. R. 4150, *et al.*, 80th Congress, 2nd Sess., pp. 20-55.

be to Assistant Secretary Brannan, who expressed the fundamental approach of the Department

"that the existing conservation programs are sound, going concerns, which already have accomplished a great amount of good; that these programs should be retained and strengthened; and that any new action should be consistent with the established policies and procedures whereby farmers themselves have a major responsibility in formulating and carrying out the program policies and procedure."

Perhaps the most significant recommendations of the Department dealt with the committee system. An additional Assistant Secretary of Agriculture was requested to shoulder national responsibility for the proposed state and county USDA committees.[13] A line was then to be perfected through state committees to the counties. State committees were to be composed of at least five farmers, appointed by the Secretary of Agriculture, plus the state Commissioner of Agriculture and a representative of the Land-Grant College. Congressman Cooley criticized the proposed secretarial appointment of farmer-members who would, he thought, become professional bureaucrats. Asserting that considerable dissatisfaction existed with present state PMA committees, he advocated "letting the farmers have a voice." As will be seen respecting the recommendations of the Hoover Commission (Chapter XII), the power of appointment of state committees is a bone of contention; it is a crucial point in the power structure of agriculture.[14]

The state committees were to be two-way links between the

_____

13. Mr. Brannan said that "the committees would have a direct and ready access to the Assistant Secretary." Reference is probably to the storm raised in 1946 when many PMA state committeemen thought that the central area of power in the USDA was being insulated against them. See above, chap. ix, sec. 2.

14. Although Mr. Brannan said that he would gladly discuss the election of state committeemen, he stoutly maintained that they should be appointed. At the county level, where the program involved actual operations on farms, the USDA favored election of committees; but, at the state level, the requirements of coordination suggest that "There must be established some more direct administrative line." Congressman Cooley declared that the USDA was interested in making programs which were then handed to the state committees whether they liked them or not. Mr. Brannan replied: "Well, that is your opinion. That is not what happens and it is not my attitude on it."

USDA and county committees. The latter were to be elected by a vote in which all farmers would be eligible. They would be responsible for the development of county conservation plans, approval of requests for assistance by soil conservation districts, determination of farm acreage allotment and marketing quotas when these programs are operating, and certification of eligible applicants for Farmer's Home Administration loans. The farmer-elected county committees were to be assisted by technical committees composed of administrators who were members of the USDA council in each county.[15]

Without going into other recommendations made in 1947, it may be said that the USDA proposals were heavily conditioned by the then existing administrative pattern. Nevertheless, they represented a kind of planned advance in the direction which current administration indicated. The proposed county committees were to be given general local responsibility for USDA action programs. A direct line was to be established from the Secretary's office to the counties. The general responsibilities of the committee system would, presumably, militate against the bureau autonomy which plagues the Department in its efforts to make general agricultural policy. The operations of pressure groups upon the committee process, hence upon the administrative process in agriculture, would perhaps be somewhat diminished; so would be the influence of the colleges of agriculture. Although the actual reorganization of February, 1951 (Chapter XIII), does not go so far, it is well to keep the question in mind whether the 1947 USDA recommendations

---

15. Later, Congressman Hope and Under-Secretary Dodd developed a clearer picture of the Department's proposals for modification of local committees. First, these committees would have broader functions than the old Triple-A committees. They would be responsible for more programs, and Mr. Dodd also predicted that as the years go on more responsibilities would be added to the committees. Second, whereas the old committees were elected by cooperating farmers, the Department now proposed that committees be elected by all farmers. Third, whereas the county committees were formerly elected by delegates to a county convention, one from each township or other community in which community committee elections were held, the Department now proposes that all community committeemen meet to elect the county committee. This was thought to be more democratic. Mr. Dodd said the present system invites politics and makes it easy for a county committee to stay in office. *Hearings*, H. R. 6054, 80th Cong., 2nd Sess., p. 34.

do not show the intentions of the Department respecting the
eventual roles of the PMA committee system.

The Department recommended consolidating the SCS and
the ACP part of PMA, but was not prepared to say just how.
The statement that the new USDA elected farmer committees
would approve soil conservation district requests was made by
Secretary Anderson on October 6, 1947; Mr. Brannan did not
repeat it in March, 1948. A statement of March 29, 1948,
suggests that the Department would recognize soil conservation
districts and service them in the traditional manner, i.e., through
SCS. But PMA committeemen knew what they wanted: "All
programs for conservation—including technical assistance to
farmers, preparing individual farm conservation plans, and related programs—to be under the administration of county and
community committees." [16] On March 30, 1948, the Hope Bill
was introduced; representing the SCS position, it would have
resolved the issue in favor of soil conservation districts. No
wonder the "Department" could not make up its mind!

Nevertheless, the Department made perhaps its most serious
effort to provide for the consolidation of conservation and related
land-use programs, certainly the most serious one that has
appeared in print.[17] This effort required an examination of
fundamental approaches at the farm level. What was developed
was a "basic appraisal." Apparently, assumptions were about
as follows: First, a certain minimum technical survey and service
background is needed for soil conservation. This background
means the consideration of a number of relatively simple physical
factors (soil type, slope, degree of erosion, drainage and water
supply, and present land-use). These physical factors would
help determine the practices to be applied on particular pieces
of land. They would suggest the technical on-site assistance
needed for the installation of complex practices. Second, it was

16. See *Congressional Record,* March 28, 1948, Appendix, p. A2034.
This is a statement of various proposals for soil conservation administration,
including the Jensen and Cooley Bills, Secretary Anderson's plan, and recommendations of state PMA committeemen.

17. *Hearings,* Oct. 6-8, 1947, *op. cit.,* pp. 112 ff. The committee, chaired
by O. V. Wells, Chief of the BAE, had representatives composed of ranking
officials of the SCS, the PMA, and the Forest Service.

assumed that the ACP approach did not sufficiently stress the technical aspects and that ACP provided too much a "cafeteria" of choices which were unaccompanied by technical advice to the farmer respecting how best to fit these practices into his farming system. Third, it was assumed that the SCS approach was too slow, costly, and complex. Fourth, the effective use of public funds for conservation was believed to require the coordination of the limited resources which could be brought to bear on the problem so that the same general objectives could be set, area by area, and farm by farm.

The "basic appraisal" represented an attempt to provide a practical, specific approach to the problem of improving soil conservation and land-use at the farm level. It drew upon, but was not wholly compatible with, the several approaches then in operation. Thus much of the physical inventory that underlay the basic appraisal followed SCS practice, but the basic appraisal was not a "complete farm plan." Moreover, the tenor of the report in emphasizing the application of relatively simple practices varies somewhat from the typical SCS approach. Again, it was declared that recommendations relating to land-use and soil practices should be based on information supplied by the National Cooperative Soil Survey, which represents the classic approach to soil mapping and typing that SCS has grown up to rival. On the other hand, the amount of technical analysis and planning involved went far beyond what ACP was doing then or has done since.

Nevertheless, the basic appraisal is none too clear. For one thing, the working group dealing with conservation did not examine the administrative organization, which was left to the Secretary's office. But this made for an ambiguity about who was to do the job. Mr. J. C. Dykes of SCS gave his opinion that the PMA committees were not sufficiently qualified and that trained technicians were required to perform the task of making the physical inventory thoroughly and economically. But Mr. Wells inserted a statement in the record, as follows:

". . . I should like . . . to call the attention of the committees [of Congress] to the fact that the conservation working group in the

Department recommended that 'The physical appraisal and development of conservation recommendations should be carried forward by technicians *or adequately trained persons* who have proved themselves competent.' We *deliberately left open the question* as to whether selected farmers, county committeemen, or agricultural workers other than full-time soil-conservation technicians could do such work. That is, we feel that the question should be answered by actual field tests, based not only on adequate training courses for selected farmers, committeemen or others, but also specific checks to see whether such individuals are in fact competent." [18]

In short, the working group could not develop a comprehensive and unambiguous approach without combining analysis of the substance of local programs with administrative analysis; but the latter was left to the Secretary's office which, at that time, had not been able to reach a formula for coordinating SCS and ACP. Furthermore, when the working group came to the crucial question of who was to do the job, it chose deliberately to leave the question open. Yet this is a problem which continues to plague SCS-ACP relationships. [19]

So much for the USDA's efforts in 1947. The Wells committee also recommended the continuance of conservation payments but suggested that Congress consider the advisability of making price supports contingent upon the performance of conservation practices. This suggestion (it was not a proposal) touched off considerable debate among Congressmen and Senators, as did a somewhat similar suggestion of Secretary Brannan in his famous statement of April 7, 1949. Rather than speculate on the future of this matter, however, the analysis will now turn to the USDA's objections to the proposals for reorganizing agricultural administration contained in the Aiken and Hope Bills in 1948.

5. THE DEPARTMENT AND THE CONTROVERSIES OF 1948

An exhaustive examination of proposals for administrative reform of conservation and related administration in agriculture

---

18. *Ibid.*, p. 146; italics supplied.
19. Cf. chap. vii, sec. 4, above.

occurred in 1948. On March 15, 1948, Senator Aiken introduced a bill which would have radically changed agricultural administration. The original draft would have transferred SCS functions to Extension and would have greatly decentralized and limited PMA committee operations. But on March 30, Congressman Hope introduced a bill which was almost diametrically opposed to the Aiken measure.[20] The result was that neither bill passed; but committee hearings on the proposals fully disclose the travails of the USDA in confronting administrative readjustment. A quotation from Secretary Anderson is illustrative. Asked for his views on the most advisable mode of decentralizing agricultural administration, he demurred on grounds that much work had been involved in reaching a common opinion within the Department. "I would not want to tear that agreement up by misstating it at this time." He added:

"You will recognize when we come to bring the Soil Conservation and ACP programs and the Extension Service together and try to get them to agree upon what we are willing to recommend, it involves some operation."[21]

The Aiken Bill proposed considerable decentralization of function upon the Land-Grant Colleges. Secretary Anderson professed some uncertainty whether the Aiken Bill proposed merely administrative decentralization or (a very different matter) a grant-in-aid program with local autonomy to decide the content of that program. Admitting that decentralization is necessary and desirable, he argued that a national program should not be broken into a large number of semiautonomous parts. W. A. Minor, assistant to the Secretary, declared that such local autonomy would mean wide variation. "Obviously there will not be a common thread that runs through them, unless the Secretary has some means of getting a common thread." He pointed out that if Congress placed some particular responsibility upon the Department, the Secretary would be powerless to see that performance was achieved except by denying funds to the states.

20. This chapter should be read with the author's article, "Current Proposals . . . ." *JFE*, November, 1948.
21. *Hearings*, S. 2318, 80th Cong., 2nd Sess., p. 41.

During this testimony, Secretary Anderson made one of the most incisive remarks anywhere in the hearing about the problem of decentralization as against the problem of responsibility in government:

"As I read this bill, it would open the door to subversion or nullification of the actions of Congress by putting operations in the hands of persons who are neither accessible nor responsible to the Congress. Democracy expresses itself through the Congress, as members of this body will quickly assert, if anyone contends otherwise. The Congress takes into account both local and national considerations in formulating farm programs. It is possible to take both local and national considerations into account in administering the programs without making them inoperative or ineffectual at state and county levels and without weakening the democratic system." [22]

This quotation had been preceded by an exchange which placed Secretary Anderson clearly on record against any further decentralization or, preferably, devolution of agricultural functions upon the state.

"Senator Aiken: You would not give the state and local people any more authority than they have now, then?
Sec. Anderson: In research?
Senator Aiken: In anything.
Sec. Anderson: That is about right." [23]

Now to the Hope Bill. Under-Secretary Dodd made a notable presentation.

First, the narrowness of the conservation farm plan was criticized. Farmers could not have two operations, one for production and one for conservation. Farmers who did not achieve a reasonable degree of financial success as a result of farm production were in no position to carry out many needed conservation measures.

Second, Mr. Dodd objected to the original Hope provision for a national advisory council with a specified membership. Discussion then reviewed the arguments for flexibility in consultation with group representatives. Mr. Dodd declared:

---

22. *Hearings,* S. 2318, 80th Cong., 2nd Sess., p. 43.
23. *Ibid.,* p. 27.

". . . I do not believe, Mr. Chairman, that you could set up a committee, having in mind, I think what I think you intended with this committee, to cover the whole broad field of agricultural problems in the United States. It is easy enough to pick out three, or four, or five, or six top-ranking organizations that you would want to have membership on that committee, but in almost every state you have some local groups that are awfully important in their own particular field. They may be a commodity group or they may be composed of a number of commodity groups. They would also feel that they were not given proper recognition if they did not have a spot on the committee. I feel that the policy that has been followed by the Department in calling in the affected groups to discuss changes in legislation and to discuss problems of administration is much better than it is to set a rigid formula whereby certain people or certain groups are to be considered on the board and others are left off."

Mr. Dodd insisted that if some groups were named and others were added as needed the committee would be large and unwieldy. He also said that if a particular group were named and then others added to it the others would feel that the five or so who were specifically named "had a little special entry into the Department of Agriculture that they would not have." Mr. Dodd also denied that Congressman Hope was right in suggesting that the Secretary sometimes appointed a committee of seven when twenty others thought they should be on the committee.

"Mr. Dodd: That is not the way, Mr. Chairman, that it is done. We have not set up committees of seven or nine or any other number. We have sent word to different organizations that we would like to discuss with them either some administrative changes or legislative changes and suggested that they send a representative. But you generally cover the whole field and those who can, who are able financially or are close by or for other reasons can send a member, are represented there.

"I think it is much better than to limit it to 5 or 7 or 10. I think it would be most unworkable from the standpoint of operation." [24]

Third, Mr. Dodd complained of the inflexibility with which the Hope Bill would organize administration within the Department of Agriculture. His criticism was reminiscent of that he

24. *Hearings,* H. R. 6054, 8oth Cong., 2nd Sess., pp. 22-23.

gave in 1946 respecting the Hope-Flannagan Act, regarding tendencies to legislate administrative changes. He declared a preference for leaving the establishment of the Agricultural Resources Administration to the discretion of the Secretary of Agriculture, who could then be held responsible for it. He argued that it had taken the Department a long time to work out the consolidation and coordination of research in the Agricultural Research Administration. Congressman Hope pointed out that he had known several Secretaries of Agriculture, all of whom seemed to feel the need to change the Department. Would it not be better to fix some things once and for all? Dodd said, "Maybe so. But if Congress sets up a bureau itself then pretty soon that bureau begins to believe it has special favors of some kind granted to it." Mr. Pace wondered if the bureaus in the Department were not so autonomous now that Congress should pass some kind of bill like this to knock their heads together and make a coordinated organization.[25]

Fourth, in illustrating the difficulty of legislating administration, Mr. Dodd pointed up an important criticism of the Hope Bill with respect to research.

"An appropriate illustration of the principle I have in mind pertains to the soil survey and those other research functions in water conservation and soil physics, which would be transferred to the proposed Agricultural Resources Administration under the provisions of H. R. 6054. These research functions are closely allied with, in fact are a part of, other phases of agricultural research relating to crop and livestock production. To properly serve all the agricultural programs they are designed to serve, including those dealing with conservation, it would be unwise to freeze them in an organizational pattern which experience might prove less than fully effective." [26]

Fifth, an interesting problem was presented by the decentralized character of soil conservation districts. Mr. Dodd argued that the Department needed local committees to perform definite functions *as integral parts of federal machinery.* Congressman Poage asserted that the Department professed its ability

25. *Ibid.*, pp. 24-28, 32-33.
26. *Ibid.*, pp. 9-42.

to work through Extension, also decentralized, and charged the Department with letting the districts "bleed to death." [27]

The ticklish underlying problem can be illuminated by a comparison of the soil conservation districts—SCS alliance with the Extension-Farm Bureau relationship and with the PMA committee system. While the Extension-Farm Bureau alliance upholds a relatively weak federal bureau, the associated soil conservation districts support a powerful federal agency operating direct from Washington to the farms in administering a highly dramatized and unique program. While the Farm Bureau is "merely" an organization of farmers, soil conservation districts represent to many the ideal of local democracy. Where PMA committees, if elected, receive per diems and are administratively responsible through the PMA hierarchy to Washington, the districts are local units of government. Criticisms of any of these alliances or agencies are freely construed by defenders as attacks upon democracy; but none can make a better *prima facie* case for this rejoinder than the SCS-soil conservation district spokesmen.

So the consequences of the federal system continuously generate difficulties for the USDA. If the USDA acquiesces to "decentralizing" proposals which strengthen Extension, it appears to be tacitly favoring one general farm organization at the expense of others; if the USDA agrees to increased cooperation with soil conservation districts, it thereby adds to the autonomy of the SCS and worsens its internal difficulties of integration and coordination. Either of these alternatives would somewhat weaken the scope and prestige of the PMA committee system. On the other hand, if the USDA prefers the PMA committees, it is charged with grasping centralization and with callousness toward local democracy. At the same time, to prefer the PMA committee system is further to enhance the power of an agency which rather continuously threatens to "take over" the Department of Agriculture. Certainly administrative proposals in this area are fraught with politics!

---

27. See chap. v, sec. 2.

CHAPTER XI

Congress Goes to the Farmer

I. THE FIELD HEARINGS OF 1947

During 1947 extensive field hearings were held by both the House Committee on Agriculture and a sub-committee of the Senate Committee on Agriculture and Forestry—the first such traveling hearings on general agricultural policy since 1937.[1] The purpose of the hearings was variously defined. Senator Aiken wanted views of farmers and their representatives on the entire range of agricultural policy—credit, conservation, price support, international trade, etc. He did not invite testimony on specific bills. Senator Thomas (Oklahoma), then ranking minority member of the Senate Committee wanted to know how the price support programs were working and what farmers thought of production controls; but he declared himself uninterested in

1. From October 20 to November 10, 1947, the Aiken Sub-Committee of the Senate Committee on Agriculture and Forestry visited Peoria, Minneapolis, Sioux Falls (S. D.), Denver, West Springfield (Mass.), Memphis, and Columbia, (S. C.). These hearings are cited as: *Hearings*, 80th Cong., 1st Sess., S. Res. 147, Part 2. The House of Representatives Committee on Agriculture visited Durham (N. H.), Lancaster (Pa.), Rocky Mount (N. C.), Montgomery (Ala.), Madison (Wis.), Sioux City (Iowa), Kansas City (Mo.), and Temple (Tex.). These will be cited as: *Hearings*, H. of R., 80th Cong., 1st Sess., Long Range Agric. Policy, Part 6, Part 7, etc. In view of the frequent longevity of farm Congressmen, it is notable that only Senators Thomas of Oklahoma and Ellender of Louisiana commented on participation in the hearings ten years previously.

answers to questions prepared by the committee's staff. Congressman Hope said that the purpose was to ascertain farmers' views on long-range agricultural policy and to acquaint committee members with agricultural conditions in various sections.[2]

No hearings were held on the home grounds of either chairman or ranking minority member, although some meetings were held in other members' bailiwicks. Congressman Hope spread his hearings more generally, holding only two of the eight here reviewed in the Corn Belt—which was the scene of six of Aiken's 13 sessions.[3] Some initial planning consisted of prepared questions circulated in advance of hearings to various interested parties. But, although some of the advance questions were discussed without reference from time to time, only one Senate witness (and perhaps two or three before the House) specifically referred to the questionnaire. Typical evidences of nonpartisanship are scattered throughout the hearings, although opportunities arose which, in view of the imminence of the 1948 election and the wide-reporting of hearings in the press, could not be passed.[4] Little House-Senate rivalry appeared.[5]

2. *Hearings*, 80th Cong., 1st Sess., S. Res. 147, Part 2, pp. 329, 340, 401, and *Hearings*, H. of R., 80th Cong., 1st Sess., Long Range Agric. Policy, Part 6, p. 708.

3. The House Committee held West Coast hearings late in 1948 as well as those examined here.

4. *Hearings*, 80th Cong., 1st Sess., S. Res. 147, Part 2, pp. 366-67, 711-12; *Hearings*, H. of R., 80th Cong., 1st Sess., Long Range Agric. Policy, Part 7, p. 853, Part 13, p. 1499. Such non-partisanship may be related to the traditional voting behavior in the rural electorate, which tends to return incumbent legislators of the same party. Legislators may accept partisan rivals as representing areas beyond the reach of their own party. Of course, as many students have pointed out, cross-party friendships and camaraderie are frequently important characteristics of legislative bodies. Among "rural" legislators in the United States Congress (those who are really influential regarding farm policy and who are well-established in Congress) something of the relationships of the club exists.

5. Other general characteristics follow. A faithful group in each committee accounted for most of the legislative attendance. The House Committee had 16 Republicans and 11 Democrats. Seven men accounted for 93 per cent of the Republican participation; seven also provided all Democratic appearances except that of Mr. Cooley when the Committee met in his North Carolina district. The Senate sub-committee included four Republicans and three Democrats. Two from each party (Aiken and Thye, Thomas and Ellender) were invariably present. Other Senators attended only those hearings held in their own states. After the first hearing, the House Committee confined itself

2. WHO WAS HEARD

Organizations dominated. It is not implied, of course, that
farm organization representatives are not *bona fide* farmers; but
a distinction is drawn between all witnesses who represented a
farm organization or who identified themselves with some other
kind of organization or institution and all other witnesses. Mis-
takes must have been made. Some witnesses appearing only as
farmers were beyond question representative of organizations,
particularly of the Production and Marketing Administration;
but some of these and other farmers no doubt failed to give
their connections because they are unassuming men. With all
qualifications, study of the field hearings further attests the organization and channeling of "opinion" in agriculture. Traveling hearings merely tap the organized opinion representation industry in its field and district offices; it is all part of the same
process.

The Peoria, Illinois, Senate hearing comprised 174 pages.
Farm organizations had 15 per cent, government agencies 48
per cent, and college professors had 21 per cent. Eventually, one
farmer who was unidentified with any association spoke for
three pages. When the committee moved to Minneapolis and
recorded 116 pages of hearings, farm organizations filled 57
pages, non-farm organizations (a sugar organization, hybrid seed
companies, canning companies, etc.) had 30 pages. Once more
a farmer "representing only himself" appeared; he proved to be
a windbag and had to be cut off by the chairman. These examples may be somewhat extreme, but they suggest the tendency.[6]

to listening to witnesses; but Senators cross-questioned witnesses and freely
engaged in discussion. Thus the Senate hearings are livelier reading; but the
House procedure divided time more equally among witnesses (who rarely had
less than one or more than three or four pages) and heard more witnesses.

6. Of the 59 statements in the House hearings at Lancaster, Pennsylvania,
15 were by farmers not identified with any organization or agency; of 58
statements in the House hearings at Madison, 16 were by farmers without
expressed associations. Southern Hearings appeared to call forth a higher proportion of witnesses without expressed organizational identifications. Thus 38
of the 86 statements in the House hearings at Temple, Texas, were by farmers who gave no organization. The comparable figures for Kansas City were
23 and 67. On the other hand, see the description by Congressman Hope of

The prevalence of the professional committeeman was demonstrated. Thus LeRoy Getting described himself as a director of the Iowa Farm Bureau and of the National Livestock Meat Board, as chairman of the Sheep and Woolgrowers Association, and as a soil conservation district director. "I think that is enough of that," he remarked.[7] Such persons are in strategic positions to be consulted whenever anyone wants to learn "what the folks at the grass roots are thinking." Any farmer one is taken to see by SCS, TVA, Farmers Home Administration, or Extension, will ordinarily be highly accustomed to such visitations—indeed, he may give the visitor a mimeographed sheet bearing upon his operations. Similarly, the "duplication and over-lapping of committeemen" is phenomenal. The field hearings support the common observation that the intensive activity in agricultural agencies and associations is confined to a relatively small circle of farmers.[8]

The heavy participation of supporters of federal agencies, especially SCS and PMA,[9] was notable; it was referred to, somewhat invidiously, as "packing." [10] Packing in the early hearings

the North Carolina hearing which represented "every official State organization dealing with the welfare of the farmers of North Carolina, all the farm organizations."

7. *Hearings*, H. of R., 80th Cong., 1st Sess., Long Range Agric. Policy, Part 11, pp. 1202, 1252, 1253, 1299; these are a few of many illustrations.

8. Cf. Ch. v, section 2 and Ch. viii, section 2. Strong efforts are in process to enlarge the circle of participants in farm programs (Charles M. Hardin, "Natural Leaders and the Administration of Soil Conservation Programs," *Rural Sociology*, Sept., 1951) and in discussions of agricultural policy (the establishment by the Ohio Farm Bureau Federation of some 1600 advisory councils is especially noteworthy; so are similar efforts by the Farm Bureau in Illinois as reported by W. Bruce Storm, *The Illinois Agricultural Association*, unpublished Ph.D. thesis, University of Chicago, 1950; as well as by *The North Dakota Farmers Union*—Ph.D. thesis by Ross Talbot, in preparation at the University of Chicago.)

9. REA and the Farmers Home Administration also marshalled support.

10. In South Dakota, witnesses claimed that the 1937 hearings had similarly been packed; then Henry Wallace was said to have attempted to manufacture public sentiment in favor of perpetuating crop control. Testimony of E. H. Everson, who was president of the National Farmers Union from 1934 to 1937, after which he was Secretary of Agriculture in South Dakota from 1937 to 1946. *Hearings*, 80th Cong., 1st Sess., S. Res. 147, Part 2, pp. 699-710. Everson declared that Wallace, fearing the hearings would be unfriendly to the administration, attempted to pack them by urging triple A committeemen to attend. An editorial from *Wallace's Farmer* was quoted to this effect,

resulted in rigorous instructions against it, but without marked subsequent diminution. Some said that packing boomeranged against the agencies. Others maintained that, even though legislators understood perfectly what was happening, they became progressively more impressed by the testimonials produced for both PMA and SCS.

A frank and rather pleasing statement of the situation was made by Jim Neal, a PMA witness: [11]

"I did not know about this committee being here. I was off at the ranch working cattle, but the secretary of the triple A called me up and says, 'Jim, the Agriculture Committee is going to hold a hearing in Temple, we can't get hold of anybody else who will go up there. Won't you go?' I said, 'I will do my best.' I got here this morning at 9 o'clock; I missed the barbecue yesterday.

"I asked those people what they wanted me to say. They said, 'Jim, we want you to go up there and take a look at that congressional committee, to see how they look. We have never seen a Congressman here and never have seen anybody from the legislative branch of the Washington Government except our junior Senator from Texas, and we want you to go up there and take a look at them.' I said, 'What do you want me to tell them?' They said, 'Tell them anything you damn please.' That is what I am here for."

In the Senate hearing at Minneapolis, five farmers favored PMA and spoke for 20 pages. In Peoria, 14 farmers favored PMA and filled 41 pages; and four spoke for SCS, using 26 pages. In the House hearings at Madison, 21 witnesses commended PMA; eleven, the SCS. At Kansas City, 12 supported the PMA; and nine statements favored SCS—of these, eight were by soil conservation district supervisors. And so it went. If anything, the written record may underrate the degree to which hearings were organized by these agencies. Thus the Sioux City hearing of the House Committee produced relatively

and it was said a large number of committeemen and other administrative officials from Nebraska, South Dakota, Iowa, and Minnesota were in attendance. Everson also quoted a poem of 1937 which parodied the "Charge of the Light Brigade." The poem was called "The Charge of Wallace's Brigade." The 600, of course, referred to triple A committeemen who were ordered to ride into the hearings and stampede them for crop control.

11. *Hearings*, H. of R., 80th Cong., 1st Sess., Long Range Agric. Policy, Part 13, p. 1497.

little testimony for either SCS or PMA; but toward the end
of the hearing, James Henry remarked:

"My observation has been that 95 per cent of the speakers have
emphasized soil conservation work by the boys of the Soil Conservation Service and the soil district committees."

Mr. Henry, a PMA supporter, may have been trying to dis-
credit SCS; [12] but another interpretation is that many farmers
who appeared at hearings without identifying themselves with
any organization or agency had really been prompted to appear
on behalf of some organized interest.

*The field hearings were dominated by larger farmers (less
diffident, better informed, better equipped to attend such meetings) and their spokesmen.* Senator Aiken's statement, made in
Memphis (of all places!), is ironical:

"It seems that farm people and their friends talk more freely when
they are on their own home ground than they do when they come
into Washington. In fact, we are out in the home territory of our
good people because so many of them couldn't get into Washington
anyway, and we wanted to give them a chance to be heard."

Generally, the hearings disclosed little Congressional interest in
the matter of farm size; the House, as noted, refrained from
publicly questioning witnesses; questions on this point in the
Senate hearings were desultory. Yet some Congressmen are
keenly disturbed by the class nature and larger-farmer orientation of public agricultural policy in this country—disturbed, yet
frustrated as they are so caught in terrific pressures in favor of
commercial agriculture that they are generally unable to adjust
policy effectively to meet the needs of low-income farmers.

Admittedly, acreage figures are not wholly reliable in establishing farm size, yet they are probably not dangerously mis-

---

12. Usually, the agency spokesmen confined themselves to favorable remarks about the work of their own agencies. Thus at Temple, Texas, the
House hearing produced 18 statements vigorously favoring SCS; many were
by district supervisors and some were by bankers and other businessmen.
Three statements criticized PMA, which, however, was supported by eight
other statements. At Kansas City, there were three anti-SCS and one anti-
PMA statements. Occasionally, witnesses praised both agencies; but it was
very rare that witnesses identified with one agency would have a good word
for the other.

leading outside of the range territory and areas dominated by rough and stony land. The following table indicates the situation in the Senate Hearings at Memphis: [13]

No. of Farmers	No. of Acres
12	Did not give their acreage
4	900 or over
2	800
1	700
5	440-600 (One was a father-son combination with 556 acres)
5	200-315
6	120-190
1	95
1	80
1	40 (cash tenant)

Moreover, there was lengthy testimony from the Delta Council, represented by Mr. Gary, who spoke for a paid-up membership of 3,000 with some 2,000,000 acres on which some 900,000 bales of cotton are annually produced, or around eight per cent of the average total cotton production of the nation. Further, there was the Agricultural Council of Arkansas, represented by two members of its Board of Directors, Messrs. Branch and Brinkley. The latter said: "I am not quite as large an operator as Mr. Branch. I only have 3,200 acres, of which 1,000 acres is in cotton."

The size of farms of the typical persons appearing at the hearings caused James M. Smith of Corinth, Mississippi, to remark: "I noticed the gentlemen that have appeared before me, they have all been operators of larger tracts of land, which doesn't exist in our county [Alcorn]. We have maybe a half a dozen or more farmers with large acreage, but the average acreage in cultivation would run around 30 acres of cropland per farm." Another witness, Mr. Levi Ayers, owning a 95-acre farm, said: "Quite a number of these farmers have come before you and have termed themselves little farmers, yet they owned from 500 to 1,000 acres or more of land. Well, I guess I am not a little farmer, then."

---

13. *Hearings*, 80th Cong., 1st Sess., S. Res. 147, Part 2, pp. 1257-1398.

The same predominance of larger farmers characterized the Montgomery, Alabama, hearing of the Hope Committee. One farmer, P. T. Hill, said: "I am not like some of the other farmers who have been talking, in one respect. I own and operate a small farm of 40 acres, which is typical of that section of the State." Another farmer, C. H. Wilhite, said, "There has been a lot said about the farmers whose land ranges from 100 to 500 acres or more, but I hail from a section of the country where I have to support myself and my family off 25 acres of crops. I am not alone in that in my section. There are hundreds in north Alabama, in the area known as the Sand Mountain area." The Memphis meeting was ideally located to draw plantation owners; the Mississippi Delta has been said to end in the lobby of the Peabody Hotel in Memphis. Yet the Hope Committee hearings at Montgomery also drew heavily from the same groups; and hearings elsewhere in the country bore out the same trend.[14]

Commodity organizations were well-represented, and there was some tendency of professional farm managers to speak for farmers. These characteristics of witnesses merit notice but are not sufficiently important to the phase of agricultural politics under discussion to require elaboration.[15]

---

14. Thus the Kansas City hearings of the House Committee recorded acreages of 19 farmers. Acreages reported were 160, 220, 13 from 400 to 800, 1100, 1800, 2000, and a stock ranch of 10,000 acres. One man who did not give his acreage said that he had been proclaimed the wheat king of Kansas. In the Sioux City hearings, 14 acreages were recorded. Omitting the two largest and two smallest, the others ranged from 230 to 480 acres. In the Temple (Texas) hearings, a number spoke up for the "small farm"; but five who did so gave their acreages as ranging from 120 to 250; but a small farm in this area would be 30 to 40 acres. In the Lancaster (Pennsylvania) hearings, 14 farmers reported farm sizes. One had 100 acres, eleven ranged from 190 to 500, one was 1,000 and another 2,000.

15. A major question for a more general study of the politics of agriculture would be, Do commodity organizations typically focus upon narrow interests in contrast to the more general orientation of the Farm Bureau, the Grange, and the Farmers Union? Cf. the remarks of Allan Kline, then President of the Iowa Farm Bureau, subsequently President of the AFBF, in *Hearings,* S. Res. 147, 80th Cong., 2nd Sess., Part 2, pp. 761-774, and Chap. xv, Sec. 2, below.

Furthermore, there was some tendency for farmers, processors, and distributors to organize and present testimony. Examples occurred in the Minneapolis hearings of the Aiken committee, with representatives of canning companies purporting to speak for farmers under contract to them. *Hearings,* 80th

3. PMA REPRESENTATIVES

We now turn to PMA and SCS in the field hearings. The bulk of the testimony on both agencies was favorable. A few of the protagonists of each favored the other; not infrequently, supporters of one criticized the other. At times, Land Grant Colleges and the Farm Bureau were brought into the testimony.

Supporters of both agencies emphasized those points which go to make up what is called the "code." [16] For example, in support of the PMA program the following were emphasized: the broad coverage, the integration between erosion control and economic policy, the social interest in and benefit from conservation—the costs of which should therefore be shared by society, the necessity for effectuating the program upon individual farms hence the value of farmer administration, etc. A frequent advantage claimed for the ACP payments was their inducement of conservation practices, even in recent years of considerably increased farm incomes. Some of these points are stereotypes, e.g., the broad coverage of the program in the sense that it "reaches everybody"; actually the regressive effects of the AAA-PMA programs have long been criticized.

The problem of regressiveness—relatively more for the larger farmers, less for the smaller ones—was not effectively considered in the hearings. The chief remarks that bore upon it were from critics of the limitations upon ACP payments to individual farms to $750. Most vehement critics were the Delta Council and the Agricultural Council of Arkansas. Spokesmen of the latter argued that soil conservation should be pursued on all productive land, regardless of ownership. The data on distribution

Cong., 1st Sess., S. Res. 147, Part 2, pp. 664-77, 684-88. It may be that as farmers perfect their ability to produce crops according to specifications of contracts with purchasers, a vertical organization tends to be created for purposes of political bargaining.

An example of farm managers' speaking for agriculture is offered by True D. Morse who led off the Peoria hearings of the Senate committee, testifying for 17 pages. Mr. Morse is President of the Doane Agricultural Services, Inc., which had been in the farm management business for 28 years and was operating in 15 states in 1947. Mr. Morse was chairman of a special corn belt committee to elect Dewey in 1948.

16. See chapters vi and ix, above.

of ACP payments in the South were said to falsify the situation by greatly exaggerating the concentration of large farms and individual payments. This statement ignored the fact that "most southern farms are an aggregation of small family farms and are in reality on what might be called a cooperative basis." No doubt many Arkansas and Mississippi tenants and sharecroppers would be delighted to know that they are really members of cooperatives with their so-called "landlords"; perhaps they might like to experiment with the "one-man, one-vote" cooperative principle. Further, as V. O. Key, Jr., shows in discussing Mississippi politics, Mississippi and South Carolina rank high in large-scale, multiple-unit agriculture; yet in each state only about 20 per cent of farm units were in multiple units (i.e., landlord-tenant or -cropper organizations) in 1945.[17] In general, not only did the field hearings fail to underscore the disparities in the operation of the PMA program, but relevant observations commonly emphasized the viewpoint of the larger commercial farmers. Congress hardly needed to journey into the counties to hear this kind of opinion.[18]

The most frequent criticism of PMA was that farmer committeemen lack authority; even so, it occurred but few times in the field hearings. It was voiced most often by Farm Bureau officials whose opposition can be explained in part by reference to the AFBF-PMA (AAA) differences which derive from 1942 or earlier.[19] Charges of Washington domination of the PMA were sometimes linked with charges of PMA partisan activity, as by W. A. Plath, president of the North Dakota Farm Bureau. But when he was sharply questioned about proof of PMA's Democratic partisanship, Plath could only assert an occasion in 1937 or 1938 when a county Democratic chairman had solicited county AAA committeemen to buy tickets to a Jefferson Day

17. *Southern Politics, op. cit.,* p. 240, n. 25.
18. Cf. *Hearings,* H. of R., 80th Cong., 1st Sess., Long Range Agric. Policy, Part 9, pp. 1020-21, 1086; also pp. 1034-35. Compare Tom Lundy's views in *Hearings,* 80th Cong., 1st Sess., S. Res. 147, Part 2, p. 822.
19. Cf. Chapter ix; as an example of farm bureau criticism in the hearings, cf. W. C. Anderson, a director of the Iowa Farm Bureau, *Hearings,* H. of R., 80th Cong., 1st Sess., Long Range Agric. Policy, Part 11, p. 1252.

dinner.[20] Finally, charges of inefficiency, favoritism, and mismanagement were extremely rare.[21]

4. SPOKESMEN FOR SCS

It is obvious that the SCS code crops up time and again in the testimony of witnesses favorable to the agency.[22] Infrequently the entire code will be presented in testimony that is pretty clearly boiler-plate, prepared by the SCS technician. More often, different parts of the code are found in the testimony of different witnesses. No doubt this is accidental, but it could mark exceedingly shrewd tactics, such as were hinted at the Missouri disclosures.[23]

Yet it is interesting to construct the SCS code from different testimonies. Thus A. L. Powell, of the Pennsylvania Friends of the Land, endorsed the idea that we need a national land policy, favored Soil Conservation Districts, called the extension service primarily educational, rejected the Cooley bill and endorsed the Jensen bill.[24] Gould Beech, editor of the *Southern Farmer,* attacked the Farm Bureau and the Extension Service in Alabama and spoke of "the specialized zeal of men with a single purpose," referring to SCS personnel.[25] Lawrence McKinney, secretary of the Indiana association of soil conservation district supervisors, criticized the Hill-Cooley Bill. He said, "The states were never concerned with soil conservation, even though one hundred million acres of good land were ruined. But when the USDA soil conservation service program received nationwide approval, the states would like to take over. This job must be a lot nearer to completion before we can break down the main

20. *Hearings,* 80th Cong., 1st Sess., S. Res. 147, Part 2, 565-75.

21. W. Graybeal, *Hearings,* H. of R., 80th Cong., 1st Sess., Long Range Agric. Policy, Part 7, pp. 907-9.

22. Cf. Chapter vi, above.

23. For the boiler plate, see Fred Sherman, pp. 733 ff., part 6 of the House Committee Hearings. For the Missouri disclosures, see *Hearings,* House Committee on Agriculture, 80th Congress, 2nd Session, "Soil Conservation," pp. 92 ff; cf. chapter vi, above.

24. *Hearings,* H. of R., 80th Cong., 1st Sess., Long Range Agric. Policy, Part 7, pp. 868-69.

25. *Hearings,* H. of R., 80th Cong., 1st Sess., Long Range Agric. Policy, Part 9, pp. 1067-70.

machine and trust 48 new ones." Thus the line is illustrated that erosion is a national problem and must be attacked by a national agency. A. P. Atkins, among other things, testified in favor of soil conservation districts, speaking of 77 of them in Oklahoma, "administered by 385 practical farmers and ranchers like myself." [26] Others, as Mr. Stackhouse of Ohio, emphasized the great backlog of farms awaiting and demanding SCS planning. Many districts, he declared, have to discourage applications because they have more than two years waiting lists ahead of them now. Then others, like Earl Elijah, president of the Iowa soil conservation district supervisors organization, asserted that Iowa county agents are too busy to help farmers with conservation programs. This is all of a piece with the frequent point that the county agents are not only overburdened but after all are general practitioners. Finally, C. W. Huntley, a member of the Iowa State Soil Conservation Committee, pointed to the lack of SCS technicians which is slowing down the SCS work.[27] Taken together, these bits of testimony fall into a consistent, complete, and symmetrical pattern.

With what size farms does the SCS work? As with the PMA this question is significant regarding the effect of governmental programs on our economy, or, more correctly, on our society, in which political power is divided. As some of the figures already shown for those testifying in favor of the SCS indicate, many large farmers and ranchers are vitally interested in the program. At the same time it should be recalled that the field hearings were generally dominated by men with large acreages. It is, of course, very difficult to get at figures on the basis of available data about the size of farms reached by the SCS. In Texas, for whatever it is worth, calculation from the testimony on the progress to October 15, 1947, indicates that the average farm and ranch plan of SCS is 432 acres. There appears more tendency for smaller than for larger operators to drop out of the program. Thus in Texas eight per cent of the land originally contracted in plans was cancelled, but approximately 10 per cent

---

26. *Hearings,* H. of R., 80th Cong., 1st Sess., Long Range Agric. Policy, Part 12, pp. 1390-92.
27. *Hearings,* 80th Cong., 1st Sess., S. Res. 147, Part 2, pp. 907-8.

of the farmers originally contracting cancelled their agreements.[28]
Perhaps even more suggestive is the testimony of Mr. Dawson,
Representative of the Business Farmers of Texas, Vice-President
and Manager of the Agricultural Department, Second National
Bank of Houston, Texas. Dawson interpreted soil conservation
as carrying out an obligation to the business men, a purpose to
which SCS is instrumental.

"I have worked with the 800 bankers in Texas, and I find that
they are becoming very much concerned about it. The banks, the oil
companies, farm-equipment manufacturers, and other forms of business are spending millions of dollars a year in an effort to bring about
conservation of our soils. It is so important to them that unless soil
and water conservation is recognized as important enough for a separate department to be established, the day is coming when they will
pool their efforts in promoting strict Federal land-use regulations, and
if the businessmen in this State are going to take part in it they
must be given the opportunity to help organize those things and take
part in solving the problems of the farmers in their local soil-conservation districts. If the initiative of the local people is killed by
letting some of the pending legislation pass, which would take the
operation of our local districts out of the hands of the local board
of supervisors and let the director of the State extension service appoint the governing bodies, this will be breaking faith with the farm
and ranch owners of this Nation." [29]

Similarly, the interest of large plantation owners in the SCS
is notable. The conception of trusteeship, wherein private owners are guardians of the land, in the interests of future generations, is admirable; but it is capable of being twisted to support
conceptions strongly oligarchic. More than one large land
owner has expressed to the writer the ideal of a landed aristoc-
racy in which the capable care not only for the land but also
for those incompetent to care for themselves. Such private pa-
ternalism has a feudal ring. Programs like that of the SCS cannot be discussed in natural science terms alone, because of their
potential influence upon the value-systems of society. The state-

28. *Hearings,* H. of R., 80th Cong., 1st Sess., Long Range Agric. Policy,
Part 13, pp. 1462-63.
29. *Ibid.,* pp. 1426-28.

ment of Hugh L. Gary, speaking for the Delta Council of Mississippi, is illustrative: [30]

> "This is an obligation of the landowner, the tenant, and all whose way of life is by tilling the soil. Titles to land are transitory. Ownership passes rapidly and is never static. Those of us who use these resources are, equitably and morally, trustees for the present and future generations. A good start has been made along this line in the past few years through the Soil Conservation Service. We think no greater service can be done the country than to continue and strengthen this service."

Yet one spokesman for the SCS took a contrary view, Price C. McLemore of Alabama. He noted that the family-sized farm was changing; it was now a mechanized family-sized farm, but the South had not kept pace. The small farm with one or two mules was uneconomic, but family-sized farms need smaller machines, and they also needed the development of group cooperatives to share more expensive machines. McLemore may have had his sights a little high respecting what constitutes an "economic unit," but he was thinking about soil conservation against the entire range of social, political and economic problems of the rural South.[31]

Criticism of the SCS, like that of the PMA, is heavily outweighed by favorable testimony. Some strictures were addressed at SCS operations by persons apparently identified with it. Ervin Bourgois, representing the state association of soil conservation districts in North Dakota, described the difficulty in planning dam-construction to meet requirements of both SCS and PMA. He remarked that: "One of the higher ups in the soil conservation [service] admitted something should be done, but they are afraid to recommend anything." Bourgois commented further upon inter-agency jealousy and efforts by agency representatives, including his own, to out-sell each other.[32] W. G. Lodwick of Iowa, who also sharply criticized PMA, declared his impatience with SCS administrative procedures. He described the experi-

---

30. *Hearings,* 8oth Cong., 1st Sess., S. Res. 147, Part 2, pp. 1276-87.
31. *Hearings,* H. of R., 8oth Cong., 1st Sess., Long Range Agric. Policy, Part 9, pp. 1053-56, 1061-63.
32. *Hearings,* 8oth Cong., 1st Sess., S. Res. 147, Part 2, p. 580.

ence of some neighbors who had developed a cooperative flood control plan.

"They were told this: first, you petition your district. Then they will take it to the district office. That isn't the county. That is some other place again. Then it will go to the region, which in our case is Milwaukee, and then to Washington, and sometimes you will get a plan, and they assured us they thought we would get around to it in five years.

"A number of these gentlemen are 72 or 73 years old, and they didn't think they wanted to wait that long." [33]

5. CONFLICTS OF INTEREST

In Pennsylvania, the State Council of Farm Organizations testified to a rather vague and ill-defined dissatisfaction with Pennsylvania State College. However, respecting administration of the state soil conservation act, the Council became more specific: "We are informed that there has not been forthcoming from State College the assistance which is necessary to make the act truly effective." Foreseeing an "intolerable" situation, if the college remained uncooperative, the Council called for an investigation.[34]

In Arkansas, C. R. Cox, a soil conservation district supervisor, mentioned recent disagreement between the new president of the state university, whom he praised highly, and district supervisors. Mutual conferences, said Mr. Cox, had achieved an agreed definition of functions of extension and of SCS and ironed out difficulties.[35] Other reports from Arkansas suggest that this statement considerably glosses over the situation.

In Alabama, Gould Beech, editor of the *Southern Farmer*, claiming 900,000 circulation, was critical of efforts, particularly the Cooley-Hill Bill, to liquidate the soil conservation service.

---

33. *Hearings*, 80th Cong., 2nd Sess., S. Res. 147, Part 2, pp. 833-39.
34. *Hearings*, H. of R., 80th Cong., 1st Sess., Long Range Agric. Policy, Part 7, p. 834. At the time, Pennsylvania had no state Farm Bureau; the largest farm organization numerically was the Grange, which has generally supported the SCS.
35. *Ibid.*, Part 13, p. 1475.

"Of course, the power of the Extension Service to force farmers to join the Farm Bureau will be increased. Likewise, its power over the politics of the Farm Bureau will be increased. Any farmer who does not go along with the idea of the Extension Service can have any Government service cut off. The farmer will live in the insecurity of not knowing what will happen to his quota, whether he will be able to get the services of the Soil Conservation technicians, and so on. Finally, the education function of the Extension Service will be endangered."

He noted that these organizations would not be subject usually to the direction of any elective official, Congress, the legislature, county boards or commissions, but could elect or defeat candidates to the same. He added, with respect to the Cooley Bill:

"We have had some disagreements in the State and I am not trying to run Walter's business, but we have offered to invest quite a sum of money in Alabama to find out whether this issue of the Cooley Bill has been discussed in the meeting of the Alabama Farm Bureau and distributed 100,000 copies of this. No man has offered that this thing was discussed and that any came out in favor of the Cooley Bill." [36]

This attack by an SCS spokesman in Alabama upon the Farm Bureau and the Extension Service is reminiscent of the 1942- and-after conflicts between the AAA and the Extension Services and Farm Bureaus of the corn belt. Perhaps it is merely the glow of past battles lingering in the sky (as some would argue); nevertheless, in the field hearings a number of corn belt Farm Bureau officials vigorously criticized the AAA's successor, PMA. Earl C. Smith, then recently retired as President of the Illinois Agricultural Association, slashingly attacked PMA; he was answered in kind by John Taylor, who apparently has made his career inside the adjustment agency.

On behalf of the SCS, a number of criticisms were made of the Farm Bureau, in a manner disclosing some, at least, of the internal dissidence of that farm organization. A. P. Atkins, a district supervisor from Texas County, Oklahoma, who owns

36. *Hearings,* H. of R., 80th Cong., 1st Sess., Long Range Agric. Policy, Part 9, pp. 1067-70. The reference to Walter is to Mr. Walter Randolph, President of the Alabama Farm Bureau.

and operates a 10,000-acre cattle ranch, was vehemently critical of Ed O'Neal, then President of the American Farm Bureau Federation.

"While I subscribe to the general principles of the Farm Bureau, to which I belong, and which I helped to organize in Oklahoma, yet I sometimes suspect that its national leaders are occasionally blinded by a desire for power—much like the leaders of some labor unions and other pressure groups. I can place no other interpretation on some of their recommendations. I recall that President O'Neal of the Farm Bureau once told a group of farmers that he had refused to run for the United States Senate, because he wanted to run the United States Senate. Although he didn't mention the House of Representatives, I assume that he would be willing to control it, too." [37]

Further, Carlos C. Palmer, an Indiana district supervisor and a Farm Bureau county president, declared,

"I have been a member of the Farm Bureau for more than a quarter of a century and was president of our county Farm Bureau for more than a decade. Last week I spent a day urging my neighbors to join the Farm Bureau. Speaking as a Farm Bureau member I deeply resent the efforts of Edward O'Neal, president of the American Farm Bureau, and those of his followers who are trying to merge the Soil Conservation Service with the Extension Service through the passage of the Cooley Bill. On their part it can only be a desire for more power and not to the interest of the Farm Bureau member. It is just one of those cases of power politics regardless of who gets hurt." [38]

More moderate, but hardly less telling criticism, came from C. V. Arnold, an Illinois farmer and district supervisor, as well as a county Farm Bureau Board director:

"But as the farm bureau grew and farming became a business instead of a manner of living, the stress placed upon the activities it pushed was toward commercial activities not contemplated in the original plan. Today an investigation would show that the varied activities of the farm bureau are predominantly commercial. Solicita-

37. *Hearings,* H. of R., 80th Cong., 1st Sess., Long Range Agric. Policy, Part 12, pp. 1390-92.
38. *Hearings,* H. of R., 80th Cong., 1st Sess., Long Range Agric. Policy, Part 10, p. 1148.

tion for membership is frequently made on the basis of how much money can be saved by joining and qualifying for patronage refunds. Understand me, I see no reason why the farmer should not engage legitimately in such business as fertilizers, seeds, machinery, gas and oil, insurance, veterinary supplies, etc., but I question using such an outlet concerned almost entirely with this commercial viewpoint as the proper or able servant to replace the SCS." [39]

These meager gleanings of differences within the Farm Bureau will confirm some critics of that organization in their conviction that it is dominated by a few insiders who manipulate the membership figures in support of their own desires. On the other hand, Farm Bureau leaders will merely remark that internal differences attest to the fundamentally democratic character of their organization. More noteworthy is the paucity of such differences which emerge in 2000 pages of hearings. Generally, state units of national farm organizations, whether Bureau, Grange, or Farmers' Union, supported the position of the national. Three state Farm Bureaus were mentioned as on record in support of the SCS program; yet apparently no state Farm Bureau leader has publicly testified against the AFBF position on this matter.

6. EXPERIENCES IN COOPERATION

In a number of states, relationships are reported as very good between the conservation agencies. In Vermont, both rural and urban leaders declared that the conservation of soil resources is partly a responsibility of society and not the total responsibility of the individual farmer. Estimates made by committeemen administering the agricultural conservation program, as well as by representatives of the Vermont College of Agriculture, indicated that only 10 per cent of the tonnage of ground limestone now being used under the agricultural conservation program would continue to be used if the incentive payments by the Federal Government were withdrawn. Perhaps only one-third of the current applications of essential minerals, superphosphate,

---

39. *Hearings*, H. of R., 80th Cong., 1st Sess., Long Range Agric. Policy, Part 2, pp. 546-48.

and potash would have been made by farmers in the absence of federal assistance. Carrying out earth-moving and land-drainage practices was largely dependent upon the technical assistance and heavy machinery available through soil conservation districts and the SCS.

"There is excellent cooperation between representatives of the Soil Conservation Service, the Production and Marketing Administration, and the Vermont Extension Service in promoting the conservation of soil resources in Vermont. The technical workers of the Soil Conservation Service assist the county PMA committeemen in giving prior approval of practices on individual farms, and the county agricultural agents work very closely with both the Soil Conservation Service technicians and the PMA committeemen. It is the feeling of agricultural leadership in Vermont that there is only limited duplication of effort between the agencies administering soil-conservation activities." [40]

7. THE ISSUE OF CONTROLS

Do farmers favor production control? This issue is closely related to the conservation phase of farm politics for two reasons. First, PMA, which administers one soil conservation program, is primarily designed to achieve parity for agriculture through price supports and (if necessary) production control. Second, the need for control is sometimes advanced as a means of ending the erosion menace. Many people believe that Midwestern and Northeastern farmers especially are unalterably opposed to control; but much opinion also holds that Western wheat farmers and Southern cotton, tobacco, and peanut farmers favor production control.

Indeed, the opposition to control has been cited by informed and thoughtful observers as the reason that Midwestern farmers began to shift away from the New Deal in 1936. Others, however, attribute the shift back to Republicanism to a growing belief that farmers were the subjects of political discrimination by an administration bound to the service of organized labor. This controversy over the cause of the political shift after 1936 among

---

40. *Hearings*, 80th Cong., 2nd Sess., S. Res. 147, Part 2, p. 1188. Cf. C. H. Stackhouse of Ohio, *ibid*, pp. 495-500.

Midwestern farmers is introduced to suggest the profound political significance of arguments about farmers' attitudes toward controls.

Most people recognize that the control programs either were not very effective, or, more profoundly, were not very necessary and very applicable in the midwest and in the northeast, except for certain special crops. The attempt to control the production and use of feed grains, especially when the bulk of these are fed on the home farm, as is true in the corn belt, is notoriously difficult. At the same time, the absence of marketing quotas does not mean that farmers and their representatives in the midwest were blind to the advantages, while seeing only the disadvantages of controls. Fields were measured in the midwest, and farmers certified for commodity credit corporation loans thereon.

The field hearings suggest that it is not the geographical area of the country, but rather the nature of the farmer's problem, which seems to influence his attitude. Generally, wherever potato farmers or tobacco growers or fruit and vegetable growers testified in the hearings, be it north, east, south, west, or midwest, these persons favored controls. Egg and poultry producers were opposed to controls, hoping for a period of competition which would weed out many small producers.

Nor is it merely the PMA which carries on the battle for controls "in the interest of maintaining its bureaucratic hold upon the American farmer." For example, Earl C. Smith, in the Senate Peoria Hearings, attacked PMA but strongly favored controls as a standby need. So long as two-thirds of the farmers were required to approve quotas, he said, dictation did not seem to be involved.

More farmers testified in favor of controls than in opposition to them.[41] Even in the testimony of those opposing controls a

41. In the Madison hearings of the House committee, nine statements favored controls (three representing tobacco and two, potatoes.) The Master of the Wisconsin Grange opposed controls except in emergencies, the typical Grange position. The Kansas City hearing produced testimony by the Farm Bureau wheat committee: "When all . . . possibilities have been exhausted in an attempt to maintain a parity price and to bring supply in line with demand, as a last resort we favor . . . acreage or production control." In the Pennsylvania hearing, David C. Bradfute, son of the second President of the American Farm Bureau Federation, acknowledged the unpopularity of controls and marketing quotas but said that "these should be held in re-

fundamental inconsistency often appeared. Thus, in the House hearings at Temple, Texas, nine statements favored controls outright; three favored controls as a last resort; and only one statement flatly rejected controls—but in the following words: "We do contend for parity, but we are not willing to submit to acreage control." President F. V. Heinkel of the Missouri Farmers' Association declared at the House Kansas City hearings: "The very nature of the business of farming precludes the possibility of farmers' restricting production." But the following paragraph said: "We in the Missouri Farmers' Association believe that in the years ahead there may be need for crop adjustment. In the case of . . . wheat and cotton, for example, there is a tendency for production to exceed consumption at a reasonable price."

Controls do not solve everything—even in tobacco.[42] Yet a reading of the field hearings supplemented by conversations suggests that farmers are prepared to ask their government to control production, to help administer controls, and to accept heavier penalties and tighter administration than has ordinarily been experienced in the past. Whether farmers generally "like" controls is certainly debatable and, in the short-run, at least, probably irrelevant.

8. CRITICISMS

The following criticisms are offered in all humility; whether they are sound can only be proved in practice and at great ex-

---

serve." In the Sioux City hearings, in the absence of spokesmen for crops in which production control has seemed most palatable (potatoes, tobacco, peanuts, etc.), three statements opposed controls; but three other statements favored them, and one would accept controls in emergencies.

42. G. W. Mitchell began a severe criticism of the present acreage control program in tobacco by saying: "Under our present control, and I hate to say it, but it is just a joke. We haven't any control." *Hearings*, H. of R., 80th Cong., 1st Sess., Long Range Agric. Policy, Part 8, p. 983. But Levy Hill was of a different mind. He had bought a farm of 70 acres in 1940 with an acre and a half tobacco base. "I went out there, 'Mr. Noyes, can you help me please sir? I ain't got no tobacco. I like to have some.' He said, 'Levy, I can't hardly help you right now . . . , but I tell you what you can do. . . . If you will stay under the AAA I will see . . . every year you get a little additional.' So now . . . I am able to tend 5 acres of tobacco on my place. By being obedient." *Ibid.*, pp. 966-67.

pense.[43] Further, if they are sound, they have been derived only
in retrospect. We are, after all, dealing with the relationship between a government and its public, a most difficult and little-
understood one. All citizens interested in good government owe
a debt of gratitude to the men in Congress who planned and
carried out even this groping effort to get closer to the people.

In light of the 1947 experience, a better method and procedure for subsequent hearings should be possible. This plan
would rest initially upon the assumption that hearings are not
only to ascertain views, experiences, and suggestions respecting
the content and administration of agricultural programs (important as this is),[44] but should also increase the public knowledge
of the process of government.

The second assumption of the plan is the obvious one that
such hearings are highly selective. Congress cannot advise with
everybody, and the fiction that it can is positively harmful. If
Congressmen would arrange for, say, 75 per cent of the hearing time by invitation, this act would frankly recognize the inevitable selectivity. It would give Congress both control over the
general make-up of the hearings as well as the responsibility for
acceptable selections which goes along with control. It should
deprive hearings of an ill-deserved aspect of "touching the well-
springs of democracy."

If hearings are to increase knowledge of the political processes,
some criteria should be employed in selecting sites other than
(or in addition to) type-of-farming areas, political sectionalism
(Senator Aiken's four corn-belt hearings), and the occasional
importance of affording a legislator a work-out on his home

---

43. The writer is well aware that the written record, on which this analysis
is based, falls considerably short of the entire "record" which would have to
be supplemented by the informal contacts between Congressmen and others
before and after the hearings.

44. David B. Truman lists three functions of such hearings. "First, the
hearing is a means of transmitting information, both technical and political,
from various actual and potential political groups to the committee. . . . A
second use is as a propaganda channel. . . . A third function is to provide a
quasi-ritualistic means of adjusting group conflicts. . . ." *The Governmental
Process, op. cit.,* p. 372. Although Truman considers the first function "probably the least important," it is the one emphasized in these criticisms.

grounds. Hearings could be located in accordance with political and administrative,[45] as well as economic, variations.

Thus the prevalence of large farmers raises some questions about the "representativeness" of the hearings. Some political scientists have observed that representation is largely subjective; if one feels represented, he *is* represented.[46] This conception of the representative relationship is essentially voluntaristic rather than deterministic; it asserts that society is not a machine but is rather composed of individuals and groups in an organic relationship which acknowledges a large role for emotional drives, individual wills, and individual consciences. Yet representation organizes itself around interests, especially property interests— and in agriculture, around those of commercial farmers who stand in organized relationships both to the market and to government. If "representativeness" cannot be determined scientifically by statistical analyses of the citizenry, it can be observed that the market orientation and the easy access to the political process enjoyed by commerical farm groups tends to diminish the influence of the less-commercial, the scattered, the unorganized, and the less fortunate.

The interest in maintaining a stable democratic polity may be cited as a reason for giving those presently unorganized more voice in public policy through their progressive organization and articulation into the process of government.[47] It is useful to know that a study of the field hearings brings out what *a priori*

---

45. Hearings might be located in accordance with variations in Extension-Farm Bureau relationships (Chapter iii); in states with two or more politically active general farm organizations of comparable strength; in states wherein commodity organizations vie with general organizations in political significance; in areas where there are relationship problems between the Departments of Agriculture and the Interior; etc. Hearings might also be located to probe particular problems of inter-regional politics in agriculture as well as such special issues as migratory labor and friction between organized agriculture and organized labor. Another possibility is systematically to probe in various areas the relationship of national policy and administration to state and local policy and administration.

46. An example occurred in the House hearings at Lancaster, Pennsylvania, where nearly all spokesmen of New Jersey organizations agreed that Charles A. Collins, who operates a thousand-acre farm and is a frequent testifier at hearings, should speak for the group.

47. Cf. David B. Truman, *The Governmental Process, op. cit.,* especially pp. xi and 524.

assumption should predict—that such hearings essentially fail to reach farmers outside the charmed circle of those already well represented in Washington by organized groups and administrative agencies.

Frequently, Congressional committees elicit brief statements from witnesses respecting the size, location, and composition of the groups they represent; or witnesses volunteer such information. It is rare, however, for Congressmen to probe such questions as the manner of formulation of the group's position, how it is modified, or how binding the general formulations are on the official spokesmen.[48] The best illustration that the field hearings disclosed of the process by which a joint declaration of policy was prepared came from the Vermont delegation. "Representative farmers, leaders of farm organizations and public officials" were invited to a meeting at the College of Agriculture. They invited Dean Carrigan to appoint a committee to prepare a statement on the basis of their discussions. This statement was "submitted for consideration to a large group of farm people representative of all phases of Vermont agriculture." Endorsed by this group, the statement was then presented to the committee.[49] A number of questions emerge. Who are "representative farmers"—how defined and by whom? How was the referendum-group selected and what was the process of submittal? What differentiates the Vermont situation from that in other states, making this joint policy statement possible? Certainly we need to know as much about the processes of democracy as about the nature of people's wants; yet none of these questions were asked.

Another example comes from South Carolina where a joint policy statement was prepared by the Farm Bureau and the Extension Service. What makes this particularly interesting is that it has been only a few years since South Carolina was held up to refute the generalization that all state Extension Services are associated with Farm Bureaus—there was no Farm Bureau in that state. What accounts for the radically changed situation

---

48. Cf. *ibid.*, pp. 382 ff. for a sketch of lobbying investigations, in which the statements made in the text are qualified somewhat.
49. *Hearings*, S. Res. 147, 80th Cong., 1st Sess., Part 2, pp. 1183-93.

in South Carolina? Why is a policy statement prepared between Extension and the Farm Bureau without other groups participating; are there no other organizations? Again, no questions were asked.[50]

Another illustration of the need for clarification of the process of policy formation occurred in Pennsylvania. Here the State Council of Farm Organizations took vigorous stands on government control, soil-conservation, the administration of Pennsylvania State College, and other questions. So controversial are the statements of this council that one is consumed with desire to know how the council is constituted and what groups and organizations contribute to its policy determinations. The statement refers to the council as "We, the farmers of Pennsylvania ..."; yet, to put it bluntly, its significance as a political influence may vary from considerable to microscopic. But the hearings offer us no guide to estimate the influence of the council.

Finally, note what F. E. Mollin, Executive Secretary of the American National Livestock Association, said:

"Our association is a voluntary organization of range cattle producers. We have 19 State organizations, 16 of them west of the Missouri River and the other 3 in Louisiana, Florida, and Michigan, and we have 3 national organizations affiliated with us and more than a hundred local and regional associations.

"Our membership is largely through these 125 or more associations with some three or four thousand individual members."

In spite of the controversy over the administration and disposal of the public range lands and forest preserves, no Senator saw fit to question either Mr. Mollin or Mr. Pauley of the National Wool Growers Association, who testified in the same hearing, about the relationships of their organizations to state member organizations and other livestock associations; about the manner in which policy is formed by such associations and their structure of internal control; or about the pattern of distribution of public benefits among their memberships. Naturally, such questions may be somewhat embarrassing; nevertheless, the public

---

50. *Hearings*, H. of R., 80th Cong., 1st Sess., Long Range Agric. Policy, Part 8, p. 941.

activities of organizations such as these should be conducted in a public light.

A traditional strength of our Congressional system with both Houses having members with widely scattered and relatively independent bases of local strength has been that it has allowed, indeed encouraged, the emergence of sharp and necessary critics. To illustrate, our industrial society has concentrated power, first private power and then more lately public power. During this development it has been important to us that our political structure has facilitated the emergence of national legislators who, standing firmly on the strength of their local and state political organizations (machines, if you will!), have been able to challenge the representatives of industrial power. One thinks of sockless Jerry Simpson and his cohorts of the Populist revolt, or of Senator Beveridge and his colleagues of the Progressive movement, or of Senators Norris and LaFollette, or currently Senator O'Mahoney of Wyoming. In light of this history, it seems clear that Congressmen should also serve in helping delineate the structure of influence in agriculture as well as in business or labor. Furthermore, there seems to be a special obligation on the agricultural statesmen in Congress to perform this task for agriculture; they should be able to do it at once more sympathetically and more effectively than others.

To make a different kind of criticism, the failure to organize the hearings as logically as possible appears to result in a mine-run of testimony with the good, bad, and indifferent all mixed in confusion. When bits of testimony that appear to the examining reader as gems are actually offered, they are not brought in in a manner conducive to their best use. Minds are not prepared for them. No way has been provided for the insights they offer to inform related arguments. One example was the analysis of Donald Christy, Scott City, Kansas, who argued an analogy between the constitutional checks and balances and the balance of power that results from competing agencies. In short, his statement was the reverse of the stereotype "avoid competition and overlapping" which falls as readily (and with as little thought) from the lips of farm leaders as the phrase "save free enterprise" from the lips of businessmen.[51] Another buried and lost gem is the testimony of H. C. Woodward of New Hampshire who began his penetrating comments with the remark:

"The main criticism that can be leveled at present agricultural programs is that responsibilities of action agencies are confined to segments of the agricultural problem instead of taking an organic approach." [52]

Another excellent example is in the testimony of the Piatt County, Illinois, group, which appears in the Peoria hearings of the Senate Committee. These farmers proposed to hinge price and income supporting assistance upon fulfillment of obligations to conserve the soil; they further proposed local delegation of discretion as to what constitutes conservation farming, in full recognition of the grave responsibilities that would have to be assumed locally if government payments or loans were denied farmers because of their refusal to follow conservation farming.

While other criticisms of a detailed nature could be offered, their listing would detract from whatever impact foregoing observations may have. In closing, however, it is appropriate to reiterate an appreciation which all of us who are interested in the preservation and strengthening of American democracy must feel to the Senators and Congressmen who conceived and carried out these hearings. There are fine flashes of humor in the hearings, and moments of that humility which is the handmaiden of legislative greatness in a democracy. Further, however ineffective it may eventually be in the final writing of policy, there is something admirable about United States Senators and Congressmen meeting with farmers and their representatives across the table of county court houses.

51. *Hearings*, H. of R., 80th Cong., 1st Sess., Long Range Agric. Policy, Part 11, pp. 1311-13.
52. *Ibid.*, Part 6, p. 804.

CHAPTER XII

The Hoover Commission and Its Sequel

1. THE HOOVER COMMISSION

Governmental reorganization is a continuous problem. President Taft and all his successors have urged Congress to empower the executive to make administrative adjustments. Congress has acquiesced with limited grants of power from time to time. In 1937, the President's Committee on Administrative Management recommended extensive changes; and a bill was drawn to vest reorganization powers in the President. Amid charges of impending presidential "dictatorship," the bill was killed in 1938; it succumbed to onslaughts of vested administrative interests and their allied private groups, including the Forest Service and its friends. In 1939, reorganization powers were granted President Roosevelt for two years, with executive reorganization plans subject to Congressional veto by adverse concurrent resolution; but a long list of agencies was exempt. Subsequently, the Farm Credit Administration and the Rural Electrification Administration were incorporated in the USDA; and the Bureau of Public Roads, the Weather Bureau, and the Bureau of Biological Surveys were removed from the Department. This chapter will examine the reports of the Hoover Commission affecting agriculture and the failure of President Truman's 1950 reorganization plan. Special attention will be accorded to the significance of these developments for soil conservation administration.

The Commission on Organization of the Executive Branch of the Government was created pursuant to a 1947 law and charged to study and make recommendations "To promote economy, efficiency, and improved service in the transaction of the public business . . ." Jointly appointed by Congress and the President, the commission of twelve well-known and generally distinguished men named Herbert Hoover as chairman. The commission employed 24 task forces. On the basis of staff studies, the task forces made reports. On the basis of task forces reports, the commission has made its own recommendations.

2. THE TASK FORCE FOR AGRICULTURE [1]

Dean H. P. Rusk, College of Agriculture, University of Illinois, was chairman. Others included Dean H. W. Martin, College of Agriculture, Rutgers University; D. Howard Doane, Doane Agricultural Service; Executive Director F. W. Peck, Farm Foundation; Professor John M. Gaus, Department of Government, Harvard University; W. A. Schoenfeld, Dean of Agriculture, Oregon State College; President Chester C. Davis, St. Louis Federal Reserve Bank; and Executive Vice-President William Rhea Blake, National Cotton Council.[2]

In view of the interests involved in the controversy over agricultural administration, it is important to note that three agricultural college deans were members; in addition, Dr. Peck had been Director of the Minnesota Extension Service. No current USDA employee was included, although Chester Davis had had experience in the AAA and Frank Peck in the Farm Credit Administration. No general farm organization provided a member, nor any other commodity organization than the Cotton Council. Only one (albeit a very distinguished one) professional student of government was included.

1. A number of other Hoover Commission and Task Force reports of general relevance for agricultural administration will not be considered here.

2. G. Harris Collingwood was Research Director; consultants were Frederic P. Lee, Washington attorney, and General H. P. Seidemann, former treasurer, Brookings.

The same tendency was borne out in consultations of the Task Force, which acknowledged the special assistance of 18 individuals. While several had held high policy positions in the USDA, only one was then so employed (W. A. Minor, Assistant to the Secretary). Eight of the 18 were in policy-making positions in the Land-Grant Colleges.[3]

Surely, a task force heavily representative of bureau chiefs in the USDA would have consulted different individuals and have produced a different report. It might be answered that to make the task force "representative" of the interests involved would have been to insure deadlock; but the appropriate re-buttal is to point out that the task force *was* one-sided in its heavy recruitment from the land-grant colleges. A way out of the impasse might have been to recruit the majority of the task force from men like Professor Gaus, uncommitted to institu-tional interests, either in the colleges, the USDA, or the farm organizations.

With respect to the USDA generally,[4] the task force employed the concept of function as a basic guide. Dean Rusk has de-scribed the procedure for arriving at this concept.[5] The task force wished to go beyond mere shuffling of existing units. The first problem was to determine a basis of reorganization. There were vigorous proponents of the *subject matter* approach—economics, chemistry, entomology, etc.; but the task force concluded that these were tools to solve agricultural problems; since several tools may be required to attack one problem, some other means to identify major administrative units must be sought. The *various programs and activities* of the USDA were considered

---

3. Acknowledgments were made to men from three general farm organi-zations, but none from commodity groups; of the vigorous farm press, only Associate Editor E. H. Taylor of the *Country Gentleman* received acknowl-edgment.

4. These observations are not intended to be exhaustive and may be sup-plemented by Lauren Soth, "Mr. Hoover's Department of Agriculture," *JFE*, May, 1949.

5. *Hearings*, Senate Committee on Expenditures in the Executive Depart-ments, "Reorganization Plan No. 4 of 1950," 81st Cong., 2d Sess., S. Res. 263, p. 31. While this and other sources will be cited further, this chapter is chiefly drawn from the Task Force and Hoover Commission Reports on Agriculture.

as "expressions of changing public policy" hence not sound bases of organization. *Commodities* were rejected as requiring an organization of as many "little departments of agriculture" as there are commodity interests.

Hence the task force turned to functional organization. Its proposals "reflect earlier tendencies to group activities within major functional fields." Reference was made to the establishment in 1923 of the Extension Service, the Office of Experiment Stations, and the Director of Regulatory work, and (1936) the Director of Research. Rapid expansion in the 1930's and the exigencies of war obscured or diverted this tendency; nevertheless, the fundamental tasks of the Department persist. Following "historical experience," the task force recommended functional divisions, each headed by an administrator, as follows: Research, Extension, Agricultural Resource Conservation, Commodity Adjustment, Regulatory Work, and Agricultural Credit.

The emphasis upon organization by function is laudable. However, the task force was chiefly concerned with the criterion of economic efficiency, i.e., employment of the fewest means to achieve given ends. This concentration excluded other considerations, such as those concerning the organization and control of political power and also concerning the purposes of power. Hence, one can applaud the preoccupation with function but deplore its narrow conception.

The task force report is long on recommendations and short on analysis. Of 130 pages, the report devoted only 57 to the functional organization of the Department. A mere 15 pages were accorded to explanatory statements. Recommendations for state and county agricultural councils (discussed later) were "explained" in one-half page! Discussion of the proposed Commodity Adjustment Administration recognized potential conflicts in that (for example) a wheat program may affect dairy, poultry, livestock, or the corn-feeding and corn products industries. To provide coordination, the chiefs of the six commodity bureaus were constituted as an advisory council in the office of the administrator. How does this differ from the contemporary function of staff conferences in PMA? The task force proposals were not supported by analysis.

Two other criticisms of the task force report concern costs of government and projected savings. The discussion of costs was misleading. The progression in round millions was shown from $17 in 1912 through $92 in 1932, $881 in 1935, $1,145 in 1939, to $2,403 in 1947. This information was repeated in various ways, e.g., in two full-page charts (pages 71 and 74). But the 1947 figure included $1,563,000,000 with which Congress restored Commodity Credit Corporation capital impaired by the food subsidy program in 1945–46. The task force did point out in the text that this was a wartime expenditure; but the use and reiteration of the figures smacks of sensationalism. The chart on page 74 shows governmental expenditures for agriculture increasing by leaps and bounds. If, however, the aforementioned billion and a half for CCC fund impairment were subtracted, the 1947 chart would be only about three-fourths as high as the 1939 chart. But this operation would destroy the dramatic showing that agricultural adjustment costs are rapidly pyramiding.

The task force predicted a saving of $44,000,000 if its recommendations were accepted. The Hoover Commission concurred; but Vice-Chairman Acheson and Commissioner Rowe dissented on grounds that the task force had failed to document the manner in which these savings might accrue. The dissent is well taken. For example, regarding the Office of the Secretary, the task force merely said: "Surely, net savings of $500,000 per annum in these costs is not an unreasonable expectation."

A more serious criticism of the projected savings has to do with the Farmers Home Administration (FHA; successor to the controversial Farm Security Administration). The task force recommended rigorous curtailment of FHA's lending operations under present circumstances. Only especially qualified borrowers, carefully screened from applicants, should be financed. FHA borrowers should be required to refinance their indebtedness through private or cooperative agencies as soon as their finanical conditions warrant. After highly praising the cooperative credit system characterizing generally the operations of the Farm Credit Administration, the task force said:

"The underlying objectives of direct lending . . . , illustrated by the . . . Farmers Home Administration . . . , are essentially different from the underlying principles of the cooperative system."

FHA had authorization to lend 75 millions in fiscal 1948—60 millions for farm ownership and 15 millions for production and subsistence loans. The task force proposed to save 30 millions of its projected 44 millions by curtailing FHA loans. It proposed to save an additional five millions in FHA administrative costs. Yet the task force proposed a reduction of only 37 employees in FHA's staff. At $5,000 each, this would amount to only $185, 000. Where is the rest of the $5 million saving coming from?

The task force did not analyze the differences in FHA credit from other credit for agriculture, both public and private— differences in method and objectives; differences, indeed, in *function*. John D. Black, for example, has called the development of farm and home planning by the Farm Security Administration one of the major social inventions of our time. Yet the task force report is innocent of any consideration of this method or of the social needs which called it forth.

How necessary is the work of FHA? The task force made no analysis; hence it did not attempt to answer statements of Dillard B. Lasseter, FHA Administrator. In the agricultural appropriation hearings (House of Representatives) on February 18, 1948, Mr. Lasseter said that, despite the high level of total farm income, demand for operating loans from FHA had steadily increased, especially on the part of veterans. He cited the 1945 farm census to show that 51 per cent of the nation's farmers annually produced but $670 worth of farm products each. He cited figures as of June 1, 1946, to indicate that 10 per cent of the farmers held 70 per cent of all demand deposits owned by farmers. Half of the farmers held no such deposits.

In view of these figures, it is unfortunate that the sketchy analysis of the task force opens its members to the charge of being unsympathetic toward low-income farmers. Many persons are intensely (and often unfairly) critical of land-grant college officials for their alleged disregard of low-income farmers. A careful "functional" analysis might indicate that agricultural policy should employ a distinction between commercial and non-commercial farmers. Had the task force done so and carefully analyzed how the needs of non-commercial farmers might otherwise be met, it might have drawn the sting of the foregoing strictures. But neither the distinction nor the supporting analysis was offered.

These comments on the task force's proposed savings at the expense of FHA seem more important to me than the more obvious retort, as follows: After all, FHA has a *lending* program. What it lends out is supposed to be returned, with interest. Despite its necessarily high-risk operations, its repayment record has been very good. How, then, can specific annual "savings" be gained by reducing FHA's lending authority by $30,000,000 annually?

3. GENERAL EVALUATION OF TASK FORCE RECOMMENDATIONS

An Agricultural Resources Conservation Administration was proposed for the USDA. Headed by a career administrator appointed by the Secretary, this agency would include a Forest and Range Service,[6] a Fish and Wildlife Service, and—what especially concerns this chapter—a Soil and Water Conservation Service. Each service would be headed by a career chief appointed by the Administrator.

The Soil and Water Conservation Service would administer federal programs on land and with respect to farm water outside the public domain. In recognition of the "regional nature" of much soil conservation work and the need for coordinating regional and state programs with a national plan, the Service was given a coordinating function. The Service would be responsible for the administration of any agricultural conservation payments, including development of the basis and standards

---

6. The Forest and Range Service would administer programs of the Bureau of Land Management, transferred from the Department of the Interior. Neither this service nor the proposed Fish and Wildlife Service (also transferred from Interior) will be discussed here. The exclusion is based upon the approach of this book which requires a rather comprehensive analysis of each agency considered. Lack of space prevents an exhaustive analysis of relationships between Interior and Agriculture in the West as well as discussion of fish and wildlife conservation.

for such payments, under the law. The Service would "see to it" that adequate technical service and needed assistance in conservation is made available to soil conservation districts, other organizations, and farmers through the cooperative Extension Service. The Service would "act for the Secretary" in making investigations and developing projects. It would bear the USDA's responsibility for water-resource surveys and the development of plans for upstream flood-control programs, although these activities would require close cooperation with other bureaus of the Agricultural Resources Conservation Administration as well as with other national and state agencies.

Respecting soil conservation, the Service's direct responsibilities were to stop at the state lines.[7] Said the report:

". . . a strong central administration will carry its educational and service programs to the soil-conservation districts and other organizations and farmers . . ."

through the "revitalized Extension Administration . . ." of the USDA and the states. State Extension Services were to be strengthened by transfer of personnel, presumably from SCS. All this would end duplication and conflict, "and will strengthen rather than weaken the driving force of the conservation movement."

Comments are as follows:

1. As elsewhere, analysis is confined to a few, brief paragraphs. Thus much conservation work is of a regional nature, says the report, but it proposes to eliminate the SCS regional offices—with no explanation. The Soil and Water Conservation Service is made broadly responsible for administering conservation payments and supervising the educational and technical-assistance program; but what sanctions the Service is to have in meeting these responsibilities is nowhere made clear.

2. Recommendations are somewhat contradictory. What is the role of the federal Extension Service? On page 78, the Soil and Water Conservation Service is supposed "to supervise operations at the state level in cooperation with the State extension

---

7. If, however, a land-grant college is unable or unwilling to cooperate where the Secretary of Agriculture believes that the law or the public interest requires action, the USDA may go directly to the farmer.

services . . ." But on page 39 the "strong central administration" is to carry its programs to soil conservation districts, etc., through the "revitalized extension administration of the United States Department of Agriculture." Which is it?

3. Several weaknesses appear respecting the recommendations on the agricultural conservation payments. The report makes the well-known criticisms that such payments are paid on a year-to-year basis without regard to the farmer's performance in improving his practices and without relation to a farm plan. The report recommends that payments be made to induce cooperation and not to supplement income. It also urges the importance of coordinating existing efforts to facilitate carrying out plans for individual farms. Unfortunately, the report does not deal with pressing problems arising when one attempts to link conservation payments to individual farm plans. Nor is the controversial question of relationship of the conservation program and the individual farm plan to the operations of the production control program recognized.

Nor did the task force make specific recommendations for reducing the conservation payment program, although noting ACP outlays of more than a half-billion dollars in 1939 and $383,000,000 in 1947.[8] In view of the commendable search for possible saving by the task force, this silence is difficult to comprehend. Most students of the USDA's budget would agree that the agricultural conservation payment program represents the most obvious possibility of reductions—although there are differences respecting the political repercussions that would follow.

4. Recommendations respecting the Extension Service require more analysis than the task force offers. Noting that the SCS field staff cost $32,000,000, the committee recommended transfer of $24,000,000 to provide 6,000 county Extension workers at $4,000 each. Presumably, some expansion would take place at the state level in Extension. But the federal Extension Service would receive only ten additional project leaders. The then current federal appropriations to extension work, some

---

8. Task Force Report, p. 77; the comparable figure for fiscal 1947 as shown in the Agricultural Appropriation *Hearings* for fiscal 1949, H. of R., Vol. II, p. 132, is only $305,000,000.

$26,500,000, were to be nearly doubled by adding $24,000,000; yet the federal Extension Service is to be "revitalized" by adding ten men. Further, nothing is said about the distribution of the $24,000,000 among the states; is it to be a matched grant? What formulae are suggested for distribution? The report is silent.

More serious is the question: What would this mean for the Extension program? Extension prides itself on a well-rounded program, including 4-H Club Work, older youth programs, home economics, balanced farming, and general assistance to farmers in marketing and production. The task force's proposal is largely to graft the SCS program on Extension. Political power and influence are not considered. Previous chapters have indicated that the soil conservation district supervisors have organized state associations and a national association. Presumably, the 6,000 county workers would be largely recruited from SCS. Presumably they would continue to work closely with soil conservation districts, both as technicians and as cooperators in the art of influencing Congressional appropriations. By the simple act of incorporating this formidable force into their organizations, do state Extension Directors believe that they can control it? If effectuation of this proposal ever appears imminent, the reaction of the Farm Bureau will be interesting to watch. The proposal, if carried out, might distort the Extension program until that agency might properly be renamed the cooperative agricultural conservation service.

4. AGRICULTURAL COUNCILS

PMA committees and all other farmer committees with federal functions would be replaced by state and county agricultural councils. County councils would be elected by farm owners and tenants, voting by administrative units. The county council would select its officers, and the county Extension agent would be eligible for secretary. Terms are for four years with the proviso that a member has to be out of office one year before he can be re-elected. The chairmen of all county councils would elect eight farmer members of the state committee, which would include, as *ex officio* members, the directors of agricultural extension and research at the land-grant college as well as the heads of departments of agriculture and of conservation in the state government. No compensation would be paid, except that state council members would be reimbursed for travel and subsistence while attending meetings.

The councils would have only advisory and consultative functions. Administrative responsibility would lie with land-grant college agencies for research and extension and with federal employees for production control, etc. The state agricultural council is broadly charged to study agricultural problems and prepare a long-range program of agricultural objectives for the state. It is to analyze and make reports and recommendations with respect to federal agricultural programs. It is to consult widely with administrators and other interested persons in order to facilitate administrative coordination and efficiency.

Further, the report specifically recommends that state and county councils shall not administer agricultural conservation programs, acreage allotments, marketing quotas, crop insurance programs, etc. Committees now operating in the administration of such programs would be abolished; all such administrative functions would be performed by USDA personnel, appointed and paid by the Department.

In three brief explanatory paragraphs, the task force justifies these recommendations. The explanation justifies the state and county councils as providing the popular consultation needed to accomplish program objectives. Consultation should help greatly to coordinate various agricultural activities. The multitude of existing farmer committees, some with administrative responsibilities, would be eliminated. Paid farmer administration of federal programs would be ended. Administrative contacts with farmers, duplication, and overlapping would be reduced. Efficiency would be promoted and administrative savings achieved.

In view of the tendency for structures of power and influence to grow up around agricultural administration, these recommendations are most significant. It is certainly important that administration of federal programs is here recommended to be handled by civil service administrators with clear-cut hierarchical authority and responsibility direct to the Secretary of Agriculture from the farm level itself. At the same time, the committees of farmers are retained but reduced to consultative and advisory positions. There is much to be said for these recommendations. Yet the implicit ideas of the task force about the nature of influence in the PMA is in striking contrast with the lack of regard for power and influence in the soil conservation districts linked with the Soil Conservation Service, as already indicated. Here, as elsewhere, the task force should have set forth its reasons in an analysis elaborated to fit the importance of the subject. The task force would then have had to face the question whether local councils of farmers and state councils should actually be elected. The committee uses terms such as "true" conservation and "real" conservation; one might also ask if this kind of election of committees, even advisory committees, by one group of the population is "true" democracy?

The task force might have considered as an alternative the appointment of committees of farmers by administrators at state and county levels. That this would not necessarily avoid the creation of a pressure group is seen from the experience of the Farm Bureau which essentially came into existence through committees to assist the early Extension Services. Nevertheless, the Farm Bureau and other farm organizations have to defend themselves as private and partial groups. On the other hand, a general and official election has all the earmarks of creating officers who speak with the voice of the people. This is one of the problems which the PMA attests. At the same time, the tendency for such committees is to become quite involved in particular programs directed toward realization of particular ends through particular policies. This raises once more the problem of the single purpose or the limited purpose pressure group against even the general purpose farm organization.

Should we make an effort to reserve the general procedures of general election, with all their possibilities for drama and conflict and symbolization, for general government? Political scientists have long bemoaned the overburdened voter; something like nine hundred thousand officers are elected in the United States.

The multiplication of elections creates confusion in the minds of the voters, and makes for indifference. Light electoral participation is a consequence. PMA elections are ordinarily light; yet there is no doubt that PMA committeemen speak with much greater authority because of their election.

We must here make it clear that we are dealing with democratic political theory. Politics involves choices in which some win and others lose. Democratic politics insists that these choices should be made in a process in which the public generally participates. Elections in which qualified persons participate secretly and individually are extremely important here. To be sure, as M. P. Follett has said, "I go to the polls to express the group man in me." This statement is based on the obvious truth that people approach their government through groups and realize themselves through group activities as well as through elections. It also recognizes that group activities influence elections. Nevertheless, although some groups are broader in their interests than others, group interests are particular interests as far as society is concerned.

But, where groups press for particular interests, elections produce governments charged with the always awe-inspiring task of making political choices. It is essentially through electoral participation that the citizen shares in the public choices involved in political life. In his groups he can press for what is right or what he conceives as good for him; through his government, he must share in the choices that compromise various interests and purposes. Elections should be used sparingly and made as significant as possible. As Frederick Watkins suggests,[9] ceremonies and ritual are needed to nurture the common attitudes necessary to enlist common support for any social institutions and social creeds—and the democratic creed and institutions are no exceptions.

These observations call for seriously questioning the continuation of elected farmer committeemen or even councils. Strong political arguments favor the retention of the elected committee system. Indeed, the task force is to be commended

---

9. *The Political Tradition of the West,* Harvard Univ. Press (1948), ch. xii.

for the courage it has shown in grappling with the subject. At the same time, a thorough analysis of different methods of committee selection against a background of democratic political theory would have been desirable. Thus state and local agricultural committees or councils might be created by administrative appointment; and the appointments might even be made from nominations of general farm organizations, where such exist.

5. THE REPORT OF THE HOOVER COMMISSION

The task force reported on October 8, 1948, the Commission on February 18, 1949. With two exceptions, the following discussion will be confined to the Commission's recommendations upon conservation policy.[10]

The Commission asserted that the Extension Service "is being increasingly bypassed" by several USDA agencies. It criticized the duplication, conflict, and confusion resulting from numerous federal agency field organizations operating direct to the farmer. It found fault with the proliferation of farmer committees which "tend to become local administrators of uncoordinated agencies . . ."

The actual recommendations of the Hoover Commission respecting administration of conservation and related activities are none too clear. The federal Extension Service would be "newly constituted." Major federal educational and joint federal-state educational, demonstrational, and informational activities of the Department would be brought into the federal Service. An Agricultural Resources Conservation Service is recommended. Services to farmers are to be administered by USDA employees through offices based on the states as units. Services at the county level are to be "merged." State and county councils should be elected to serve only in advisory capacity and without compensation, except for expenses.

Comments are as follows:

---

10. The Hoover Commission accepted the agricultural task force's recommendation that the Bureau of Land Management be transferred from Interior to Agriculture; other task forces had recommended a reverse transfer of relevant agricultural functions to Interior.

1. The Commission is even briefer, and consequently more cryptic, than the task force. Questions of regional offices are not discussed. No clear-cut recommendation that SCS regional offices be liquidated is made. A consequence of the telegraphic and ambiguous nature of the Commission's recommendations was that SCS interpreted its proposals to imply that SCS continue functioning about as before.[11] Further, relationships between the USDA and state agencies are brushed over. Apparently the Commission saw no problem in the election of local committees.

2. The Commission avoided the flier into substantive policy which the task force made in endorsing the flexible price support system embraced in the Agricultural Act of 1948.[12] Consideration of substantive policy in an administrative study was criticized, for example, by the Washington *Post*. But it is hard to see how the two can be divorced, either in light of administrative theory [13] or actual practice. Any consideration of reorganization of the PMA should recognize that many PMA state officials have strongly favored a guarantee of 90 per cent of parity on basic crops.

3. The Commission's recommendations respecting the Commodity Credit Corporation are almost undiscoverable and when discovered are incomprehensible. The task force discussed the agency somewhat and placed it within the proposed Commodity Adjustment Administration for "financing only." The Commission recommends creation of a Commodity Adjustment Service in 35 words; but it also provides an Agricultural Credit Service. Then it includes, without comment, the Commodity Credit Corporation in its list of agricultural credit agencies. The CCC is a major engine for making agricultural programs work. Its organization has been controversial for many years. Limitations upon its power to erect storage facilities were apparently an important factor in the 1948 elections. Its capital stock of $100,-000,000 and borrowing authority of $4,750,000,000 (raised to $6,000,000,000 in 1950) makes it an extremely powerful

11. In an internal memorandum, one of a number prepared by USDA agencies after issuance of the Hoover Commission reports.

12. Task Force Report, p. 47.

13. E.g., Paul Appleby, *Policy and Administration, op. cit.*

agency. In light of all these points, the Hoover Commission's slight consideration to the CCC is truly astounding.

6. THE AFTERMATH—DEFEAT OF THE PRESIDENT'S REORGANIZATION PLAN FOR AGRICULTURE

Under the Reorganization Act of 1949, President Truman submitted Reorganization Plan Number 4 for the Department of Agriculture, March 13, 1950. After Senate Hearings, the Senate resolved against the plan by 63 to 1,[14] on May 18, thus killing the measure.[15] The plan contained five brief paragraphs. It vested all functions of the USDA in the Secretary.[16] It provided for two additional Assistant Secretaries, appointed by the President with Senatorial confirmation, and an Administrative Assistant Secretary of Agriculture appointed under the classified civil service. It vested full powers of delegation in the Secretary and provided for transfers of records, property, personnel, and funds necessary to carry out Secretarial reorganizations.

Opponents of the reorganization plan included representatives of the AFBF and state Farm Bureaus,[17] the National Grange, the National Council of Farm Cooperatives, and (it was reported) [18] all members of the Hoover Commission's agricultural task force except Professor Gaus. Messrs. Rusk and Blake of the task force testified against the plan, and Mr. Doane opposed the plan by letter. Only Budget Director Lawton and Secretary Brannan testified for the plan.

Apparently some members of the USDA worked with Con-

14. As reported by the AFBF *Official News Letter,* cf. issues of April 24, May 1, May 8, and May 29, 1950. The Senate Report, No. 1774, Reorganization Plans of 1950, 81st Cong., 2d Sess., merely records that the plan failed by a voice vote.

15. Whereas previous reorganization acts have required adverse concurrent resolutions to defeat reorganization plans, the act of 1949 requires an adverse resolution in only one House.

16. With exceptions unimportant to this chapter.

17. Vice President Short, accompanied by six other Farm Bureau leaders, appeared in opposition. Adverse communications were recorded from seven other state Farm Bureaus.

18. But Dean Rusk pointed out that he spoke with certainty only for the four task force members present. *Hearings,* S. Res. 263, *op. cit.,* p. 33.

gressmen against the plan. Senator Schoeppel (R., Kan.) told
Secretary Brannan:

"Some of your own people that work in your Department all over the
country have come to us, as Members of this Congress and members
of this committee, indicating apprehension because no suggestions
have been made, no blue print, no pattern to work toward . . ." [19]

A familiar occurrence, indeed!

The Hearings on the plan and the Report of the Senate Committee on Expenditures in the Executive Departments clearly
support a major thesis of this book, namely, that administrative
organization cannot be separated from substantive policy. For
example, the Report states: [20]

"The majority of the committee feels that Reorganization Plan
No. 4 deals primarily with 'matters of substantive policy' which have
been established by the Congress after many years of study."

To grant the Secretary these powers

". . . would mean that the Congress is abjectly surrendering its legislative authority. . . ."

The chief objection to the plan was that it constituted no
plan at all but was rather a "blank check" to the Secretary who
could thus reorganize the Department at will. The plan was
criticized for not committing the Secretary to a reorganization
in accordance with the Hoover Commission report. Some inconsistencies in the opposition were to be expected. For example,
many expressed fears that the Secretary would wield his power
in a manner unacceptable to the Congress (and others, of
course). But again it was stated that absence of specific directives would place the Secretary in a "very weak position with
regard to vested interests" in the USDA.

Perspective upon the real reasons for opposition to the plan
can be gained from Budget Director Lawton's testimony. He
pointed out that the Secretary of Agriculture

19. S. Res. 263, *Hearings, op. cit.,* p. 82.
20. Senate Report No. 1566, 81st Cong., 2d Sess., which contains the
minority views of Senators Humphrey, Leahy, and Benton, as well.

". . . has always enjoyed a more considerable degree of administrative control than most other department heads." [21]

Other than corporations, exempt under the plan, the USDA includes nine major operating units. So far as *legal* authority goes (which is all the proposed plan could give anyway) the Secretary could considerably reorganize the USDA now.[22] The real question was with respect to authority over the Farmers Home Administration, the Soil Conservation Service, the Farm Credit Administration, and the Rural Electrification Administration.

Hence the real problem emerged, which is the same as the problem underlying this book. What to do about relationships among the SCS, PMA, and the Extension Service? Secretary Brannan put his finger on the issue in a colloquy with Senator Thye who had been persistently pressing him to "bring in a blueprint" of his proposals for three agencies.[23] "Why is it," asked Secretary Brannan, "that we must answer the question with respect to SCS and PMA?" He added:

"You know very well if we ever bring that out, if you ever invite the expression of public opinion on that subject, you will never close these hearings during this session of Congress or the next one. There are very strong points of view on both sides."

The Secretary repeated the intention of the Department to put the SCS and PMA together. The Congressmen wanted a blueprint. The Secretary said that the Department had been studying the matter continuously and offered to show Senators five reorganization charts which propose to handle the matter in as many ways. He clearly indicated that he lacked legal authority to reorganize the Soil Conservation Service. He implied that no concrete plan could be expected to go into effect if it had to be published in advance so that opponents could marshal supporters against it. This means, in effect, that reorganization of conservation and related administration can only be accom-

21. *Hearings,* S. Res. 263, *op. cit.,* p. 58.
22. Secretary Brannan cited nine different reorganizations and administrative changes made since 1945 in the USDA under existing authority, some of them quite sweeping, such as creation of the PMA in 1945. *Ibid.,* pp. 79-80.
23. *Ibid.,* p. 76.

plished by administrative fiat. The Secretary might have cited the inability of Congress to deal with the problem, as witness the diametrically opposed Hope and Aiken Bills of 1948, both of which failed. He might also have cited Herbert Hoover's statement, quoted by Dean H. P. Rusk, that

"if the overlap and waste in the Federal Government is to be eliminated it must be handed down from on high. . . ." [24]

The President proposed, Congress disposed; the situation remained as before except that the intimate relationships between substantive policy and administrative organization were further clarified—and except that we now know that governmental reorganization involving vital interests of powerful groups and agencies cannot be easily brought about even through the intercession of so august a group as the Hoover Commission.

There was indication that reorganization of agricultural conservation programs had been postponed two years. The logical time for such action was immediately after the 1948 elections. Then Secretary Brannan's prestige was extremely high, and the Soil Conservation Service had lost face through its miscalculated overtures to the Republicans. But legislative authority was lacking. Subsequently, President Kline expressed a hope that the conservation program might be coordinated in two years, in conformance with the basic principles of the 1936 Soil Conservation and Domestic Allotment Act, namely, on a grant-in-aid basis to the states.[25] But these calculations failed to acknowledge the potentialities of the House Appropriations Committee and the USDA, if they could unite their efforts toward reorganizing the Department.

---

24. To be sure, Mr. Hoover was referring to the President or Congress; but Secretary Brannan might well have argued that the Secretary of Agriculture could at least be given the opportunity to try his hand, free from legal restrictions.

25. AFBF *Official News Letter*, July 17, 1950. See Appendix.

CHAPTER XIII

The 1951 Reorganization

I. IMMEDIATE BACKGROUND

The three preceding chapters provide background for the 1951 reorganization, but the immediate stimulus appears to have come from the House Subcommittee on Agricultural Appropriations, chaired by Jamie L. Whitten of Mississippi. In 1949 the subcommittee authorized use of 5 per cent of ACP funds in counties to acquire additional technical assistance if needed and desired; but evidence multiplied that "there was little effort made to coordinate the work of ACP and the Soil Conservation Service." [1] In March, 1950 the Appropriations Committee of the House directed a field investigation to be made of various USDA activities. Forty-six counties in 13 states were visited. In placing part of the voluminous report in the record, Chairman Whitten declared that the committee did not necessarily subscribe to all its findings; but he stressed his confidence in the ability and objectivity of the investigators.

The report declared that despite the existence of many USDA programs and field offices, the farmer usually finds that "no coordinated agricultural program exists in his county." Particulars

---

1. House *Hearings*, Agric. Approp., fiscal 1952, Part 2, p. 687. The following is largely drawn from this source, pp. 687-99, which includes excerpts from the field investigation, the Secretary's memorandum No. 1278, and testimony by Secretary Brannan.

of inter-agency conflict were given in an incisive paragraph.[2] The persistent animosity of many Extension Services toward the SCS was noted,[3] but the complaints of Extension workers about SCS and ACP-PMA were also recorded. Thus in one state meeting, the Extension Director was followed by the Chief of the SCS in Washington who

". . . completely ignored the comments of the State extension director and left the impression with his audience and the press that nothing worth while had been done in the field of Soil Conservation until SCS was established."

Extension also complained of "high-pressure tactics" by SCS personnel in establishing soil conservation districts. Farmers in one area told the state Extension Director that

". . . they had been told that if they did not sign up for the complete farm plan, 'it will only be about 5 years until you will have to do this whether you want to or not.'"

The report lists the typical chronology if a farmer wants to establish terraces. *First,* the farmer will go to the county agent (Extension) who may refer him to the local ACP office. However, the county agent may also attempt to convince the farmer that Extension can do everything that he wants more quickly and at less cost than the others. The farmer may also find that requirements of SCS and ACP differ so that, if he follows the advice of SCS technicians, he cannot qualify for ACP payments. *Second,* at the local PMA office, the farmer learns whether funds are available for defraying terracing costs and what the ACP requirements are before payments can be made. In addition, PMA may tell him that SCS technicians are impractical, that they will require him to sign up for a complete farm plan which he neither wants nor needs in order to get his terraces, that he will be far down the priority list and will have to wait long for SCS technical services. *Third,* if the farmer then goes to the SCS office, he is told that no terracing work can be done until a land-utilization survey is made of his farm and a plan prepared, whereupon an SCS technician will lay out the neces-

2. Chap. i above.
3. Chap. iii, sec. 1, above.

sary terrace lines. *Fourth,* the farmer then goes back to PMA which sends a representative to check the terrace lines laid out by SCS and issues a "formal permit" upon which the farmer will be eligible for PMA payments. However, the PMA representative may require the terrace plan to be remodeled to meet its own specifications. *Fifth,* the SCS technician may then assist the farmer in terrace construction. *Sixth,* the farmer returns to PMA who sends another man to check compliance and certify payments; but again, at this point PMA can and sometimes does refuse payment because terrace construction does not meet its standards.

In the light of this situation in the field, which is probably not greatly overdrawn, and in the knowledge of a determination upon part of the House subcommittee, Secretary Brannan moved toward action. Preparations were fairly quiet. The chief consultation seems to have been with SCS, the National Association of Soil Conservation Districts, and the PMA organization, including representatives of state PMA committees. Informal consultation was carried on, largely in terms of suggesting the general direction of reorganization; advisedly, however, no blueprint was distributed. A few days before the order was issued, available national farm organization leaders were given copies of the memorandum and asked for comments. But the order apparently came as a surprise; a few hints had been heard; but none of the journals of the general farm organizations evinced any advance knowledge of the order or even that one was contemplated.[4]

2. THE REORGANIZATION ORDER

The "agricultural resource conservation services" of the United States Department of Agriculture were consolidated by Secretary Charles F. Brannan on February 16, 1951. Following

4. The *National Union Farmer,* the *National Grange Monthly,* and the *Official News Letter,* and *Nation's Agriculture* of AFBF. With the exception of a brief story in the AFBF *Official News Letter,* February 26, 1951, none of these journals has taken note of the reorganization—farmers' major interest in agricultural policy has been in price control, manpower, mobilization, and related matters.

the declaration of purpose the Secretary's memorandum declares the "basic soil conservation objective"—that each acre shall be used within its capabilities and treated according to its needs for protection and improvement. The Assistant Secretary acquires "supervision and direction" of all departmental activities touching forests, lands, and water. He is charged to encourage and develop soil conservation districts and to supervise Departmental relationships with these and other relevant state and local agencies. Under his direction the Soil Conservation Service, the Production and Marketing Administration, and the Forest Service will jointly determine practices and payments respecting the Agricultural Conservation Program of PMA.

State and county SCS and PMA offices are to be consolidated. The state PMA committees, the SCS State Conservationist, and the Forest Service official in charge of farm forestry shall jointly determine state soil conservation and related programs. County programs are to be formulated by county PMA committees, local SCS technicians, and soil conservation district supervisors. Presidents of the Land-Grant Colleges are invited to assign members to participate at the state level and county agents are invited to participate locally. Farmers Home Administration officials also are invited to share in program formulation. State and county offices of PMA and SCS are to be physically consolidated as rapidly as this can be "efficiently accomplished."

Actually, the duties of the Assistant Secretary, as designated on February 16, have been assigned to the Under-Secretary, Clarence J. McCormick. These duties include, among other things, supervision and direction of the following activities:

"(a) The development of departmental policy with respect to agricultural resources conservation;

(b) Conservation, utilization, and management of forest, range, soil and water resources, including watershed management, irrigation, drainage, and disposal of water, flood control, and river-basin investigations;

(c) The acquisition, management, and disposition of lands under the jurisdiction of the Department;

(d) Representing the Department on governmental, quasi-governmental, or private boards, committees, commissions, or other bodies relating to these responsibilities;

(e) *Encouraging the creation and development of soil conservation districts;* [italics supplied; this is the first statement of USDA policy to encourage the creation of districts].

(f) Executing on behalf of the Secretary, departmental memoranda of understanding with boards of supervisors [of soil conservation districts] and with State soil conservation committees, or with other State or local agencies covering activities related to the work assigned to him."

The Under-Secretary is authorized and directed to make a continuous survey of relevant USDA functions and to determine with the Secretary such actions, including transfers, as will expedite and lend efficiency to the work. The Under-Secretary is empowered to delegate freely, and the land and water resources staff of the Secretary is assigned to him.

Finally, under Mr. McCormick's direction, the SCS, the Forest Service, and PMA

". . . will jointly determine the soil conservation practices to be included in the agricultural conservation program, and the rates of payments for soil conservation practices, by meetings and consultations at the national, State, and county levels. All agencies shall be guided by the Department's basic soil conservation objective."

Precisely where the memorandum leaves SCS and PMA is none too clear. Since SCS rests upon the statute of 1935, the Secretary of Agriculture is somewhat inhibited in his powers of direction over it. The February 16 order exercises the powers enjoyed by the Secretary under existing law. As Secretary Brannan said:

"It is not possible under existing authority of the Secretary of Agriculture . . . to set up at this time one sole arbiter at the State or county level. It is a matter of people having a common objective doing their job in such a way that they can achieve that result."

The order declares that the SCS state conservationist "shall be responsible for all technical phases of the permanent type of soil conservation work, except forestry," undertaken by the SCS and the PMA within a state. He shall, further, "carry out his duties

and responsibilities under the direction of the Chief of the Soil
Conservation Service but shall coordinate and integrate the performance of his work with the PMA State Committee." At the
same time, the state PMA committee

". . . shall continue to administer the agricultural conservation program and to carry out such other duties as are now or may be hereinafter assigned to it."

In formulating the state policies for guidance of PMA and
SCS, the state PMA committee, and the SCS conservationist
(and the Forest Service representative, as noted, and others
who respond to the Secretary's invitation) shall proceed by conferences or other means "as initiated by" the state PMA chairman. Within the ambit of this state program, "the PMA County
Committee and the local technicians of the Soil Conservation
Service shall, working with the governing body of the soil conservation district, formulate and determine the soil conservation
policies and programs by conferences or other means to be initiated by the Chairman of the County PMA Committee." The
PMA county committee shall continue to administer the ACP
program; but payments for "permanent type improvements" require that the PMA committee "secure the recommendations
of" the local SCS technician "as to the proper performance of
this type of work." The SCS technician shall direct "technical
phases of the permanent type soil conservation work"; but he
shall receive "program guidance from the PMA County Committee in consultation and cooperation with the governing body
of the soil conservation district."

Study of this memorandum reveals that PMA and SCS appear to be nicely balanced. As Chairman Whitten remarked,
"We are not trying to put any of these agencies on top of the
other." [5] Secretary Brannan stressed one thing "above all else"
determined by the order, namely,

"That . . . there is going to be but one source for the technical opinion of the Department of Agriculture on the *engineering* aspects
of conservation activities." [6]

5. House *Hearings*, Agric. Approp., fiscal 1952, Part 2, p. 691.
6. *Ibid.*, p. 695 (Italics supplied.)

The National Association of Soil Conservation Districts is on record as approving the order. One informed observer characterized it as a draw between SCS and PMA. Nevertheless, what victory there is in the order seems to be a victory for PMA.

First, it will be noted that the order does not mention SCS regional offices; rather, the line is from the Under-Secretary through PMA and SCS to the states and thence to the counties. As Chapter III indicated, the SCS regional offices have had important policy-determining roles. Little of these would appear to remain if the intentions of the order are actually achieved.[7]

Second, the state PMA committee may be able to dominate proceedings at the state level through weight of numbers and their authority as farm spokesmen; it is notable that the state PMA chairman has the authority of initiation of conferences, as does the county PMA chairman at his level. Students of Congressional procedure, for example, have long recognized the authority given committee chairmen by their ability to call meetings.

Third, in view of N. E. Dodd's testimony [8] respecting the effect upon the relationships to the USDA which results from the independent nature of soil conservation districts, the February memorandum goes a long way in incorporating such districts into the policy making process. Nevertheless, the activities of districts remain essentially cooperative, consultatory, and advisory; and it is hard to see how much more could be provided for them in the memorandum.

Another handicap of districts in contributing to county conservation policy is the fact that many of them do not correspond to county lines.[9]

3. THE CONSEQUENCES

The writer gathers that the Farm Bureau is much opposed to the order of February 16. Moreover, most of the state Extension

7. This interpretation has been strongly criticized by a ranking USDA official, but the writer is unable to read any other from the document.

8. See above, chap. iv, sec. 3.

9. See above, chap. iv, sec. 1.

Services are apparently very critical. Although the Extension Directors have issued no statements, drafts of criticisms have reportedly been circulated, particularly a most unfavorable draft prepared by southern Extension Directors. Meanwhile, Senator Aiken, for himself and twelve other Senators—including Douglas and Benton, Democrats—has introduced a bill which would substantially enact the recommendations of the Hoover Commission for agriculture. If this bill passed, as seems unlikely, it would undo the Brannan reorganization.[10] It is too early to do more than speculate about the consequences of the February 16 order; [11] yet the following points are offered:

First, Secretary Brannan's order to consolidate the "agricultural resource conservation services" of the USDA under the "supervision and direction" of the Assistant Secretary (February 16, 1951) marks the most vigorous steps toward integration in ten years.[12] Any critical analysis of this move must acknowledge that the Secretary went as far as he could unilaterally. To have gone further—that is, to have enlisted the effective cooperation of the colleges of agriculture in developing a program with different objectives and procedures—would have required a long negotiation, agreement through memoranda of understanding, and the development of unwieldy and cumbersome administrative forms and procedures full of the kind of contingencies which mark most joint efforts of quasi-independent organizations on both sides of the federal system. In this connection, the fate of the cooperative state and local land-use planning program (1938–1942) bears recalling.[13] SCS and

10. S. 1149, 82nd Cong., 2nd Sess.

11. On November 11, 1951, Secretary Brannan announced that state offices of SCS, PMA, and Farmers Home Administration had been consolidated in 12 states; nine other states had arranged consolidations. Office consolidation had also been accomplished in 1289 counties. In a number of states, one apparent result has been the effort by SCS to get closer to colleges of agriculture. Another possible result is that both SCS and PMA may take considerable interest in each other's elections—that is, elections of soil conservation district supervisors and community committeemen of PMA.

12. Further analysis of this order is found in the writer's article (which should be consulted generally on this chapter) "Land or People?" in *Land Economics*, May, 1951.

13. Cf. Chapter ix, section 2 (above) and the writer's article, "The Bureau of Agricultural Economics Under Fire . . . ," *JFE*, August, 1946.

AAA—now PMA—are still going concerns, are at least as conscious of their political interests as formerly, and (if anything) have grown in political skill. Both agencies would probably be hostile to any new cooperative federal-state program which was designed to coordinate their activities but over which they did not exercise major control. The question remains whether the colleges of agriculture and the Farm Bureau have changed sufficiently since 1942 to support a new cooperative program. Reviewing these considerations, it appears that the development of a cooperative federal-state program would have been most difficult under the best of circumstances. Given the apparently irreconcilable differences which divide Secretary Brannan from the Farm Bureau leadership, its development would appear currently impossible. In view of this analysis, it is difficult to see that the Secretary could have acted otherwise.

Second, what are the political potentialities inherent in the present reorganization of USDA conservation programs? The forced union or "shotgun wedding" of SCS and ACP may fail, as its predecessor failed in 1942. Or it may be superseded, if Congress moves effectively to reduce and then eliminate the ACP fund. This action might be accompanied by the assignment of mobilization duties to the PMA committee system sufficient to give that organization a reason for existence. It would, in effect, leave one federal action program in soil conservation on private lands—that of the SCS in cooperation with soil conservation districts. Requirements of war or near-war food production, coupled with the mounting criticism of the ACP program, might precipitate this move. If so, the colleges of agriculture and the Farm Bureau could be expected to redouble their efforts to have the SCS program as it now operates acknowledged as essentially an educational approach and therefore to have it assigned to the colleges of agriculture. A dingdong battle in state capitols (since soil conservation districts now compete with agricultural extension services appropriations) as well as in Washington, would follow. If the Farm Bureau and the colleges won, the colleges would have to face the problem of digesting the SCS program. If the SCS and the soil conservation districts won, a new major farm organization would emerge in the National Association of Soil Conservation Districts. In this event the NASCD would almost certainly have to broaden its present rather narrow interests; the nature of its orientation would be most important in the future politics of agriculture.

But the Secretary's consolidation may succeed. If it does, either the SCS or the ACP will probably become the superior partner. So long as ACP retains its appropriations for conservation payments, important questions will be: on what criteria will the payments be made and who will determine these criteria? Will the PMA committee system succeed in establishing its fiat over the state and county conservation programs, controlling the operations of the SCS technicians accordingly? Or will the SCS and the soil conservation districts succeed in taking control of the ACP funds? If so, they will probably have to elbow the PMA committees aside.

In any event, the success of the present coordination of USDA soil conservation programs will present the colleges and the Farm Bureau with a formidable fact. Generally, the colleges and the Farm Bureau have fought both SCS and the PMA committee system. So long as SCS and PMA were fighting each other, the prospects of the colleges and the Farm Bureau seemed brighter than they can possibly be if the two federal programs are effectively merged and retain control of their heavy appropriations. In short, if the consolidation of USDA conservation programs is successful, it will produce a formidable consolidation of political power—power which is nationalized in some respects but which also rests upon the strong local support inherent either in the PMA committee system or in the associated soil conservation districts.

Third, the possible effective consolidation of USDA soil conservation programs should not be interpreted as merely a consolidation of administrative political power. If the upshot is to strengthen the PMA committee system, the question of the partisan activity of the PMA, especially in the midwest, will be uppermost in many minds.

PART THREE

RECOMMENDATIONS
AND GENERAL INTERPRETATIONS

CHAPTER XIV

Farm Family Living

I. A POLICY GOAL [1]

Charles E. Kellogg, Chief, Division of Soil Survey, USDA, has stated:

"Generally, erosion is one of the symptoms of some deep maladjustments between the soil and the farming system. Rarely can we achieve control by simple direct means; rather we must get back of the immediate symptoms and find the cause. Frequently we find weak plant cover and declining soil fertility resulting from unstable economic conditions, bad tenure relationships, overcrowded land, poverty, disease, and wars. . . ." [2]

The breadth of this statement is staggering. It implies that soil erosion and related problems can be approached with ultimate effectiveness only in light of comprehensive understanding of human nature, human relationships, non-human resources, and the relationships of human beings to such resources. No such complete grasp of all facets of the problem as would provide criteria for judging present conservation programs is possible. Dr. Kellogg's challenge, however, enables us to ask whether erosion control and related programs should not be

1. This chapter draws heavily upon the writer's papers "Land or People," in *Land Economics*, May, 1951, and "The Politics of Conservation: An Illustration," *Journal of Politics*, August, 1951.

2. Lecture, Graduate School, United States Department of Agriculture, November 15, 1948.

oriented toward a different goal than the "basic soil conservation objective" as stated by the Secretary. An alternative goal is proposed—the improvement of farm family living on a soil-conserving base.[3] Without overlooking the significance of conservation, this orientation assumes that natural resource policy will be appraised in terms of human values.

The humanistic objective urges us to look to the conditions which bear upon improved farm family living. Much farm policy, it is assumed, roots back into decisions of the farm family —what enterprises to include and how much, whether to acquire more land, what division of farm income will be made among farm and home claims, etc. There is an implicit assumption that considerable farm and home planning either does or should take place. But is "rational" planning facilitated or hampered by land tenure? By the availability of credit? By attitudes toward credit? By the presence or absence of skills and managerial understanding?

The SCS employs the "complete farm plan," of course; and the ACP program has often attempted to fit its annual payments into some kind of plan for the farm. But neither approach is organized to consider the various conditions of tenure, credit, taxation, agricultural instability, or available skills and managerial

---

3. This goal is not put forward as a "scientific" conclusion, but as a proposal derived in part from value judgments and in part from analysis. No detailed examination of the "family farm" is required since the writer accepts the views set forth in Chapter V of T. W. Schultz, *Production and Welfare of Agriculture*, Macmillan, New York (1949). True, Professor Schultz maintains that the family farm is not viewed as "an end of agricultural policy" but "as an instrument through which agriculture and rural life can be made a rich and satisfying experience . . ." That this statement is not incompatible with the writer's position, however, may be seen by examining section 4 of the present chapter. Nor is the present chapter inconsistent with A. Whitney Griswold, *Farming and Democracy*, Harcourt, Brace, and Co., New York (1948). President Griswold has cut the specious intellectual underpinnings from under the "agricultural fundamentalism" that still finds frequent expression in agricultural policy statements. The criticism by the Farm Bureau and a number of agricultural college representatives which greeted the Family Farm Policy Review in 1951 reflects in large part the animosities which have been created against the present administration of the USDA; but they also show the soundness of Griswold's question whether the "dominant political forces in American agriculture" are behind the family farm as a policy goal. (p. 177). Nevertheless, the concluding pages of Griswold's book are compatible with the conclusions of the present chapter.

ability—conditions which in some combination often delineate the problem of improving farm family living on a conservation base. The February 15 memorandum proposes to accelerate and improve soil conservation on private land; but it fails to make the improvement of farm living an explicit objective. No criticism is implied of Secretary Brannan who went about as far as he could go under the circumstances.

2. DIFFICULTIES OF FARM PLANNING

Three obstacles exist to the attainment of improved farm family living on a conservation base. Do farmers think of their farms as wholes; are farm families prepared to undertake farm and home planning? If the answer is largely in the negative, what can be done to educate farm families to make farm and home plans, with assistance from various technicians? Second, how can the services of government be organized to stimulate farm and home planning in these terms? Further, how can the organization and administration of such services be related to other functions, both public and private, so that all the assistance possible can be marshalled in support of the policy? Third, how can the ideal of highly productive farming with high levels of farm-family living on a conservation base be substituted for the ideals which have been strongly implanted in the thinking of farmers and others by the SCS and AAA-PMA programs?

Consider the orientation of farm families. Let us assume that a desirable orientation would be for them systematically to plan to use their resources to obtain the largest monetary returns with the least expenditure of effort. This is a tremendous assumption. Even in the fortune-favored corn belt, many if not most farmers operate at a low level of efficiency in terms of their potential production.[4]

If the restraints of tradition are weak in rural America (relative to their effect in most other rural areas),[5] they are by no

---

4. Cf. John Strohm, "Are You Wasting Labor?" *Country Gentleman*, May, 1951.
5. Carl C. Taylor, *et al.*, *Rural Life in the United States*, Knopf, New York (1949), p. 13, and Index, under "tradition."

means negligible. Furthermore, increases in returns must be balanced against increased expenditures of effort—including effort spent in analyzing, planning, and managing. But many farmers and others are obviously loathe to spend effort in planning.

Farm and home planning programs inevitably encounter the unpreparedness, the inability, or the unwillingness of many farmers to plan. The experience of TVA and the colleges in the Tennessee Valley with Unit Test demonstration farms is in point, likewise that of the Missouri Extension Service, in attempting to spread the effects of balanced farming. The carefully made SCS farm plans often come to rest in bureau drawers, there to remain undisturbed. The Program Surveys Division of the Bureau of Agricultural Economics analyzed experience of the "tenant purchase" program and found that the concept of a long-term farm and home plan was almost non-existent in the minds of these borrowers—the most highly selected and intensively serviced group in the Farm Security Administration.[6]

One may nevertheless recommend a program of farm planning toward the end of improving farm family living, stimulating agricultural production, and conserving resources. The program might proceed through the selection of typical farms upon which adjustments are needed; the analysis of obstacles to adjustments; and provision for overcoming these obstacles. Demonstration and pilot farms could be vigorously used;[7] aids and benefits offered by various public programs might be made flexible enough to fit into the recommendations for typical farms. Yet all these steps would come to little if the essentially educational problem is not recognized and solved, namely, how farm families can be educated to make and carry out farm and home plans.

---

6. Reference is to what is now the farm ownership division of the Farmers Home Administration.

7. Charles E. Kellogg, "The Natural Sciences and Farm Planning," *Journal of Farm Economics*, Feb., 1947 (Proceedings number).

3. INSTITUTIONAL OBSTACLES

We are confronted by the hard fact of federalism. The February 16 order combines the SCS and ACP programs, thereby moving to incorporate the intensive technical services of SCS into the mass coverage of farms achieved by ACP. Secretary Brannan noted that there is henceforth to be but one source in the USDA on the *engineering* aspects [8] of conservation activities—the SCS. Much more is involved, however, than engineering aspects. So much is involved that even the genius of Secretary Brannan (who was hailed by Chairman Cannon of the House Committee on Appropriations as having "perhaps the greatest administrative capacity the Department has enjoyed for many years") is sorely challenged.

What is needed ideally is a well-rounded county staff. At first blush, the cost of placing such a staff in every agricultural county in the United States appears staggering. It would be even larger if we include the additional money needed in the county Extension program to bring the benefits of this staff effectively to the maximum number of farmers. Nevertheless, the annual expenditures of government for the *local* provision of *technical* services *direct* to farmers (not counting clerical and other help) probably approach $80,000,000 at present. Even double this amount would not be exorbitant in view of the following. First, we are dealing with the whole agricultural industry in which net income to farm operators has been fluctuating between 13 and 18 billion dollars since World War II. Second, while farm businesses have greatly improved their financial positions, farms remain typically too small to provide such technical services entirely by themselves. Third, governmental policy has recognized this inability of farmers to provide such services in the past; the present proposal would merely be an extension, not a departure. Fourth—and most compelling—the aims of this program would be to place agriculture in a sounder economic position so that the need for conservation payments and other subventions would be considerably diminished.

---

8. House *Hearings,* Agric. Approp., fiscal 1952, Part 2, pp. 695-698.

It is important to recognize that the February 16 memorandum proposes to provide *a part* of these technical services to farmers through combining the SCS and the ACP. So long as only a part of these services—those primarily concerned with the engineering aspects of controlling soil erosion—are offered, public programs in this area will fail to come to grips with the fundamental adjustment problems in agriculture noted by Dr. Kellogg in the opening quotation of this chapter. At the same time, the SCS has maintained itself and contributed to its own development by emphasizing its uniqueness. In offering a program like the one here described, however, the USDA would meet the colleges of agriculture head on.

Hence, the fact of federalism looms as the major institutional obstacle to the successful development of a general agricultural conservation and adjustment program aimed at stimulating production, maximizing farm family living, and maintaining the resource base. There are two dilemmas in this situation.

The first dilemma is this: on the one hand, the intensive planning program as a means for showing the way to agricultural adjustment must be an integral part of the PMA program to be effective; on the other hand, this incorporation of the planning program into PMA can take place only with the greatest difficulty. The preceding chapter has shown the travail of the drafters of the February 16 order in "consolidating" SCS and PMA-ACP without "putting either on top of the other." Secretary Brannan acknowledged the possibility of a stalemate.[9] If one occurs,

". . . the chairman of the meeting [i.e., the county PMA chairman] would report that to the State. If the State people are not able to resolve the differences in the county—or are not able to point out to the county people that there is a common ground for understanding within the framework of the conservation program for the Nation, as generally defined by the agencies here in Washington—then we will have to ask the Assistant Secretary [read Under-Secretary McCormick] to send someone in to resolve the difference."

Note that these difficulties are foreseen in operating a program in which only SCS and ACP are involved. If, however,

9. House *Hearings,* Agric. Approp., fiscal 1952, pp. 695-96.

the recommendations of this chapter are followed, a local administration would be developed that would involve the colleges
of agriculture. For the colleges would either have to play vigorous roles in such a program or be prepared to withdraw from
the field.

The compelling nature of the dilemma further is exhibited
in considering the PMA program. Traditionally this program
has been aimed at securing parity for farmers. The methods have
been price supports, subventions, *and* production control. Operation of this program through the far-flung committee system
engenders in the minds of its administrators strong adherence
to its purposes. One of the purposes is to control production.
This purpose derives its strength from experience with the
failures of farm cooperatives as bargaining agents, unaided by
government, and even with the program of the Federal Farm
Board, which had federal funds but no powers to control production. When the belief that agricultural price support logically involves the ability to control production is reinforced by
participation in the operation of a control program, "control-
mindedness" develops. As John Dewey has remarked, "Thinking is secreted in the interstices of habit."

The present proposal rests upon the assumption that the rigid-
ities in the PMA approach can be removed by incorporating in
the program itself its own mechanism of adjustment—namely,
the intensive farm planning program to show the way so that
progressively more farmers can achieve a situation which requires the minimum of governmental support and subvention.
If this analysis carries the ring of probable truth, then the
dilemma is very real; for the incorporation of the one program
into the other presents formidable difficulties.

The second dilemma lies in the possible role of the colleges
of agriculture. If the program contemplated is established and
the colleges are pushed out of it (or retreat from participation
in it), their influence individually and collectively respecting
agricultural policy will certainly shrink. If the analysis in the
writer's article, "Programmatic Research in Agriculture," is
sound,[10] this development would be most unfortunate. For in-

---

10. *JFE,* May, 1947.

dependent analysis of farm policy by the colleges of agriculture provides a valuable counterweight against the concentration in Washington of governmental power over agriculture. How are the colleges to retain and strengthen their influence if they are outside the major stream of agricultural policy and administration? How are the colleges to participate in these without losing their independence?

A possible resolution of these dilemmas may be achieved through a joint formulation of a common program by the colleges and the USDA, to be followed by its shared administration by the same. Joint administration might be achieved, in part, by making the colleges of agriculture initially responsible for *all* the technical aspects of the intensive farm planning program in somewhat the same way that the SCS is now responsible for the *engineering* aspects. This recommendation would require transfer of SCS functions to other agencies in the USDA and to the colleges of agriculture, an action which would necessitate legislation.

The recommendation would be successfully carried out only if most colleges of agriculture whole-heartedly shared in the joint formulation and administration of the program. The colleges would have to accept an identification in farmers' eyes with federal programs—an identification which, outside the South, has been almost universally rejected by the colleges. The success of the recommendation would also depend on the effective establishment of intricate administrative procedures, separating initial responsibility for administration of technical experts from responsibility for administering price supports, commodity loans, and production control. On the other hand, the program would have to be so administered that the payments and supports of PMA would be used as levers to facilitate the adjustments indicated by the farm planning program. Otherwise, the intensive planning program would not become an integrated part of PMA activities, with its consequent effects upon the thinking of PMA personnel. At the same time, this degree of incorporation in PMA would hardly be effective unless PMA were given considerable authority over the actual operations of the technical planning program—for example, over the use of the various parts of the PMA program, as incentives to get production shifts in the direction indicated by the farm planning program.

Will the colleges accept some such program and administrative organization as this? Acceptance would certainly be reluctant. But what are the alternatives? One alternative is to let the present reorganization stand, thus incorporating SCS with PMA, but attempting through participation in the state and county administration, as established by the February 16, 1951 order, to replace the intensive farm planning along SCS lines by more rounded whole-farm planning. This is the most feasible present alternative. But its potential effectiveness is doubtful, and it is certainly not attractive to the colleges. A second alternative is to replace the Secretary's memorandum with the Hoover Commission's recommendations, as embodied in the current Aiken Bill, noted earlier. This alternative might be practicable in the event of a Republican victory in 1952; but it is noteworthy that the overwhelming Republican control in the 80th Congress failed to produce a measure along these lines. It should not be overlooked that a third possibility is for the colleges to be directed by the Congress to cooperate along lines laid down essentially by the USDA. Congressman Whitten has taken note that the February memorandum only invites, and does not require, the colleges to participate. "Whether or not some modification could be made so that he [the county agent] could be called on, that is a possibility." [11]

Deep involvement in administrative analysis may blind the eyes to the limitations of programmatic and administrative changes. Successful agricultural adjustment may depend upon the availability of agricultural credit, appropriate kinds of credit, and the willingness of farmers to contract debt; the laws and customs pertaining to tenure of agricultural land; and farm real-estate taxation.[12] It may also involve the development of marketing outlets and marketing facilities.

On a number of these matters, the development of effective

---

11. House *Hearings,* Agric. Approp., fiscal 1952, Part 1, p. 551. Cf. chap. ii, sec. 7 above.

12. Cf. the writer's "Land or People?" *op. cit.*

programs will require cooperation of independent public agencies, of agricultural cooperatives, and of private agencies. Under present circumstances, the provision of farm enlargement and farm improvement credit, for example, must largely depend on private banks. On other matters, state and local political and administrative action may be required. If tenure forms are the obstacles to the development of sound rural economies that they are often argued to be, the primary source for relief—over and above the educational approach to the problem—is the state legislature. If farm real estate taxation again becomes the obstacle to agricultural adjustment that it often was in the 1930's, then both state and local political administrative action may be involved. Administrative organization, even if supplemented by redefinition of national policy, is insufficient to cope with the range and variety of the problems encountered in agricultural adjustment.[13]

4. THE IMPORTANCE OF IDEOLOGY

Soil conservation is a cause. It lends itself to the elaboration of programs which are more than expedient actions to serve human and social interests—which are, indeed, highly moral and righteous. The true conservationist often considers anyone who disagrees with him not merely misinformed and wrong-headed, but wicked and possibly vicious. Further, moral righteousness is combined with a highly scientific approach in both the analysis and the solution of problems—an approach extremely attractive in a science-worshipping age.

Thus we get analyses which purport to show that "one hundred million acres have been ruined." And we are confronted with an unhappy picture of ourselves as greedily destroying the very foundations of our civilization. Then the Messiah appears and offers us a creed—"to use each acre according to its capabilities." This creed might easily be expanded into "from each acre according to its capabilities, to each according to its needs—and damn the expense!" Moreover, an irreproachably scientific

---

13. Cf. the writer's "Reflections on Agricultural Policy," *American Political Science Review,* October, 1948.

solution is offered—conservation surveys, land-use classification, and complete farm plans.

Likewise the PMA program is firmly rooted in a great moral imperative that "farmers deserve a fair share of the national income." This, too, employs a highly scientific analysis which is spelled out in the mysteries of the parity index. A "priesthood of parity" arises as guardian and administrator of the program designed to achieve economic justice for the farmer.

The political implications of this moral infusion of conservation and price supporting programs, coupled with their elaboration in scientific terms, are significant. An ideology is created which lends itself to elaboration in administrative codes that define the functions of those who serve the programs directly—and define these functions in ways that satisfy the human urge to feel that one's job is not just a way to make a living but is a means to the service of high moral purposes.[14] The realization of these purposes requires a high degree of conformance on part of affected individuals.

The resounding moral purposes of soil conservation and agricultural parity have another political significance in the mass support that they appear to elicit for their respective programs. Mass support is believed to come from persons who are not united by a direct interest in their maintenance but who respond favorably to the appeals. The parity program has many supporters among farmers who get very little direct benefits, since some 20 per cent of the farmers have traditionally received 60 per cent of the ACP payments and, supposedly, an equally disproportionate share of the other AAA-PMA benefits, such as parity payments (to 1942) and commodity loans. Nevertheless, parity for farmers is believed to have heavy public support, in and out of farm circles, as an ideal. By the same token, wide support by persons not directly concerned as farm operators has apparently been engendered for soil conservation programs by horrendous pictures of the "farms that washed away" and stories of "continents sliding to ruin."

The magnitude of this mass support can only be determined by political events; but it is an element in all political calcula-

---

14. For further analysis, see "Reflections on Agricultural Policy," *op. cit.*

tions about conservation and adjustment policy. Persons whose political interests would dictate sharp opposition to the SCS and PMA programs are careful to modify their attacks in order to avoid being characterized as enemies either of soil conservation or parity for agriculture.

The possibility is now open for someone of sufficient genius to combine the high moral purposes of both soil conservation and parity for agriculture into an ideology which will unite and solidify the mass support of both camps. If this trick can be turned, it will constitute a major political stroke.

The ideological content of soil conservation and adjustment programs, together with the mass support that they engender, must be examined in another light. Inherent in both programs is the concept of detailed and continuous planning of individual farm operations. This planning can be vindicated in part by circumstances. If economic instability in agriculture causes farm prices to fall precipitately, price supports become effective. But price supports are coupled with production control. For a number of years culminating in 1942 we had production control through marketing quotas on cotton, wheat, tobacco, and peanuts, and, through acreage allotments, on corn.

Since the war, with the exception of tobacco, we have had marketing quotas only upon cotton and only in one year (1950). Present needs are for all-out farm production; if the cold war gets hot, these needs will be greatly sharpened. Under these circumstances, production control can be set aside. But the agricultural production picture can change rapidly. In the long run, and even the middle run, falling agricultural prices may again call price supports, production control, and the detailed and continuous regulation of farms into play.

The soil conservation approach also implies detailed farm planning. Conservation farm plans have now been prepared for perhaps 15 to 20 per cent of the farms in this country. It is true that these plans at present have no coercion behind them. Nevertheless, coercion has been implicit in much thinking about soil conservation. Chief Bennett of the SCS [15] has foreseen the "coming technological revolution on the land." He writes that:

---

15. From its inception to Nov. 15, 1951.

". . . too much of the land traditionally has been in the hands of the untutored and the inept . . . Under the names of peasant, farmer, rustic, and country fellow, these individuals have been synonymous, for generations, with all that is naive, uneducated, and backward . . .

"In the long run, the overwhelming urge of mankind for survival will dictate that every remaining productive acre be handled in such a way that it will continue to produce indefinitely. . . .

"For these and other reasons, the application of land technology will spread around the world, either voluntarily or by decree . . .

"Development of land and water resources for agriculture, as by drainage and irrigation, will be governed primarily by factual, technological elements of land-use and land maintenance rather than by promotional, exploitive, or political standards. . . .

". . . It is not impossible that the prospective farmer of the future will be required to satisfy society that he is qualified by training and experience to take on the trusteeship of a piece of productive land." [16]

If the SCS, governed by such ideas, can be thoroughly integrated with the PMA program, with its great stress upon production control, the organization will be prepared for a managed agriculture in the United States—if conditions for a managed agriculture again become favorable. In light of this possibility, let us examine how the colleges might respond to Secretary Brannan's invitation to participate in the "agricultural resource conservation" activities of the USDA. The questions are: to what ends and with what means will the colleges participate?

The writer suggests that the colleges cannot meet the challenge of the ideals of the achievement of parity and the handling of each acre according to its capabilities without offering an ideal of their own. What kind of ideal can be offered? It ought to be clear by now that the elimination of waste in government is not sufficient. As Paul Appleby has remarked: "To a person of liberal convictions, liberal administration is more efficient; for a conservative the opposite is true." [17] Nor can the colleges successfully argue the virtue of decentralization in their favor. What could be more decentralized than soil conservation districts—the "most local of local institutions"? For that matter,

16. "Development of Natural Resources: The Coming Technological Revolution on the Land," *Science,* January, 1947; cf. the consideration in *Farm Policy Forum,* October, 1948, and the writer's comments thereon.
17. *Policy and Administration, op. cit.* p. 130.

what could be more local than the community elections of PMA committeemen?

The ideal of the educational approach, long sponsored by the colleges, is very attractive to professional educators. It stresses self-help and self-determination. It puts the emphasis in agricultural programs upon building the kind of self-reliance in farmer citizens that may carry over with good effect into all sorts of decisions which these same citizens are called upon to help make in this exacting world. Nevertheless, the idea of education for its own sake is a pallid abstraction unless it is given some concrete content in terms of a goal which is meaningful in the life experience of citizens.

Such content can be provided by asserting the ideal goal of *improved farm family living on a conservation base.*[18] This conception can challenge directly the ideals of farm parity and conservation of the land. Since it embraces both, it cannot be effectively criticized as denying either of the others. Yet it is capable of being made very concrete and real in terms of better diets, better instruments of production, more economic security, and greater self-confidence for farm families. Furthermore, the means to crystallizing this ideal in visible "good works" are in the hands of the colleges—in the programs of farm and home planning and community development that several state extension services have been shaping up in recent years.

Numerous obstacles exist, however, to the effective enunciation and prosecution of this kind of ideal by the colleges of agriculture. Many colleges are conservative, set in their ways, and determined in their extension services to continue in their single-practice approach—for example, to improve farm breeding herds, or to establish better practices of caring for livestock, or to further the adoption of hybrid corn, or to stimulate shifts to improve pastures, etc., etc. All these improvements may be admirable in themselves, but as single practices they fall short of the integration of what the college has to offer which is implied in the balanced farm and home planning program. Furthermore,

18. That this idea is by no means a monopoly of the Land-Grant Colleges may be seen, for example, by referring to the Annual Report of Secretary Charles F. Brannan for 1950, "Family Farm Policy Review," pp. 33-36.

colleges are subject to vigorous and effective demands by well-organized, special-purpose groups. It is difficult for various departments of the colleges which are effectively integrated with various clientele groups to acknowledge the importance of over-all strategy for the college in developing and implementing a common program designed to improve farm family living on a conservation base. Further, individual colleges are very much entities in themselves and are often little less jealous of their fellow colleges than they are of Washington; this situation makes difficult the joint action essential to the success of the present proposal. It may be significant, however, that a new generation of college administrators is rapidly emerging in place of those who came to maturity before the New Deal, and whose fundamental political views were often conditioned by deep desires for an impossible return to something like the 1920's.

The ideal of "improved farm family living on a conservation base" has implications which may disturb the equanimity of many college officials. In the first place, it requires an orientation to all farmers and not merely the commercial farmers. Because they are members of educational institutions, college personnel find a continuing challenge in non-commercial farmers. To reach these farmers, however, is difficult, partly because the resources of the colleges are already heavily committed in what they are doing now; partly because there are unsolved methodological problems in reaching farmers who are extraordinarily diffident, whose education is frequently low, who are physically less inaccessible, and who are not motivated in the same way that both college officials and commercial farmers are; and partly (it must be admitted) because some college personnel tend to believe that not much can be done with these rural people who are on the fringes of society.

In the second place, if the colleges are going to get behind "the immediate symptoms and find the cause" of erosion in the "deep maladjustments between the soil and the farming system," this will require probing into "unstable economic conditions, bad tenure relationships, over-crowded land," and the rest of Dr. Kellogg's list. The report of the college Committee on Post-War Agricultural Policy fully acknowledged these dimensions of the problem.[19] But the gap between acknowledgment and a systematic attack upon these fundamental maladjustments is difficult to close. One of the great strengths of the SCS program has been precisely its glossing over of such difficulties. To attack rural poverty, inadequate credit facilities, and present tenure relationships will often mean to challenge powerful vested interests. Whether publicly supported educational and research institutions can mount an attack like this remains to be seen. So far they have not done it.

Finally, the ideal goal of improved farm family living is, paradoxically enough, concrete and specific, yet also vague and general. It is concrete in that it can be presented in terms of real increases in productivity and real gains in the ability of farmers to manage their resources and control their environment. It is specific in given situations in which typical farms can be analyzed. At the same time, it is general in that nothing more than the most-overall objectives and methods can be developed nationally or even regionally. The real test lies in the adaptations at the farm level where local differentiations require imaginative variations in cropping systems, soil management, the development of lines of credit, the adjustment of tenure, the employment of crop insurance, and the like.

Furthermore, the ideal has a certain vagueness and generality. If it is to be reflected in real accomplishments in the rural social scene, it will have to be accepted by the pattern of social and political groups and interests therein. In the process, these groups and interests may and probably will undergo change; but in a free society, they will not disappear. In an even more ultimate way, the ideal cannot be made viable by the expertness of technicians; it can only become viable through being taken over by farm families—a process that will require its adaptation in terms of their general ways of living and their outlook upon the purposes of life.

In sum, the great strength of the ACP and SCS programs teaches the importance of defining goals in ideal terms. Both programs operate toward simple objectives—parity for agriculture and the use of each acre within its capabilities, respectively.

---

19. See above, chap ii, sec. 3.

The history of mass political movements reveals the paramount importance of simple, concrete, intelligible goals by which all actions and eventually all thoughts can be measured, accepted, elevated, enshrined—or rejected and suppressed. In the science-worshipping modern world it greatly strengthens such goals if they can be described as "scientific." Both the drive for price supports and for soil conservation are mass movements; both gain strength from oversimplification of objectives; both have developed simple criteria by which the faithful are easily distinguished from the heretics; both are elaborately "scientific." [20]

In contrast, the proposals for orientating toward improved farm family living are deliberately general, vague, and open-ended. This goal cannot be defended "scientifically" in the simple terms that its rivals are. If (for the sake of the argument) we grant that the capabilities and limitations of each acre can really be "scientifically" ascertained, who will pretend to calculate the capabilities and limitations of human beings? Indeed, the program proposed invites dissension; it incorporates factionalism and confesses itself often unable to tell the sheep from the

---

20. This statement should not be read as an indictment of individuals involved; it is essential to lift our political analyses to the level of analyzing processes, institutions, and values—as these influence and are influenced by individuals and groups. It is argued that the federal programs, SCS and ACP, separately or in combination, tend to have the characteristics noted. It is further argued that the continuous concern of administrators, farm leaders, and farmers with programs so oriented tends to produce habitual responses and conceptions which favor the simple "scientific," inexorably right goal. It is finally argued that these habitual responses and conceptions may be carried over into other fields—may contribute to attitudes that answers to complex political problems can always be scientifically found and simply expressed, that positions can be reached so clearly that what is good and what is bad will be self-evident. Then it can truly be said that "he who is not with us is against us." In stressing the role of the colleges of agriculture to broaden and generalize the goals of farm policy in this field—to insist on the human orientation of this policy, even at the expense of simplicity and clarity with respect to what ought to be done—the writer does not imply that the college folk are more virtuous than federal administrators. Rather, he implies that this breadth of purpose is something which the colleges can hardly escape attempting to express, by virtue of their orientation as *educational* institutions. In contrast, the breadth of purpose here advocated is all but impossible for certain federal agencies to incorporate by themselves, given their orientation to the program objectives which they have, and given the partial approach which they are charged to employ.

goats among the warring factions. It invites attention to conflicts
between owners and tenants, debtors and creditors; it stirs up
differences and goads antagonists. But it does none of these
things in the spirit of the revealed truth; rather the ideal that
it offers is man-conceived, man-directed, man-criticized, man-
changed. The definition and provision of this kind of ideal is full
of difficulties. But make no mistake, we will have ideals. The
question is whether they will be simple, hard and fast, inex-
orable, and (in the end) intolerant—or whether they will be
flexible, full of difficulty, productive of compromises and expedi-
encies, and always unattainable. It is vital to recognize that
this kind of alternative, which pervades much modern politics,
manifests itself in agricultural policy.

CHAPTER XV

General Political Implications

I. FOR THE CONSTITUTIONAL SYSTEM

Constitutionalism as used in the West means limited government. The constitution defines the scope of governmental power, confines somewhat the action of the government, and sets some limits to public action which the government of the day (or the administration) cannot ordinarily overstep. Sometimes these grants of, and limitations on, power are set down in writing; sometimes they are contained in bundles of precedents and constitutional usages. Always (it is believed) the vitality of the constitution rests upon its acceptance by a significant number of the citizens concerned who have some grasp of what the constitution means, who are responsive to charges that it is being violated, and who insist that it be observed.

The study of politics, however, is only partly concerned with the limitation of power; it must also deal with the organization of sufficient power. Sufficient for what? There the debate begins. To keep order (but does this mean to break strikes?). To provide for the common defense (but who is the enemy, how imminent the danger, how best to ward it off?). To provide for the general welfare (to support farm prices? to require minimum wages? to provide free education? medical care?). So politics embraces both the organization of power and its control. Many (including the writer) believe that the problem of politics will never be finally solved. Nevertheless, some working solution has to be found for it month by month and year by year in constitutional governments, at least—if they are to remain constitutional.

One way to examine the political problem is to study what is happening to the governmental arrangements in a given polity. Thus the constitutional system in the United States includes the separation of powers, checks and balances, the rule of law, the bill of rights, and federalism. Since policy for agriculture is one of the major constituents of public policy in the United States, one may ask: What effect does the politics of agriculture have on the American constitutional system? [1]

In this book, however, it is only appropriate to ask: What are the effects of the soil conservation phase of agricultural politics on the constitutional system? The major effect of this phase of politics is upon federalism. [2] Much of the instant controversy is over centralization or decentralization of power. Thus to enact the present Aiken Bill or the recommendations for agriculture of the Hoover Commission would decentralize power to the states and strengthen both the colleges of agriculture and the Farm Bureau. On the other hand, successful consummation of the reorganization of February, 1951, will probably tend toward the centralization of real political power.

---

1. For a preliminary essay, see Charles M. Hardin, "The Politics of Agriculture in the United States," *Journal of Farm Economics*, Nov., 1950.

2. A general study of the politics of agriculture would emphasize its effect upon the separation of powers and checks and balances. This would be especially true if one studied agricultural price policy, in which the relationships between President and Congress are apparent in issue after issue. The conservation phase has some relevance for this matter, of course, since conservation and price policy are closely related; but the significance of conservation policy here should not be stretched too far. The same can be said for the rule of law. General agricultural politics have raised important questions to the Supreme Court from time to time. (One might begin with *Fletcher* v. *Peck* 6 Cranch 87 [1810] and come down to *Wickard* v. *Filburn* 317 U.S. 111 [1942]). It is also significant for the development of administrative regulation and adjudication, both of which have been related through Supreme Court decisions to the general legal and political processes. (*The St. Joseph Stockyards Co.* v. *U.S.* 298 U.S. 38 [1936]; the Morgan Cases, summarized in *U.S.* v. *Morgan* 313 U.S. 409 [1941]). But the politics of soil conservation has not contributed significantly here, although it might if land-use regulations were used vigorously by soil conservation districts. Cf. P. M. Glick, "The Soil and the Law," in *Soils and Men*, Yearbook, USDA, 1938, and chap. v, sec. 1 (above).

Analysis of the issue has been pressed.[3] The present concern is to point up the significance for American federalism. Political judgments on centralization versus decentralization will reflect group interests. So long as soil conservation remains linked with price supports and production control, the working answer will probably continue to be found in some uneasy combination of federal and state administration. As participants debate and act on these matters, they may profitably recall John Marshall's statement when he was developing the doctrine of implied powers. "In considering this question, then, we must never forget, that it is a *constitution* we are expounding." As Marshall well knew, however, the political question cannot be confined to formal constitutional aspects.

2. GROUP POLITICS

Much of this book has emphasized the group process of policy formation and execution. The significance of the various groups involved for the internal politics of agriculture hardly needs recapitulation. But some notice is required respecting more general political issues involved. Examination of soil conservation policy underlines the tendency for "private" groups to emerge and grow strong through their association with public agencies. The alliance between the Extension Service and the Farm Bureau is in point as is that between the SCS and the National Association of Soil Conservation Districts. The PMA has developed a strong farm organization in its committee systems. It is of some importance to add further demonstration of the tendency of organized group influence to parallel the growth of public administration. But there are more general political issues in this development.

First, the creation of the PMA committees and the formation of a career ladder for farmer-bureaucracy represents a considerable departure in public policy. One may acknowledge the apparently inevitable tendency of administrative organization to stimulate the growth of pressure groups. Nevertheless, these

3. Chapter xiv, above, and Charles M. Hardin, "Programmatic Research and Agricultural Policy," *Journal of Farm Economics,* May, 1947.

groups remain separate organizations, essentially "private" in
nature. In contrast, the PMA organization tends to speak for
farmers as a social class, and to speak with an authenticity which
is enhanced by the fact that the broad bottom of the PMA
pyramid rests upon local elections. Furthermore, the PMA organization is directly financed by Government, including the
payment of per diems to county and community committeemen
for the days that they work. The AAA and subsequently the
PMA have understandably grown to become the primary challenge to the American Farm Bureau Federation respecting
which shall constitute the major organized voice in agricultural
politics. Whether the preservation and further strengthening
of the PMA organization is sound public policy is largely a
matter of political judgment—assuming that, at this late date,
there is any choice in the matter.

The writer's judgment would be that the retention of the
present PMA committee system is not sound public policy. This
judgment assumes that government should not directly create
and finance an organization of farmers. To do so is to emphasize
the distinctiveness of farmers as a political class. Carried further,
the PMA organization may lead to syndicalism in agriculture.
By this is meant that the formulation and administration of agricultural policy would be devolved upon farmers as organized by
government itself. Finally, the PMA organization tends to become "the voice of agriculture" in a way that private farm organizations cannot match. Theoretically, PMA embraces and
represents all farmers in every agricultural county and subdivi-
sion. Not even the Farm Bureau can match this claim. If it is
urged that the Farm Bureau has come off rather well in its tilts
with PMA, the reply can be made that PMA has been fighting
under adverse circumstances since 1945, with production control
virtually non-existent. In view of the possible reintroduction of
production control, the writer would recommend shifting from
election to appointment of all PMA committeemen.[4] This shift

4. Appointments of county and community committeemen might be made
from panels of nominees prepared by general farm organizations, soil conservation district boards, extension organizations, and commodity organizations which are interested in the PMA program.

would preserve the essential values of the committee system while deflating PMA's political significance.

Second, however, one cannot make this recommendation for PMA without examining its effect upon the Farm Bureau-PMA rivalry. The writer would make the PMA recommendation contingent upon the legal separation of Extension from the Farm Bureau, as suggested in Chapter III. This is consistent with the principle that when a series of inter-related issues present themselves, a general settlement should be worked out. It is assumed that, if PMA committees are shifted from election to appointment and if Farm Bureau and Extension are legally separated, enough colleges of agriculture will dissociate themselves in fact from the Farm Bureau so that a significant change in the configuration of power will have been accomplished. Many of the colleges have become inherently strong enough to achieve separation if they want to. The present threat which they read into the PMA's activities drives them to a closer union with the Farm Bureau. If this threat can be reduced, the colleges will be prompted by the nature of their function to dissociate themselves.

A third question of general political significance concerns the orientation of farm organizations. It is true that the so-called general farm organizations, the Grange, the Farmers Union, and the Farm Bureau, have strong commodity interests. The primary concern of the Farmers Union is wheat and, of the Grange, dairy products. The Farm Bureau has been called a "union of cotton and corn." Nevertheless, all three organizations are typically interested in the entire range of agricultural policy as well as in many other public policies. (Examination of their resolutions as well as the articles in their official journals will bear this out.) All three organizations habitually testify before Congress on all major agricultural issues and many others besides. The same statements cannot be made of special purpose organizations in agriculture, whether organized by commodities or in some other manner. These organizations profit from the very narrowness of their objectives. They can invest all their resources in influencing the determination of those issues in which they are vitally concerned.

Hearings on the Hope Bill in March and May, 1948, demonstrate how well narrow-purposed groups can be marshalled to support measures in which they are intensely interested. Thirty-four witnesses appeared in March; 21 were representatives of state associations of soil conservation district supervisors or of the National Association or were in some way associated with soil conservation districts. A representative of the Mississippi Valley Association also supported similar points of view. The Farm Bureau was represented by six witnesses, the Grange by two, the National Farmers Union by one. Two representatives of land-grant colleges appeared. Assistant Secretary (now Secretary) Brannan of the Department of Agriculture testified. In the May hearings, omitting both those who spoke to provisions of the Hope Bill touching the Department of the Interior and also several Congressmen who appeared, there were 59 witnesses. Of these, 34 were associated with soil conservation districts or associations of district supervisors. This time the Farm Bureau got out its opposition in greater force, counting 13 witnesses. The Grange again had two representatives and the National Farmers Union had one. One man appeared from a land-grant college. Undersecretary Dodd commented for the Department of Agriculture. Six witnesses came in, apparently with the stimulation of the Production and Marketing Administration, the PMA, to oppose the Hope Bill.

In contrast, the Washington hearings in 1948 on the Aiken Bill convened the general farm organizations in force but called out only President Kent Leavitt of the National Association of Soil Conservation Districts.[5] Title II of the Aiken Bill dealt with agricultural price policy in which the organizations concerned primarily with soil conservation are less interested. Furthermore, the National Association of Soil Conservation Districts made no appearance in the hearings on the "General Farm Program" in the first session of the 81st Congress.[6]

Much agricultural politics stimulates the aggressive action of organized groups with narrow purposes. The question is, Do

5. *Hearings*, S. 2318, 80th Cong., 2nd Sess.
6. Hearings before a Special Subcommittee of the House Committee on Agriculture, Serial R, Part 3, Testimony of Farm Organizations, and Part 5, Testimony of Producer Groups and the Congress.

general farm organizations with their rather comprehensive orientation toward agricultural and related policies provide broader political education for their officers and members than groups with more narrow and special interests, such as interest in particular commodities or in some policy like soil conservation or rural electrification? If so, Does this broader political education contribute to the service of the national interest or the general welfare? The writer believes that these questions are not subject to "scientific" examination, at least as such examination is often understood. But as a matter of judgment, the writer would tentatively answer both questions in the affirmative. This judgment does not require one to deprecate the emergence of special purpose groups; but it supports efforts to develop general agricultural policy in a manner which requires that the several component parts of that policy be considered in terms of their mutual interrelations. Examples are the Aiken Bill in the 80th Congress, the several reports prepared by the USDA on "Long-Range Agricultural Policy" in 1947, or the 1944 Report of the Committee of the Association of Land-Grant Colleges and Universities on *Post-War Agricultural Policy*. By the same token, the writer would also favor (not exclusively, but on balance) the general farm organization over the special purpose association.

3. POLITICS AND ADMINISTRATION

Pendleton Herring quotes the Supreme Court: "The theory of our government state and national is opposed to the deposit of unlimited power anywhere," [7] and adds a metaphor of his own:

"Power must be finally identified with no one class or group; it must be handled like a loving cup and passed about lest one of the company grow drunk."

When organized groups press for favorable laws and administrative agencies to carry them out in the American system, they frequently succeed in creating new nuclei of power. Administrative agencies thus created often stimulate the further organiza-

---

7. *The Politics of Democracy, op. cit.,* p. 46.

tion of groups among their clientele. This action, in turn, often activates other groups opposed to the policy in question or suspicious, at least, of the organized power which it has created. The political process is enriched. Many examples appear in the foregoing chapters.

One effect is that administrative agencies become part of the representative process of government. Who speaks for farmers? Among others, the PMA, the SCS and the National Association of Soil Conservation Districts, Deans of Colleges of Agriculture, and Extension Directors speak for farmers. Who should represent farmers? This question is answered with variations in accordance with the group interests concerned. Meanwhile, the fact of representation goes on; interests will employ any and all spokesmen who have access [8] to the Secretary of Agriculture, strategic Congressmen, and others who figure in making policy. The representative process has also been enriched.

Another effect of the link between politics and administration is to create obstacles to the development of general policy. When administrative agencies join hands with interest groups, they frequently gain considerable independence from the general direction of the department in which they are located as well as from the more general coordinating agencies like the Bureau of the Budget.[9] Examples in the soil conservation area of policy include the difficulties experienced by the land-use planning program, 1938–1942, by the Department of Agriculture in coordinating soil conservation administration in 1940–1950, and by the Secretary of Agriculture in developing a comprehensive plan for the Missouri Valley since 1949.

If freedom to organize and press political demands exists, integration of the programs achieved by the several interests will be largely the result of compromise and accommodation. Can we improve somewhat the processes of policy formation so that those responsible at the more general levels of government for examining group claims in light of the "public interest" are in

8. For the concept of access, see David B. Truman, *op. cit.*

9. For the case of the civil works function of the Department of the Army, see Arthur Maass, *Muddy Waters,* Harvard University Press, 1951. For an example in agriculture, see Charles M. Hardin, "The Tobacco Program: Exception or Portent?" *Journal of Farm Economics,* Nov., 1946.

stronger position to influence the shape of the final decisions? To draw a leaf from Edmund Burke, can we improve our governmental arrangements so that the discretionary powers of executives shall be exercised "upon public principles and national grounds, and not on the likings or prejudices, the intrigues or policies, of a court"? [10]

Can we do this—or should we even raise the question? So long as the important values of free speech and free association continue to be realized, is this not enough? Properly to explore these matters is beyond the scope of this work. It should be emphasized, however, that Secretaries of Agriculture are regularly confronted by the claims of some bureaus which are all but independent. Yet it is also clear that strong political forces oppose vesting sufficient power in the Secretary fully to coordinate such bureaus.

At the same time, a similar issue emerges at the state college level. The analogy is not perfect because the colleges are essentially research and educational organizations within which effective coordination can be had only at the price of stultifying these functions. Yet colleges of agriculture might take a "programmatic view" of agricultural policy and some of them have; [11] but the colleges, too, are plagued by the politics of administration. If a department of dairy husbandry becomes closely interlocked with the dairy interests it serves (to take one example among several), and if these interests (including the dairy husbandry department itself) begin to take a jaundiced view of the activities of the "damned economists" in "turning a perfectly good cow college into a tax-supported blueprint of Harvard University"—what has happened to the general outlook, the universal view, of the college?

So politics and administration are combined at various levels and with various consequences. The problem invites nice, full, and continuous analysis which is adapted to the numerous situations involved. The present book is intended to contribute to an understanding of these problems in the area on which it focuses;

10. Quoted in John M. Gaus, *Reflections on Public Administration,* University of Alabama Press (1947), p. 14; see this source generally.

11. Cf. Charles M. Hardin, "Programmatic Research and Agricultural Policy," *Journal of Farm Economics,* May, 1947.

but it also serves to point up the nature of problems which are manifested in many other political situations.

4. PARTISAN POLITICS

In analyzing the relationship of PMA to Democratic politics, the writer insisted that a complementary examination be made of the Republican orientation of state Farm Bureaus and Extension Services in the Midwest. If both inquiries can be made together, some of the tendencies toward mutual vilification can be mitigated. Rather, attention can be focused on political issues. What is the role of political parties? What is their relationship to pressure groups?

The analysis can be pressed a little further. Consider the Brannan Plan as an effort to make farm policy a partisan issue. If most farm leaders deplore the Brannan Plan, both in content and in manner of formulation, they must grant that the plan broke farm policy out of the hands of the "insiders" in agriculture and made it the subject of a general—and quite profound—debate. The debate dealt not only with economics but with the way farm policy is made. Once the Brannan Plan was introduced, farm leaders evinced an unprecedented interest in the role of the parties, the nature of representation, and related political questions. This interest opens the way for suggesting to persons in agriculture that political parties play a role to which pressure groups cannot aspire. Only parties provide citizens with the opportunity to substitute one government for another. Parties thus safeguard an essential democratic principle.[12]

One can suggest to farm leaders that, just as the parties police each other, the pressure groups have an interest in policing the parties—and an obligation to the same end. Recognition of its own interest should counsel organized agriculture to do what it can to counter the unwholesome tendencies in our society for partisan opposition to turn upon questions of loyalty and patriotism. Organized agriculture, in its own interest, can join with

---

12. Cf. Pendleton Herring, *The Politics of Democracy, op. cit.,* and E. E. Schattschneider's penetrating observation that "Democracy is not to be found *in* the parties but *between* the parties." *Party Government,* Farrar and Rinehart, New York (1941).

other groups in insisting that both parties keep their mutual accusations within certain bounds. Beyond questions of interest, organized agriculture has a moral obligation so to act. This is a role that agricultural pressure groups are well fitted to play because their membership is divided between the two major parties.[13]

5. THE DRIVE FOR POWER

Hans J. Morgenthau declares that politics is not a science but an art, that any political analysis must begin with power, and that the elimination of the destructiveness of power politics requires "rational faculties . . . which are different from, and superior to, the reason of the scientific age." What is needed is "not the rationality of the engineer, but the wisdom and moral strength of the statesman." [14] The researches of the present writer have led him to much the same conclusion.

Elsewhere, however, Professor Morgenthau seeks to explain the phenomenon of modern nationalism as follows: [15]

"We have learned from our discussion of the ideologies of international policies that in the mind of the individual the aspirations for power of others bears the stigma of immorality. While this moral depreciation has one of its roots in the desire of the prospective victim of the power of others to defend his freedom against this threat, the other root stems from the attempt of society as a whole to suppress and keep in bounds individual aspirations for power. Society has established a network of rules of conduct and institutional devices for controlling individual power drives. These rules and devices either divert individual power drives into channels where they cannot endanger society, or else they weaken them or suppress them alto-

---

13. A common resolution by the Grange, the National Farmers Union, The American Farm Bureau Federation, and the National Council of Farm Cooperatives was recorded in favor of the display of the United Nations flag beside the flag of the United States on United Nation's day—a ceremony that had been condemned by what Albert Goss of the Grange called the " 'smear tactics' of the national heads of the VFW and the DAR and the McCormick newspaper interests . . ." *National Grange Monthly*, Nov., 1950, pp. 4, 8.

14. *Scientific Man versus Power Politics*, University of Chicago Press (1946), pp. 9-10.

15. *Politics Among Nations*, Knopf, New York (1948) p. 74.

gether. Law, ethics, and mores, innumerable social institutions and arrangements such as competitive examinations, election contests, sports, social clubs, and fraternal organizations—all serve that purpose.

"In consequence, most people are unable to satisfy their desire for power within the national community. . . . Not being able to find full satisfaction of their desire for power within the national boundaries, the people project those unsatisfied aspirations onto the international scene. There they find vicarious satisfaction in identification with the power drives of the nation. . . ."

Without detracting from the soundness of Morgenthau's general position, the present book suggests some modification in these conclusions. The politics of soil conservation is only one of many areas of domestic politics in which opportunities are multiplied for many people to work off their aggressions and to fulfill their desires for a share in the organized power and influence in this country. The issues, agencies, and interests involved in numberless controversies provide a multitude of people with the opportunity to "get into the act." The effect is fortunate if one believes that the drive for power is one of the indispensable dynamics of a free society as well as a component of that individualism of which the ethics of democracy requires considerable recognition.

Appendix—State Administration
of National Soil Conservation Programs

This appendix is prompted by the submission in 1952 of a plan by Mississippi for state administration of the Agricultural Conservation Program of the Production and Marketing Administration. A provision of the Soil Conservation and Domestic Allotment Act of 1936 thus became active for the first time. That act provided for administration of the program by agencies designated by the state and approved by the Secretary of the USDA according to mutually acceptable plans.[1] Appropriations were to be apportioned among states as grants-in-aid. USDA administration was to continue until the states qualified but was to terminate in two years. Twenty-four states have passed enabling laws; but in the absence of state plans for administration, Congress has granted several extensions of the termination date. The USDA has made repeated efforts to have Congress eliminate the provision for state plans. But the Senate Committee on Agriculture and Forestry has favorably reported a bill which merely extends USDA administration until 1955. (S. 2659 as reported with amendments, Senate Report No. 1305, 82nd Cong., 2nd Sess.).

The American Farm Bureau Federation has supported extensions of the terminal date for USDA administration but has opposed

---

1. The provision for state administration may have been in anticipation of a possible invalidation by the Supreme Court of direct federal aids to agriculture.

elimination of the provisions for eventual state administration. The AFBF is currently stimulating the submission of state plans. The March, 1952 meeting of Southern Farm Bureau state presidents agreed to work on this matter in each of their states, and Midwestern state presidents were slated to consider the matter.

If grants-in-aid and state administration of ACP replace the present mode of operation under the 1936 Act, the USDA will be in a strong position relative to state administering agencies. The Secretary of Agriculture must approve the designated state agency. The state plan must provide such methods of administration and participation of committees or associations of farmers as the Secretary finds necessary to effective administration. The Secretary must require reports on the administration of state plans and may require measures to assure the correctness and verification of reports. There appears to be no *legal* reason to prevent the Secretary from stationing employees in the states to verify state reports, although he may find this action *politically* impracticable. The Secretary also controls the scheduling of funds to the states and thereby could rather effectively influence the budgetary procedure of the state agencies concerned. The Secretary may cut off funds to any state in which there has been a "substantial failure" to carry out the plan or in which the plan fails to further the objectives of the law. In the Smith-Lever, Hatch and other Acts for grants-in-aid for agricultural research and extension, there are provisions for the USDA to withhold grants to states. But states have a statutory right to appeal to Congress before such withholding becomes final. No such provision appears in the Act of 1936 (Act of Feb. 29, 1936, ch. 104 Sec. 1, 49 Stat. 1148, as amended).

The agitation for submission of state plans raises serious questions. If colleges of agriculture are to be designated state agencies, they will find themselves in a very different relationship to the USDA from what they have commonly known. Most of the colleges traditionally have been loath to accept responsibility for administering federal "action" programs. Yet if the colleges do administer ACP funds, it is difficult to see how financial accountability can be maintained without rather strict administrative controls from Washington. But some other agencies, such as state departments of agriculture, may be designated. Very few state departments of agriculture now have anything like the field organization which would be necessary to administer ACP funds to individual farmers. If new state agencies are created (and there is some talk of it), the relationship of such agencies to colleges of agriculture will pose serious problems. Will such agencies move to create Extension Services of their own? Further, those desirous of reducing and eventually eliminating the ACP payments may well ponder the effect of transferring these payments to the states as grants-in-aid. The history of such grants indicates that they are exceedingly hard to reduce. With all the difficulties of reducing present ACP funds, such funds are probably more vulnerable now than they would be if they became grants-in-aid. In addition to the political backing comparable to that now enjoyed by the ACP funds, such grants-in-aid would presumably have the powerful support of state governments.

Finally, there is some indication that the proponents of state administration of the ACP funds are dissatisfied with the present federal law (the Act of 1936). If wholesale revision is demanded, will the question be enlarged to include re-examination of all existing legislation for agricultural grants-in-aid? Are colleges of agriculture anxious for such re-examination now and in this context? Some interpret the political trends as favorable to decentralization, and they express no fear that the reopening of a large part of agricultural legislation will produce results which they neither anticipate nor desire. It is well to recall, however, that interpretations of political trends are notoriously unreliable; the most recent example was in 1948.

A Note on Abbreviations and Terms

AAA—Agricultural Adjustment Administration (occasionally referred to as the Triple A); became the Production and Marketing Administration (PMA) in 1945.

ACP—Agricultural Conservation Program of the AAA to 1945, subsequently of the PMA.

AFBF—American Farm Bureau Federation; sometimes referred to as the Farm Bureau.

BAE—Bureau of Agricultural Economics.

CCC—Commodity Credit Corporation.

FHA—Farmers Home Administration, before 1946, the Farm Security Administration.

FSA—Farm Security Administration.

MFA—Missouri Farmers Association.

NASCD—National Association of Soil Conservation Districts.

NFU—National Farmers Union.

PMA—Production and Marketing Administration, replaced the AAA in 1945.

SCS—Soil Conservation Service.

USDA—United States Department of Agriculture.

APSR—American Political Science Review.

JFE—Journal of Farm Economics.

PAR—Public Administration Review.

The term *colleges of agriculture* or sometimes merely *colleges* refers to colleges or schools of agriculture which are part of Land Grant Colleges or Universities. The term *Extension* usually refers to the Extension Services of colleges of agriculture in the 48 states; occasionally it refers to the Cooperative Federal-State Extension Service. *Farm Bureau* is used to designate particular state Farm Bureaus, the state and American Farm Bureaus taken together, and occasionally the American Farm Bureau Federation. It is believed that these various connotations will be clear in the context and that the usage in this book reflects the common employment of these terms.

Acknowledgments

Professional debts accumulate, and my obligations to fellow political scientists are incompletely expressed in footnotes. Edward C. Banfield, Charles R. Cherington, John M. Gaus, and W. Robert Parks have read parts of the manuscript at various stages, and I have profited from their comments. I am particularly glad to thank Norman I. Wengert who, in addition to constructive counsel on what I have written, supplied thoughtful and informative chapters on the Tennessee Valley Authority for an earlier manuscript, chapters which unfortunately had to be eliminated as the book was cut down and re-oriented. Among agricultural economists, my debts are especially heavy to John D. Black and T. W. Schultz and considerable to many others. My thanks are due to a host of public servants of agriculture at all levels of government, many farm organization officials, and farmers. The insights and interest of M. L. Wilson have always been most helpful, and I am glad that he has consented to write a foreword. Any errors of fact or judgment in the book are, of course, my responsibility.

I wish to acknowledge the generous assistance of the Social Science Research Committee of the University of Chicago in supporting some of the research, all the typing, and the publication of this book. The editorial advice of Jeremiah Kaplan is appreciated. The encouragement and assistance of my wife, Sallie Gibson Hardin, have been invaluable.

I am indebted to W. Robert Parks and Robin Williams for permission to quote their Ph.D. theses, to Ralph Goldman for the use of his Master's thesis, and to Ernst Kneisel for the use of his Honors thesis. The *American Political Science Review*, the *Journal of Farm Economics*, the *Journal of Politics*, and *Land Economics* have permitted use of material previously published therein. Quotations from works copyrighted by the following are by permission: Alfred A. Knopf, Inc., University of Alabama Press, Harcourt, Brace and Co., Inc., Rinehart & Co., Inc., McGraw-Hill Book Co., Inc., Cornell University Press, the Macmillan Co., Public Administration Service, University of Chicago Press, Columbia University Press and Ginn and Co. (for Little, Brown, and Co.).

Index of Names

Subject-matter Index

"action" programs in agriculture, 26, 30, 134; defined, 27

advisory committees, problem of use in public administration, 176-7

Agricultural Adjustment Administration (AAA), 29, 48, 67, 101 ff., 163; and agricultural extension service, 115, 132 ff.; in group politics, 116-17; struggle with agricultural extension and the Farm Bureau, 135 ff. See also: Production and Marketing Administration (PMA)

Agricultural Conservation and Adjustment Administration, 87, 164

agricultural extension service, 22, 37 ff., 60, 65, 68, 132 ff., 175-6, 226-7; and AAA, 115, 132 ff.; and Hoover Commission, 214-16, 220; and Republican Party, 153-5; and SCS, 68, 72-3, 168-9; organization, 30-31; relationship to conservation administration of PMA and SCS, 113-14; response to federal programs, 31-33. See also: Association of Land-Grant Colleges and Universities, balanced farming, colleges of agriculture, Extension-Farm Bureau relationships, federal-state relations, True-Howard agreement

agricultural price policy, related to conservation policy, 108-9

Aiken Bills (1948), 26, 87, 88, 160, 174 ff., 262; (1951-2), 233

American Bankers Association, 91

American Farm Bureau Federation (AFBF), 37, 42, 44, 131, 135 ff., 222; and partisan politics, 153. See also: Extension-Farm Bureau relationships, Farm Bureau, general farm organizations

Appropriations Committee, sub-committee on Agriculture, H. of R., 34, 161-4; field investigation, 1950, 18-19, 34, 226 ff.

Association of Land-Grant Colleges and Universities, 23; and the reorganization of 1951, 229; and the Hoover Commission, 208-9; Committee on Post-War Agricultural Policy, 25, 28, 253-4, 263; joint committee with United States Department of Agriculture on Extension Work, 41-2, 50. See also: colleges of agriculture, Land-Grant Colleges and Universities

balanced farming program; Missouri Extension Service, 32-3, 65, 242

Brannan Plan, 266

Bureau of Agricultural Economics, 88, 134-6

Civilian Conservation Corps, 27, 57

colleges of agriculture, 245-7, 261,